FORGOTTEN HOLLYWOOD

BEWARE OF THE BLOG

MANNY PACHECO AND VIRGINIA VANDEWOUWER

bookhouse
PUBLISHING

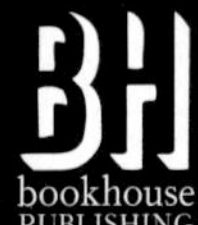

2950 Newmarket St., Suite 101-358 | Bellingham, WA 98226
Ph: 206.226.3588 | www.bookhouserules.com

Beware of the Blog

10 9 8 7 6 5 4 3 2 1

Library of Congress Control Number: 2025908900

ISBN: 978-1-967874-02-6 (Hardcover)

Editor: Julie Scandora
Cover design: Richard Adkins
Book design: Melissa Vail Coffman

Contents

Foreword by Notable Readers v

Preface by Virginia Vandewouwer vii

Introduction by Virginia Vandewouwer viii

Chapter One Vox Populi 1

Chapter Two Quill and Parchment 11

Chapter Three Panning for Gold 21

Chapter Four Shop and Compare 39

Chapter Five Standing Room Only 51

Chapter Six Filibuster 57

Chapter Seven Seventh Inning Stretch 69

Chapter Eight Ripped from the Headlines 77

Chapter Nine Across the Pond 91

Chapter Ten Time Capsule 99

Chapter Eleven Fibber McGee's Closet 113

Chapter Twelve Year in Memoriam 123

Afterword 139

Appendix: Disclaimers 141

About the Authors 147

The *Forgotten Hollywood* series of books is owned by noted entertainment personalities, such as Oscar-winning actress Margaret O'Brien; actor Steve Coogan; the late actor Hugh O'Brian (who proudly kept his copies on his coffee table); television actor Erik Estrada; singer and archivist Michael Feinstein; award-winning screenwriter J. Michael Stracynzki; the late Pulitzer Prize–winning historian David McCullough; the late former eight-term congressman Esteban Torres; President Richard Nixon's brother, the late Ed Nixon; and the late former *National News Syndicate* columnist Bonnie Churchill. The Southern California television and radio broadcasting community have also been quite supportive, including the late Tony Valdez, the late Bret Lewis, Ted Ziegenbusch, Diane Thompson, Val Zavala, Dominick Garcia, Lisa Osborne, Mike Daniels and the legendary radio personalities Roger Carroll and Art Laboe (who both died recently).

Forgotten Hollywood has achieved global success. Here are a number of everyday readers sharing their personal thoughts:

I LOVE your work!! Wish you all the continued success that you DESERVE!!

– Jeffrey Bordner, Utah (Emmy-winning voice actor. His credits include ***Hard Copy*** and *Puppy Bowl* on ***Animal Planet.****)*

I have just been reading your Forgotten Hollywood site. I am going to make a point of picking up a copy of Forgotten Hollywood Forgotten History. It looks like my cup of tea.

– Chris Whitely, Bournemouth, England

Beautifully illustrated and written, Manny Pacheco's Forgotten Hollywood book series took me as a reader on a journey through history with memorable actors. I savored each chapter, relishing the facts and memories. Pacheco's works are a must read for anyone who has watched a movie.

– Jacquie J. Ream, Seattle, Washington

Manny Pacheco is a student of the movies and he knows Hollywood. He concentrates on the character actors. And he includes photographs and stills from the movies. This is a different look at Hollywood than we usually get, and it is fascinating.

– Amos Lassen, Little Rock, Arkansas

I opened the book and I was hooked immediately. You wrote a marvelous history of many of the film actors I grew up with. It took me back to a long-ago Saturday afternoon matinee of the 1940s.

– Ivan Smith, Nova Scotia, Canada

Your books are terrific and have excellent production values.

– Barbara Ardinger, PhD, Long Beach, California

I found your book a thoughtful and an in-depth look at the lesser-known faces of Hollywood. . . . I completed reading your work whilst on vacation in Cyprus, the island in the Mediterranean. . . . I trust it won't be your last foray into Forgotten Hollywood. Your book will take pride of place in my bookcase of Hollywood reference material.

– Basil Nelson, Hednesford, Cannock, Staffordshire, England

I just wanted you to know that I have had the opportunity to read your book and I congratulate you for your contributions in keeping old Hollywood alive. And the many actors are an important part of where our movie history stems from. I wish you continued success.

– Sharon Roberts, Richland Creek Publishing

The book is great! Just finished it today. I hope you sell lots more of them.

– Theresa Holmes, Colorado Springs, Colorado

I have been having a terrific time reading your books. What a nice look at how Hollywood and history influenced each other. I highly recommend reading your work!

– Wendy Grose, California

The *Forgotten Hollywood* book series and blog site have also received wonderful five-star reviews from *The Midwest Book Review*, *Reader's Favorite*, *Recommended Reads*, *The Buzz Magazine*, *ShowMag.com*, *Trailer Life eNews* and various Amazon readers.

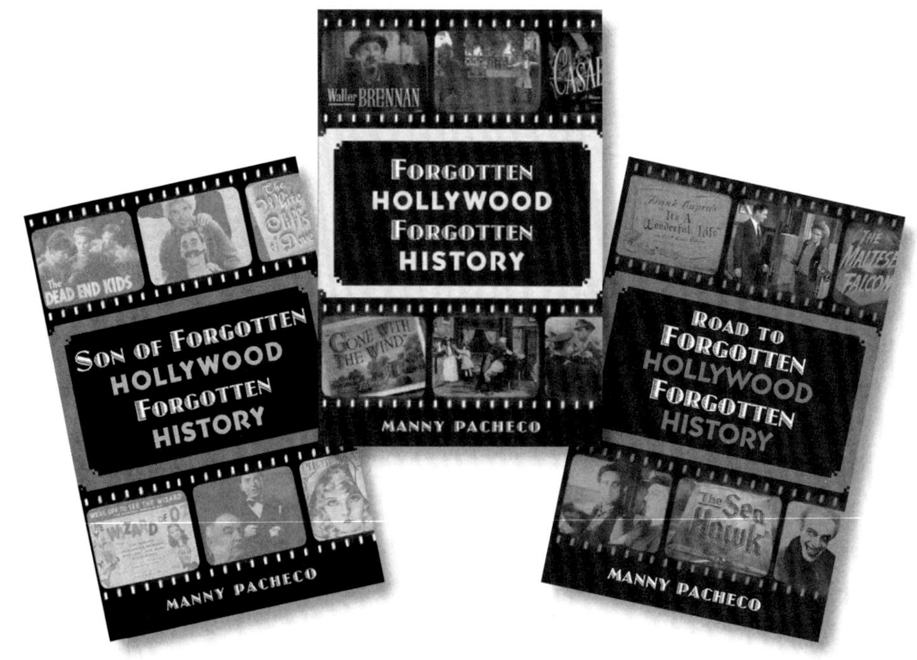

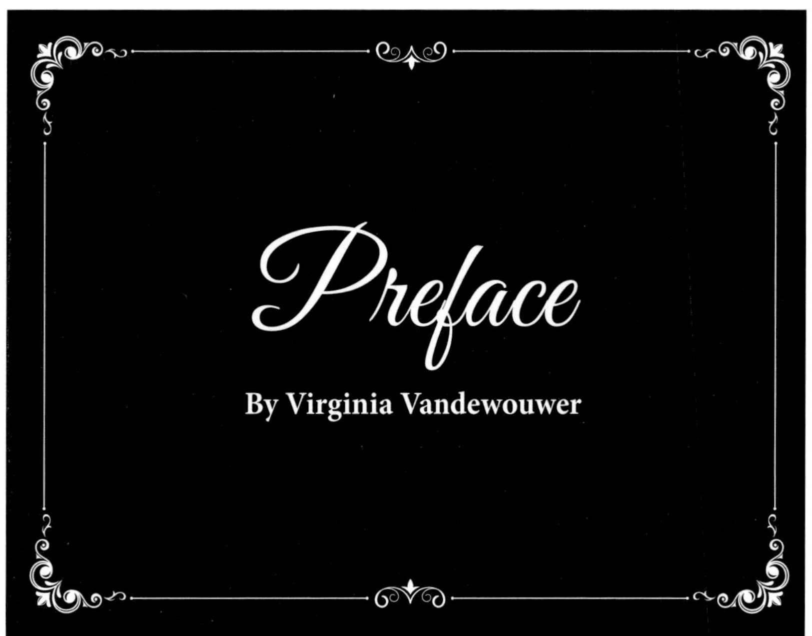

Preface

By Virginia Vandewouwer

On our journey to write *Beware of the Blog,* I can recall the first real conversation about the concept of the *Forgotten Hollywood* book series. It was on April 15, 2009, at our grandmother's ninetieth birthday celebration. Manny and my son, Matthew, were discussing the way to promote the book series. Matthew suggested that an active blog was needed to complement the initial paperback.

Manny had no idea what the heck that was. He asked: "*What is a blog? It sounds like a monster movie . . . BEWARE OF THE BLOG!*"

Hence, the title of our latest collaborative work! Oh, and by the way, Matthew did explain the blog concept and expressed the importance of writing a blog every day, much to my brother's initial dismay. That week, Manny went to the movies and saw ***Julie Julia***, which is a cinematic blueprint on how to write a blog. Now, I call that kismet!

More than two thousand blogs later—I can officially say—Manny has learned to appreciate the art of blogging! In 2012, he was awarded by the Los Angeles Press Club, Fifth Annual Journalism Awards – *Third Place, Entertainment Blog by an Individual.* (By the way, second place was awarded to actor James Franco and his blog.)

After careful deliberation, I decided that a companion blog book would be a nice addition to the *Forgotten Hollywood* franchise. When I approached Manny with this idea, he was fine with it. However, he asked: "*Who is going to be willing to read all two thousand-plus blogs, since that would be such a daunting project?*" Without hesitation, I volunteered for the task; thus, beginning the selection process for the first book in this new series. I have chosen 150 of my personal favorite blogs for you to enjoy.

And when you are done reading, visit www.forgottenhollywood.com for more recent entries.

May I remind you, *Manny is still writing . . .*

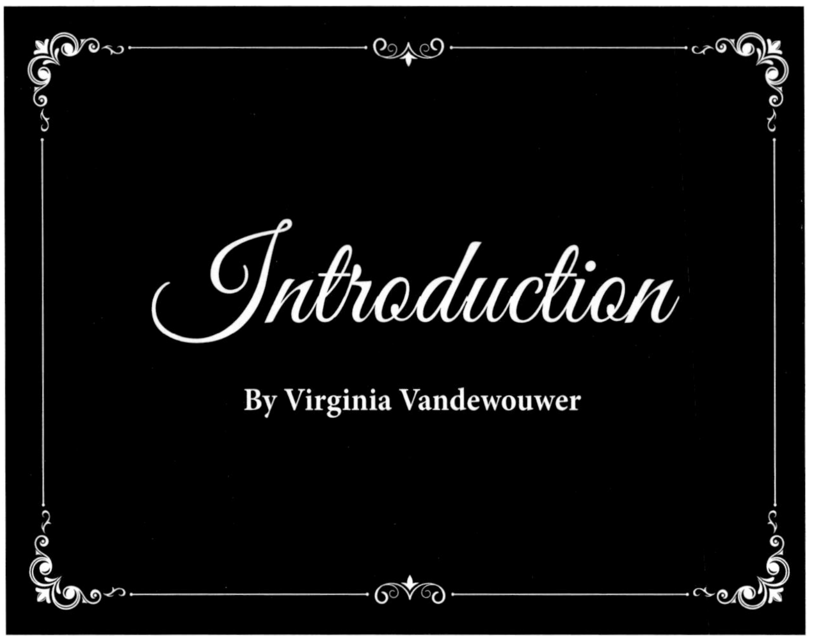

Welcome to the first installment of the *Forgotten Hollywood: Beware of the Blog* series. For those of you who have followed Manny Pacheco from the beginning stages of his book series, you understand that it has been a labor of love from the very start. The process of writing his *Forgotten Hollywood* book series has turned into quite a fruitful venture. Starting with his initial work to his just-released fourth book in the series, the franchise has expanded into an award-winning blog site, a syndicated weekly radio broadcast (and podcast) and a documentary currently in production.

I am his younger sister, Virginia Vandewouwer, and I have read through eleven years of blogs to find fascinating and delightful Hollywood and Americana-related tales. I have selected a broad range of essays from this written diary. In Manny's writings, the reader will capture the spirit for his love of country, the people in it and elements of Hollywood's Golden Age. Plus, he contributes related sports stories and his irreverent humor.

Manny had the privilege of meeting esteemed historians David McCullough and Doris Kearns Goodwin. They were clear in their concern about the importance of the written word not being lost in today's modern communication platforms of tweets and emails. They felt strongly about preserving the individuality of one's writing, being able to communicate in a thought longer than 147 characters. Simply referring to these personal messages will be a problematic issue for future historians as they look for posterity from the first half of the twenty-first century. McCullough and Kearns Goodwin had come to the realization that these tweets and emails are highly disposable, and historical reference could be lost in the process. This is the sermon they have been preaching, and a substantive goal of preserving modern history is worth a shout of hallelujah (and maybe a contribution to their cause as you tithe in support to save the American backstory for future generations). Our literary offering is dedicated to their efforts in order to save the collective stories of the masses.

That said, we have compiled this book of Manny's blogs for you to enjoy, learn and be entertained. It can provide you with a timeline that binds our rich past. Or it simply generates a few moments of escapism! Either way, let us hope you find something in this collection that will resonate with your personal journey through life.

Enjoy and keep on reading . . .

— CHAPTER ONE —

Vox Populi

The voice of the people, or *vox populi*, is the evocation of a national dialogue, relating through regional manners from a polite society. At the forefront of such a cultural reference are actors, scribes and politicos who shape this narrative in print, on stage and through the implementation of policy and referendum. Historically, an early acknowledgement of this public voice came from the work of Benjamin Franklin in his publication, *Poor Richard's Almanac*.

Today, this conversation is dispensed through tweets, emails, blogs and podcasts. Over the years, the *Forgotten Hollywood* blog site has proudly co-mingled Americana and tinsel-town as an online chronicle of past and present for the altruistic sake of posterity. Here are notable examples of *vox populi* that have captured the imagination of a public starving to be entertained.

— Virginia Vandewouwer

HAPPY BIRTHDAY TO YOU

June 27, 2016

Manny P. here . . .

A judge has approved a settlement putting *Happy Birthday to You* in the public domain. United States District Judge George King approved the agreement. It ends the ownership claims of Warner/Chappell Music, the music publishing company that has collected royalties on the song for years.

The company has agreed to pay back fourteen million dollars to those who have paid licensing fees to use the song. Last year, King ruled the company did not own the lyrics, one of the best-known and most beloved songs in the world. He said the company has no right to charge for the song's use.

The origins of *Happy Birthday to You* date back to the late nineteenth century, when sisters Patty and Mildred J. Hill introduced *Good Morning to All* to Patty's kindergarten class in Kentucky. The complete printed text of *Happy Birthday to You* first appeared in Edith Goodyear Alger's poem *Roy's Birthday*, published in her book, *A Primer of Work and Play*, copyrighted by D. C. Heath in 1901, with no reference to the lyrics.

In 1935, a piano arrangement and an unused second verse of *Happy Birthday to You* were copyrighted as a work-for-hire, crediting Preston Ware Orem for the piano arrangements and Mrs. R. R. Forman for the lyrics by the Summy Company. A later corporate restructuring in the 1970s saw Summy-Birchard becoming a division of a new company: Birch Tree Group Unlimited. Warner/Chappell Music acquired Birch Tree Group Unlimited in 1988 for twenty-five million US dollars. The company continued to insist one cannot sing the *Happy Birthday to You* lyrics for profit without paying royalties. In 2008, Warner collected around five thousand dollars each day (roughly two million per year) in royalties for the song. Warner/Chappell claimed copyright that stated:

> *For every use in film, television, radio, anywhere open to the public, and for any group where a substantial number of those in attendance are not family or friends of the performer of the song.*

On June 13, 2013, documentary filmmaker Jennifer Nelson filed a class action suit in federal court for the Southern District of New York against Warner/Chappell because the name of her film company, Good Morning to You Productions, was libel for payment to the subsidiary company. As part of a documentary she was making about the song and its history, she paid fifteen hundred dollars to secure the rights. This week's decision finally puts the tune in the public domain.

Warner/Chappell said it tried to collect royalties from not just anyone singing the song but those who use it in a commercial enterprise. Finally, the ditty will now be able to appear on television and on the big screen without fear of a financial backlash.

According to the 1998 Guinness World Records, *Happy Birthday to You* is considered the most recognized song in the English language.

ONE HUNDRED CANDLES

December 9, 2016

With boxing gloves in every table centerpiece and the *Rocky Theme* blaring, one of Hollywood's real legends walked into the Sunset Room at the Beverly Hills Hotel to celebrate his one hundredth birthday at a gathering of friends and family. Kirk Douglas made a real entrance. Images from his many cinematic credits, such as ***Spartacus***, ***Lust for Life***, ***Paths of Glory*** and others, played on a screen behind him.

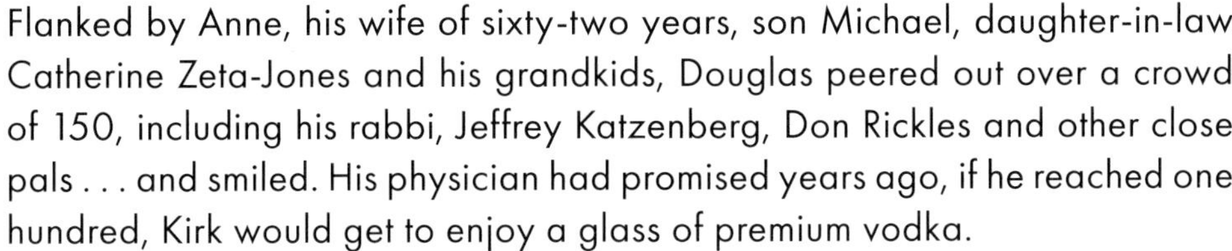

Flanked by Anne, his wife of sixty-two years, son Michael, daughter-in-law Catherine Zeta-Jones and his grandkids, Douglas peered out over a crowd of 150, including his rabbi, Jeffrey Katzenberg, Don Rickles and other close pals . . . and smiled. His physician had promised years ago, if he reached one hundred, Kirk would get to enjoy a glass of premium vodka.

Charley King's Bluebell Events oversaw the afternoon tea, where each table was designated, not by numbers, but by Kirk Douglas's films. The birthday boy was seated at the *Lonely Are the Brave* table, his favorite role. Michael kicked off the proceedings by saying it is not about age but about what he has accomplished. Kirk kept his remarks brief, thanking everyone for coming and marveling at seeing most of his family in the crowd. Zeta-Jones lit twelve candles on his cake and led the room to sing *Happy Birthday to You* with a string quartet accompaniment.

Rickles lightened a reverent and respectful mood, quipping to the crowd from his seat that he wanted to go home. He poked fun at Kirk Douglas's good looks and physique. Katzenberg reflected on the generosity of the Douglas family, who are famous for their charitable giving. Steven Spielberg arrived fashionably late, and on crutches, having recently broken his foot. Kirk Douglas closed the festivities by offering a toast and downing remnants of his vodka.

Here is to a life well lived!

VAN NUYS HIGH CELEBRATES ONE HUNDRED

October 6, 2014

My alma mater is celebrating its centennial. Van Nuys High School in the San Fernando Valley is a school with notable grads from Hollywood's Golden Age and other fields of endeavor. This gala event takes place on the weekend of October 17.

The festivities include a homecoming game that will blast music that was popular from each graduating class, a homecoming parade, an alumni event on the quad and a homecoming dance. I plan on being there for a portion of the weekend. The dignitaries will include former students, teachers and administrators.

Famous cinematic folks who graced the classrooms include Marilyn Monroe, Robert Redford, Natalie Wood, Jane Russell, Stacy Keach (***Nebraska***) and Kim Darby (***True Grit***). Television alumni include Steven Kanaly (***Dallas***), Joseph Gordon-Levitt (***Third Rock from the Sun***), Tony Dow (***Leave It to Beaver***), Ed Begley Jr. (***St. Elsewhere***), Jamie Rose (***Falcon Crest***) and Vincent Van Patten (who graduated the same year as yours truly). Other famous names are Paula Abdul, Don Drysdale, Bob Waterfield, Julie Brown and fellow broadcast personalities Peter Demetriou, Chuck Cecil and Scott Mason. ***Fast Times at Ridgemont High*** was one of the many movies filmed at VNHS over the decades.

I will be there for the alumni event on October 18 with copies of my *Forgotten Hollywood* Book Series to autograph.

You gotta love colloquial festivities!

A MAJOR SEVENTY-YEAR ANNIVERSARY

December 11, 2009

On December 15, 1939, the premiere of ***Gone with the Wind*** took place in Atlanta, after three days of celebrations. Clark Gable almost boycotted the opening when he found out the Black actors were not allowed to attend (due to *Jim Crow* laws). Hattie McDaniel decided to intervene on behalf of the event. Gable relented, appearing with his wife, Carole Lombard.

The film won eight Oscars. TCM will screen the film exactly seventy years after the initial premiere. This presentation climaxes a year of anniversaries of superior films produced in 1939, including ***Mr. Smith Goes to Washington***, ***Of Mice and Men, Beau Geste***, ***Stagecoach, The Roaring Twenties***, ***Son of Frankenstein***, ***Babes in Arms, Juarez***, ***Jesse James***, ***Destry Rides Again***, ***Golden Boy***, ***Ninotchka, Goodbye Mr. Chips***, ***Dark Victory***, ***The Hound of the Baskervilles***, ***Wuthering Heights*** and ***The Wizard of Oz***.

Three of my actors in *Forgotten Hollywood Forgotten History* co-star in the epic: Thomas Mitchell, Eddie Anderson and Ward Bond. I also spend much of *chapter 6* writing about the careers of Clark Gable, Vivien Leigh, Olivia De Havilland, Hattie McDaniel and the author Margaret Mitchell. Jane Darwell, who has a small role in the motion picture, is a projected subject in the book's sequel.

TWO BUSY DUDES

May 3, 2018

Universal Pictures and The Film Foundation have announced a multi-year partnership to restore handpicked selections of classic productions, with Oscar-winning directors Martin Scorsese and Steven Spielberg lending a hand. Universal will fund the restorations, as well as provide research and technical services. Through The Film Foundation, Scorsese and Spielberg will be personally involved in the process, contributing their unique artistic expertise and historical knowledge throughout the restoration process.

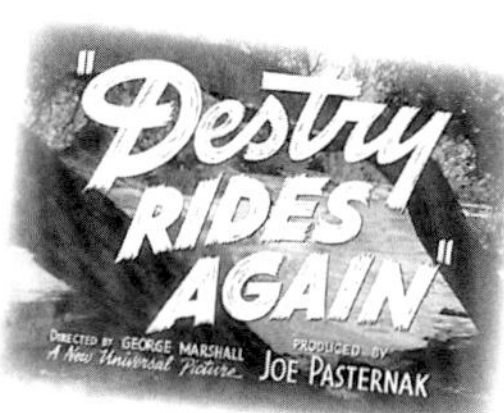

The 2018 restoration slate will include ***Destry Rides Again***, ***Winchester '73***, ***My Little Chickadee*** and both cinematic versions of Hemingway's ***The Killers***, with additional titles announced in the coming months.

The Film Foundation was established in 1990 to protect and preserve celluloid history. By working in partnership with archives and film studios, this nonprofit foundation has helped restore more than eight hundred movies, which are made accessible to the public through programming at festivals, museums and educational institutions around the world.

A collaborative partnership marks a step in Universal's film restoration initiative announced during the studio's centennial in 2012. Over seventy works have been fully restored, including ***All Quiet on the Western Front***, ***Dracula***, ***Double Indemnity***, ***Frankenstein***, ***Touch of Evil***, ***Schindler's List***, ***Jaws***, ***Out of Africa***, ***High Plains Drifter***, ***Pillow Talk***, ***Bride of Frankenstein***, ***To Kill a Mockingbird***, ***Spartacus, Duck Soup***, ***The Sting***, ***The Birds*** and ***Holiday Inn***.

In 2015, Universal launched a silent film initiative. The company has so far restored fifteen titles, including ***Outside the Law***, ***Sensation Seekers*** and ***The Man Who Laughs***. The restored versions will be screened at film festivals and archives around the world.

A MOVIE STUDIO WITH SUBSTANCE

November 2, 2013

Since its inception. one Hollywood film studio has commanded A-list talent—Elizabeth Taylor, Morgan Freeman, Sandra Bullock, Michael Douglas, Nicole Kidman—and they all have worked for free. What studio head has such pull? It is Rabbi Marvin Hier, the mini-mogul of Moriah Films, the movie division of the Simon Wiesenthal Center.

Founded by Hier in 1981, Moriah Films has won two Academy Awards for their historical documentaries. He established the movie studio a few years after opening the Wiesenthal Center in 1977. He had planned a slide show about the Holocaust when Fay Kanin, then president of the film academy, suggested he consider making a movie instead. United States Senator John Warner was involved with the Wiesenthal Center at the time while married to Elizabeth Taylor. She became the narrator for ***Genocide***, which won the Oscar for Best Documentary Feature.

The dozen movies Moriah Films has made attracted such notables as Michael York, Kevin Costner, Whoopi Goldberg, Brooke Shields, Dustin Hoffman, Anne Bancroft, Richard Dreyfuss, Patrick Stewart, Ed Asner, Martin Landau and Ben Kingsley. Its latest production, ***The Prime Ministers: The Pioneers***, featuring the narration of Sandra Bullock and Christoph Waltz, opens Wednesday in Los Angeles and travels to more cities next month. Kingsley, Douglas and Waltz have offered their talents a couple of times.

The Wiesenthal Center, a human-rights organization providing Holocaust education and fighting anti-Semitism, began its deep ties to Hollywood when Frank Sinatra and Taylor were on the original board of directors and made introductions throughout Hollywood. Today, movie moguls Jeffrey Katzenberg and Ron Meyer link the Wiesenthal Center to the film community. Moriah's productions have been screened theatrically and broadcast around the world on Showtime, HBO, Starz/Encore, as well as German, French, Russian, Chinese and Israeli television outlets.

Hier has fond memories of watching Roy Rogers's pictures at New York's Palestine Theater as a boy and remains a movie fan today. But Moriah Films aims to do more than entertain. Hier stresses the importance to put Jewish history on film to reach worldwide audiences for years to come.

We have to agree . . .

WARNER BROTHERS TOUR IS HIDDEN TREASURE

June 27, 2011

Movie mogul Carl Laemmle created the *Movie Backlot* tour in 1915 at Universal Studios. Back in the day, you would start out at the commissary and enjoy the seldom-told stories about the pictures of Hollywood's Golden Age. You might actually stroll around the sets of motion pictures such as ***Psycho***. Today, the tram ride that evolved in 1964 feels like an amusement park attraction.

GOOD NEWS! Warner Brothers offers the kind of adventure that was popular during the Studio Era. Located at 4000 Warner Boulevard in Burbank, a VIP Tour will give you a complete feel of what it was like to mingle with their stars of yesteryear. Their tram is more like a golf cart, and it moves at a casual pace. You can also ask substantive questions of your friendly guide about the history of this iconic film studio and get the appropriate answers.

Among the tour highlights:

- A fifteen-minute visual retrospective taking you back to the historic ***The Jazz Singer***
- The forest where Errol Flynn scampered during ***The Adventures of Robin Hood***
- A French street where *Rick* first told *Ilsa*: *"Here's looking at you, kid"* in **Casablanca**
- The jungle used during the 1932 version of ***Tarzan*** with Johnny Weissmuller
- The actual street where Robert Preston sang *Ya Got Trouble* from ***The Music Man***
- ***High Sierra***, ***Yankee Doodle Dandy***, ***King's Row***, ***Damn Yankees***, ***My Fair Lady*** sets
- Television sets from ***The Waltons***, ***Bonanza***, ***Fantasy Island*** and ***The Dukes of Hazzard***

They also have a museum with artifacts like the actual *Maltese Falcon* and *Sam's Piano* at *Rick's Café Americain* from **Casablanca**. And Spanish-speaking tours are available (*se habla Espanol*).

Recent cinematic releases and television programs are also discussed. The tour is very affordable . . . just forty-nine dollars per person (ten years of age or older). You can visit Warner Brothers, Monday–Friday, 8:20 a.m.–4 p.m. The VIP Tours run continuously. And now, they have limited Saturday times for the summer. Pamper yourself with this two-hour jaunt.

For the classic movie buff, this is the exact nostalgic thrill ride you will want to experience. BTW, I'm looking for *Sam* to *play it again*!

BACALL TO BE HONORED FOR FASHION

August 14, 2014

Next spring, the Museum at the Fashion Institute of Technology—with the help of FIT graduate students learning how to curate—will focus on five designers who helped define Lauren Bacall's subtle seductiveness, her sophisticated mix of classic femininity and raw masculine authority in fashion. Hundreds of personal garments she donated will be turned into an exhibit about her style.

The exhibit on FIT's Manhattan campus will focus mostly on Bacall's looks from the 1950s and 1960s. She was a model at sixteen, a pal of Yves Saint Laurent and a frequent wearer of designs by Norman Norell, some of her clothes by these designers will be joined by other designs Bacall donated from Marc Bohan for Christian Dior, Yves Saint Laurent, Pierre Cardin and Ungaro. Bacall gave FIT roughly seven hundred garments.

Much like Marlene Dietrich and the treatment of her fashion, Bacall was never elevated to muse for any one designer. Plenty, though, were touched by her style over the decades: Bill Blass, Perry Ellis, her friend Yves Saint Laurent, Donna Karan and Ralph Lauren, among them.

Lauren Bacall's only condition on the exhibition . . . make it a high-quality process. After her recent passing, it will be elevated as a tribute to the actress.

THE LEGACY OF LOUIS ARMSTRONG

May 23, 2012

The final recordings of Louis Armstrong can be yours through the Smithsonian Institute. Six months before Satchmo died, he made one final appearance in 1971 at the inauguration of incoming National Press Club President Vernon Louviere, a fellow native of New Orleans. Armstrong's signature voice and trumpet playing were captured and put on vinyl a year later after his passing. Only three hundred album copies were initially pressed. David Frost can also be heard, since he was the emcee at the event.

These rare moments are now widely available for the first time from Smithsonian Folkways Recordings as part of its eleventh annual celebration of Jazz Appreciation month. The CD is entitled *Satchmo at The National Press Club: Red Beans & Rice-ly Yours*. Notable live versions include *Hello Dolly*, a theme from *The Threepenny Opera* (*Mack the Knife*) and *Boy from New Orleans*. Own a piece of its cultural history!

His health in decline, Louis Armstrong died in his sleep of a heart attack on July 6, 1971, a month before his seventieth birthday. What a wonderful world of jazz he left behind. His body of work in music and cinema is considered immeasurable.

IN REMEMBRANCE OF ELLA

April 14, 2017

The Smithsonian's National Portrait Gallery has put on display a rarely seen photograph of iconic jazz singer Ella Fitzgerald, fondly nicknamed *First Lady of Song*. This portrait is currently on view. Ella died in 1996, and she would have marked her one hundredth birthday on April 25.

Representatives of the gallery chose the photograph of Fitzgerald in performance, flanked by Dizzy Gillespie, Ray Brown and Milt Jackson. It was taken in 1947 by William Gottlieb, who learned to shoot a camera and take pictures to accompany his weekly music column for the *Washington Post*. Ella was actually in the audience to hear her boyfriend, Ray Brown, perform with his group. But as expected, everybody wanted to hear Ella croon. Once she held the mic, Gottlieb got into position to take his picture. His photos of musicians of the 1930s and 1940s are generally considered vibrant visual records of jazz's golden age.

Fitzgerald topped *DownBeat* magazine's annual readers' poll as the Best Female Vocalist for seventeen consecutive years (1953-1970). She was a teen when she won an amateur contest at Harlem's famed Apollo Theater. This led to a chance to sing with Chick Webb's orchestra in 1935. Fitzgerald soon secured her standing as the leading swing-era performer and scored a hit with *A-Tisket, A-Tasket* in 1938. After Webb's passing in 1939, she led his orchestra for three years before moving to a successful solo career. With a voice spanning three octaves and a great knack for improvisational scat singing, she developed a wide-ranging repertoire encompassing many genres of music. Ella's long and fruitful association with jazz impresario Norman Granz resulted in a legendary series of songbook recordings that marked Fitzgerald as one of the great interpreters of American popular music.

The striking photo was given to the museum as a gift from Lisa Ruthel and Anup Mahurkar, and the Ella Fitzgerald Charitable Foundation has helped make it possible for this portrait to be on view in honor of *Ella at 100: The Centennial Celebration*. It is the first time the photograph has been displayed at the museum.

BILL HOLDEN LEGACY INVOLVES WILDLIFE

April 13, 2014

The William Holden Wildlife Foundation (WHWF) was founded in 1982 by actress Stefanie Powers in memory of the late William Holden to continue his work as a conservationist and co-founder of the Mt. Kenya Game Ranch. The estate is located on the equator at seven thousand feet above sea level on the slopes of Mt. Kenya. It was founded to carry on his important efforts and meet the increasing demand for alternatives to animal extinction.

Captive breeding is an important tool for species conservation. This highly focused and labor-intensive endeavor is accomplished by a system of worldwide organizations participating in cooperation with one another. The International Species Inventory System keeps genealogical information on individual animals of twenty-five hundred species of mammals and birds that are located in Europe and North American zoos, making it possible to arrange mates by computer and minimizing problems caused by inbreeding.

Throughout his life, William Holden continued his wholehearted support of the game ranch and often referred to this as the greatest work of his life, over and above his motion pictures. Considering that he won an Oscar for Best Actor for his performance in ***Stalag 17***, that is saying something. Virtually 100 percent of tax-deductible donations goes directly to the never-ending work of WHWF.

The William Holden Wildlife Foundation Education Center offers an opportunity to experience the outdoors in a communication with nature often unavailable in a public environment.

DUMBING DOWN OF FILM AUDIENCES!

December 30, 2011

Back in 1951, MGM released a fine sequel to the successful ***Father of the Bride***, a motion picture starring Spencer Tracy, Elizabeth Taylor and Joan Bennett called ***Father's Little Dividend***. This was a reference to the pregnancy of Taylor's character. Executive producer Dore Schary presumed the intelligent metaphor would resonate with movie audiences.

A few years back, I was quite disappointed by Touchstone Pictures' decision to follow up its 1990's remake of ***Father of the Bride*** with ***Father of the Bride Part II***. My reasoning was simple. In the latter sequel, Steve Martin's character dealt with his daughter's impending motherhood, not a second wedding. The motion picture was mistitled in a shameful marketing ploy!

In 2011, Steven Spielberg practiced a similar ruse. In the just-released animated film ***The Adventures of Tintin*** (pronounced *tahtah*), our gallant hero has a fox-terrier named *Milou*, popularized in Belgian comic books and created by Georges Remi in the 1920s. Inexplicably, Spielberg changed the name of the furry white canine to *Snowy* to relate to American movie-goers.

My concerns have more to do with the lost opportunity to teach our youngsters another language, than with obvious decisions to reach the public with sure-fire strategies. Provincial marketing of a cute pooch named *Snowy* should induce monetary dividends at the expense of education and life-lessons from cosmopolitan attitudes outside the United States. Neither example of studio decision-making is an earth-shattering issue facing our nation. In the final analysis, our society is a little bit worse from these kinds of decisions. The dumbing down of consumers does not help us on a global-economic level and keeps us isolated from the world's beauty. Plus, I simply believe in the potential classroom opportunities provided by the cinematic experience.

This is a humble opinion. Now I am waiting for *Tintin* and *Milou* to help me off my soapbox!

This blog was an award-winner at the 2012 Los Angeles Press Club's Fifth Annual Entertainment Journalism Awards – Entertainment Blog by an Individual.

MARGARET O'BRIEN TO BE INTERVIEWED

April 7, 2013

Margaret O'Brien is set to appear in the *Forgotten Hollywood* documentary pilot about Lionel Barrymore's story on how he influenced our country's view of the disabled. Suffering from advanced degenerative arthritis, his decision to carry on with his career from a wheelchair motivated the American public to champion the Roosevelt administration's *March of Dimes* campaign, the most successful effort to fight disease in our history. O'Brien was the first poster child for the *March of Dimes*.

Beginning a prolific career as a child actress in feature films at MGM, O'Brien became one of the most popular young stars in cinema. She made her first film appearance in ***Babes on Broadway*** at the age of four, and she was honored with a Juvenile Oscar as the Outstanding Child Actress of 1944 for her stint in ***Meet Me in St. Louis***.

Her career included roles in ***Madame Curie***, ***Jane Eyre***, ***The Canterville Ghost***, ***Three Wise Fools***, ***Our Vines Have Tender Grapes***, ***Little Women*** and ***The Secret Garden***. O'Brien co-starred with Judy Garland, Elizabeth Taylor, Peter Lawford, June Allyson, James Cagney, Ann Southern, Charles Laughton, Edward G. Robinson, Greer Garson, Walter Pidgeon, Orson Welles, Mary Astor, Robert Young, Thomas Mitchell, Joan Fontaine, Marjorie Main, Red Skelton, C. Aubrey Smith and, of course, Lionel Barrymore. In her later career, she appeared on television, on stage and in supporting motion picture roles. In 1990, O'Brien was honored by the Young Artist Foundation with its Former Child Star Lifetime Achievement Award, recognizing her outstanding achievements within the film industry as a child actress.

Our production team is thrilled over the addition of the legendary Margaret O'Brien to our documentary.

Until next time . . . *never forget.*

— CHAPTER TWO —

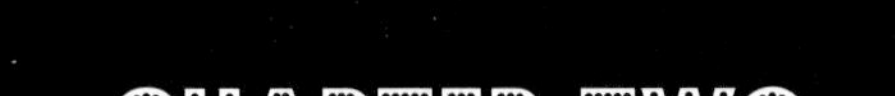

Quill and Parchment

The words we read in literature often have a profound impact on society. So much so, movie makers have been inspired to create memorable cinematic productions. The impact dates back to the *Elizabethan* era when quill and parchment were used to draft imagination. These works were often made into plays and performed in front of live audiences and sometimes including a royal court.

In this chapter, we have included *Forgotten Hollywood* blog stories that could inspire the making of great motion pictures. Like the Golden Age directors, celebrated authors put their words to paper in order to document Hollywood history, as does Manny, who also puts his own creative spin on the interpretative blogs he writes.

—Virginia Vandewouwer

AUTHOR INSPIRED BY BARRYMORE STORY

June 18, 2013

Manny P. here . . .

Craig Inglis, a children's author who has written a tender story called *Lucky*, is citing additional inspiration from the story of Lionel Barrymore, the subject of our documentary. According to his blog site:

> *Lucky follows an irrepressible terrier and his compassionate owner who work together to find happiness after an unfortunate accident leaves Lucky missing one of his limbs. Lucky learns to overcome his disability to gain a fruitful life. I was reading a chapter in Manny Pacheco's book Forgotten Hollywood, Forgotten History about the career of Lionel Barrymore. Lionel suffered a broken hip and then arthritis, which confined him to a wheelchair. But that didn't stop his career. He went on to play many more roles, the most well-known being Mr. Potter in* ***It's a Wonderful Life*** *He did not try to hide his handicap and was an inspiration to other actors who came later to portray people with disabilities.*

He was inspired to write the book from those who faced and overcame physical disabilities in their own lives. The book features fifteen beautiful illustrations by actor and artist Richard Kinsey that depict *Lucky*, his owner and his courageous recovery.

The Orange County scribe continued to recount in a recent related blog:

> *It is an inspirational book that helps children understand they can overcome obstacles in life and even make a better life than before. It's also a book that can win the hearts of readers of all ages. Reading Lucky with your children can be a starting point for talking about people you might know who are disabled and have triumphed over their disabilities.*

I thank Craig Inglis for his kind acknowledgment of my sharing the Lionel Barrymore story. The *Forgotten Hollywood* documentary is currently in preproduction.

NEW MILLION SELLER

July 20, 2015

Most critics dismissed it as just a rough draft for *To Kill a Mockingbird*, and readers despaired over an aging, racist *Atticus Finch*. But Harper Lee's *Go Set a Watchman* is still a million seller.

HarperCollins has announced that *Go Set a Watchman*, in its combined print, electronic and audio formats, has sold over one million copies in the United States and Canada, a figure which includes first-week sales and months of pre-orders. The publisher stunned the world in February when it revealed that a second novel was coming from Lee, who had insisted *To Kill a Mockingbird* would be her only book.

HarperCollins, whose award-winning authors have included Michael Crichton and Veronica Roth, is calling *Watchman* its fastest seller in history. Truth be told, other books have sold much faster. *Harry Potter and the Deathly*

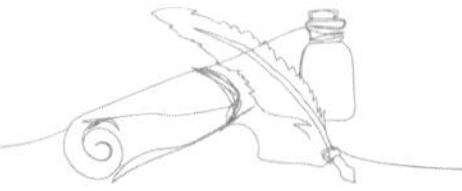

Hallows, published by Scholastic in 2007, sold eight million copies in its first twenty-four hours.

Watchman was completed before Lee's Pulitzer Prize–winning *Mockingbird* but is set in the same Alabama community twenty years later. Critics and readers were startled to find *Atticus* disparaging blacks and condemning the Supreme Court's decision to outlaw segregation in public schools.

Watchman was released July 14 and, as of early Monday, remains at #1 on Amazon.com and Barnes&Noble.com, with *Mockingbird* also in the Top Ten. HarperCollins has increased an initial print run of two million copies for *Watchman* to over three million.

LIFE AND TIMES OF CAROLE LOMBARD

April 22, 2014

Fireball: Carole Lombard and the Mystery of Flight 3 is a new book that chronicles the tragic death of the gifted actress. The book also offers a day-by-day look at the struggles of her husband, Clark Gable, and Lombard's family, friends and fans as they coped with the tragedy.

On January 16, 1942, Hollywood's *Queen of Screwball* stepped onto a Transcontinental and Western Airlines DC-3, designated as *Flight 3* in Indianapolis, with her mother, Elizabeth Peters, and MGM publicity man, Otto Winkler. Lombard had just completed the first sale of war bonds and stamps in the nation, following its entry into World War II. Exhausted from five days on the road, Carole intended to return home to California by the quickest means possible. Fourteen hours into the trip, *Flight 3* lay a flaming pile of debris, strewn across the side of Potosi Mountain, Nevada.

Fireball is a fresh look at Carole Lombard's life and presents a first-ever examination of the events leading to the final flight and her death. Lombard became the first Hollywood star who sacrificed her life in World War II. The War Department offered Gable a funeral service with full military honors. But he refused, knowing his wife would have declined such a spectacle.

But *Fireball* goes further and explores the lives of the twenty-one other passengers on the plane, including fifteen members of the United States Army Air Corps, and addresses one of the most enduring mysteries of World War II. . . . On a clear night full of stars, with TWA's most experienced pilot at the controls of a ten-month-old aircraft and under the power of two fully functioning engines, why did *Flight 3* crash into that Nevada mountainside? Author Robert Matzen visited the wreckage site, looking for clues to further the tragic story. He also spoke with Robert Stack (a close pal of Lombard's) for insight on this sad event.

Life magazine sent photojournalist Myron Davis on the road to capture Lombard's day of selling bonds for an uplifting photo essay. Davis made thirty-two negatives on January 15, 1942, and returned to Chicago to process the film, only to receive the call that Lombard was dead. *Life* subsequently killed his story and used only one of the photos in its obituary of the actress. A few others made newswires or surfaced for high-quality reproduction, while the rest remained in a trunk for seventy years. The entire group was acquired from the Myron Davis estate, and many of these fascinating photos will be published for the first time in *Fireball*. All photos chosen for print have never been seen and offer a glimpse of Lombard's hectic last full day of life.

Fireball: Carole Lombard and the Mystery of Flight 3 by Robert Matzen is published through Goodnight Books.

LIZ AND MICKEY

October 13, 2015

The *Forgotten Hollywood* blog site is not one to engage in idle gossip. But the following story is lurid and ultimately intriguing, considering the cinematic royalty involved.

Hollywood legend Elizabeth Taylor had a carnal encounter with Mickey Rooney when she was just fourteen years old, claims a new book. *The Life and Times of Mickey Rooney* is by Richard A. Lertzman and William J. Birnes. They interviewed the actor just before his death, and he revealed the pair met when she was only twelve when they starred in ***National Velvet***. The book claims that two years after their work, the actors were caught engaging in a sex act by twenty-four-year-old Rooney's second wife, Betty Jane. She was a backup singer for the likes of Elvis Presley, Frank Sinatra and Sam Cooke. She and Rooney divorced in 1949. Her friend Pam McClenathan describes the incident in the book, which occurred in 1944.

Taylor's sex life has been well documented over the years. According to reports, she was just twelve when she had her first encounter with a man, future movie actor/director John Derek, who was six years her elder. At the age of fifteen, she was reportedly involved with future president Ronald Reagan, who was married to actress Jane Wyman at the time. Her next political sexual encounter was with future chief executive John F. Kennedy.

Rooney, who died last year, married eight times in total. But this is the first time he has been linked to Elizabeth, who eventually wed seven men. Mickey bragged that he managed to get women into bed with his sense of humor. His conquests included Lana Turner and Judy Garland. One of his wives was Ava Gardner.

The Life and Times of Mickey Rooney is due out on October 20.

STAN LAUREL LETTERS TO AUCTION

September 12, 2015

Hollywood legend Stan Laurel wrote how he was lost after the death of Oliver Hardy in an amazing collection of letters that are about to go on sale in Britain. The type-written correspondence, written by Stan to his cousin in Cumbria, are expected to generate huge interest when they are auctioned in Newcastle. He writes of the terrible loss of his comedy partner and life after Hardy's death on August 7, 1957.

Laurel had confided that the illness of his comic partner had seen him lose ten pounds in weight. It also left Stan with little work to do as he moved with his wife Eda to Malibu during the summer of '57. A note from Oliver Hardy's widow, Lucille, is also for sale. His widow tells of the star's great suffering in the final months before he died.

Stan Laurel was born in Ulverston in 1890. He appeared in more than one hundred short films, feature films and cameos with Oliver Hardy. One of these

letters was written only days before his own death. Other subjects he referred to in his letters included the death of George VI and succession of Elizabeth II, sailing on the *Queen Mary* at the same time as Winston Churchill and personal family matters.

A total of forty-one letters sent to his cousin in Ulverston between May 1947 and January 1965 are going under the hammer. The collection will be sold at Anderson and Garland in Newcastle on September 15 to September 17.

ACADEMY LIBRARY ADDS SILENT STRAINS

December 3, 2013

Throughout the silent era, sheet music for cinematic-inspired tunes brought together the public's fascination with the silver screen and their love of popular music. Written by Tin Pan Alley songwriter Charles McCarron in 1915, *Those Keystone Comedy Cops* capitalized on the popularity of bumbling policemen who had been introduced by Mack Sennett just a few years earlier but had already become an audience favorite.

Illustrated by Hungarian-born artist André De Takacs, this beautiful sheet music cover makes subtle reference to the world of moving pictures. The focal point includes a photo from the film ***In the Clutches of the Gang***, featuring Ford Sterling, Edgar Kennedy, Al St. John, William Frawley and Roscoe *Fatty* Arbuckle.

This tinted image mimics a movie screen, while the Keystone company logo glows behind dramatic silhouettes of stylized policemen. The silhouettes are also depicted on the two oversized clubs adorned with tassels that frame the image like theater curtains, evoking the elegant movie palaces of the era.

This item is one of hundreds of pieces of silent-era sheet music donated by Robert Cushman to the Margaret Herrick Library and is archived in Special Collections. Other examples of silent-era sheet music may be viewed in the library's digital collections. The library is also home to the Mack Sennett's papers, featuring scenarios, production materials and photographs relating to the career of this prolific producer. While ***In the Clutches of the Gang*** is believed lost, the Academy Film Archive preserved a fragment of the production, recently discovered at the New Zealand Film Archive as part of the *New Zealand Project*.

This iconic music score is one of the treasured artifacts to be featured in the new Academy Museum of Motion Pictures, scheduled to open in 2017.

DIRECTORS AT WAR

March 25, 2014

A new book chronicles the work of studio-era directors and their participation during World War II. *Five Came Back* was written by Mark Harris and tells the stories of John Ford, George Stevens, Frank Capra, John Huston and William Wyler and their attempts to bring the war back to the home front. Incidentally, a 1939 flick was produced called ***Five Came Back***, and it starred Chester Morris, Allen Jenkins, John Carradine, C. Aubrey Smith and a very young Lucille Ball.

Films during this era were developed to boost public morale, educate millions of troops and stoke anti-German and anti-Japanese sentiment. The studios cooperated with the government to ensure that cinematic propaganda carried the right message. Besides churning out training pieces, filmmakers in uniform also sought to tell inspiring stories through documentaries.

Frank Capra (***Mr. Smith Goes to Washington*** and ***Meet John Doe***) joined up shortly after the attack on Pearl Harbor. His major contribution was the ***Why We Fight*** series, designed to explain to recruits why they were going to war. His colleagues were challenged to come up with persuasive arguments aimed at black recruits, given segregation. Depictions of the Japanese were so racist, even the United States government balked at approval, knowing it would complicate postwar relations with Japan.

John Ford (***How Green was My Valley*** and ***The Quiet Man***) was under fire at the battle of Midway Island, for which he created a memorable documentary out of his color footage, and again at Omaha Beach, when the Allies invaded mainland Europe on D-Day. He turned to Henry Fonda and Jane Darwell to interpret compelling narration. President Roosevelt openly wept after a screening of one of his movies.

John Huston (***The African Queen*** and ***The Treasure of the Sierra Madre***) embellished his own personal war stories. Huston went beyond the accepted practices of the documentarian when he passed off reenactments for ***The Battle of San Pietro*** as actual battle footage. John Huston was on more stable ground with his piece on shell-shocked troops and their treatment. ***Let There Be Light*** proved so unsettling that the government kept it under wraps for decades.

William Wyler (***The Best Years of Our Lives***) learned he had received an Oscar for the wartime drama ***Mrs. Miniver*** while serving overseas. His film crew flew on B-17 missions over Europe for one of the best-received documentaries, ***The Memphis Belle***. Wyler used footage from multiple bombing runs, and he assembled the plane's crew in Hollywood to record dialogue for the film because their words could not be heard over the roar of the bomber's engines. Wyler lost much of his hearing while trying to film aboard a B-25 flight.

George Stevens (***A Place in the Sun*** and ***Shane***) was less interested in making documentaries than in filming events as they happened. He was in Normandy for D-Day and in Paris during the celebration of liberation. Significantly, George Stevens and his cameras passed through the gates of the concentration camp at Dachau two days after its liberation. He spent weeks filming life and death among the tens of thousands still at the camp, footage later used in documentaries that served as evidence during the Nuremberg trials.

These directors faced their wartime fears with little more than spit, cameras and courage. Their frustrations were due to the indifference of government bureaucracy, mostly by the military that made things exceedingly difficult for them to obtain equipment and supplies required for them to do their jobs.

Of the five, only Frank Capra failed to find his footing when he returned to Tinseltown. His colleagues, however, achieved their best work after the war. Their post-war films turned more realistic, serious and profound. The directors were never the same.

Five Came Back is published through Penguin Books.

EARLY HITLER LETTER UNEARTHED

June 12, 2011

The Simon Wiesenthal Center has acquired a rare document confirming Adolf Hitler's long-standing anti-Semitic bigotry. A spokesperson for the Jewish center calls it, *"the most significant document in its thirty-four-year history."*

Hitler's obsessive hostility can be directly linked to his unique ability to galvanize troops as a corporal in the German army during World War I.

He expressed his success through virulent writings in a personal letter to his superior officer. Dated September 16, 1919, this four-page note openly espoused his political philosophy . . . an inner hatred of Jews and his desire to see them exterminated. This correspondence was written six years before the publication of *Mein Kampf.*

His ideas were galvanized after the Treaty of Versailles, when Germany was made to pay heavy reparations by the Allied Powers. While Jewish businesses thrived, despite widespread poverty throughout the Fatherland, the rise of extremists like the Nazis were inevitable.

According to Rabbi Marvin Heir, Wiesenthal Center dean and founder:

> *What began as a private letter, one man's opinion, twenty-two years later became the "Magna Carta" of an entire nation and led to the nearly total extinction of the Jewish people. This is an important lesson for future generations.*
>
> . . .

Demagogues mean what they say and given the opportunity, carry out what they promise. In terms of the Holocaust, we have nothing that would compare to this document.

SCHINDLER ON DISPLAY

November 13, 2016

The Leatherby Libraries is now home to the most complete set of Oskar Schindler's archives and documents, including copies of the original *Schindler's lists* that protected over a thousand Jews during the Holocaust. About fifty people attended a ceremony on November 10 at the grand opening of a room in Leatherby Libraries. It now includes twenty-two boxes of Schindler's letters, photographs and architectural drawings that Chapman presidential fellow David Crowe donated to the Chapman Holocaust Memorial Library.

Crowe's collection, which took him seven years to accumulate, was given to Chapman because of its proximity to the Beverly Hills home of the late Leopold Page and his wife, Mila, the latter attending the event. The documents were among those Schindler saved from concentration camps. Leopold convinced author Thomas Keneally to write the book that inspired Steven Spielberg's production of ***Schindler's List*** after Keneally visited Page's Southern California leather shop.

Crowe, who was on the education board of the United States Holocaust Memorial Museum in Washington, DC, for fourteen years, said he wanted to put the letters and archives in a smaller location, where it would be available for anyone interested in Holocaust study. President Danielle Struppa, who gave a speech at the ceremony, said Marilyn Harran, director of the Rodgers Center for Holocaust Education, emailed him asking if he would like to include Crowe's archives. But the contents of the room were kept a secret until Thursday. The ceremony culminated with a champagne toast and a ribbon-cutting ceremony, where Struppa, Crowe and Harran gathered around Mila Page. Marie Knecht, the Pages' daughter, was excited to see photos of her mother and father and hopes the exhibit will help ensure that scholars never forget the history of the Holocaust.

The archives are on display in the Brandman Survivor's Room, adjacent to the Samueli Holocaust Library. They will be available by appointment to Chapman students, faculty and visiting researchers.

In a related story, the dilapidated factory that Oskar Schindler once used to save his Jewish workers from Nazi death camps during World War II will be restored into a Holocaust memorial, Czech officials have announced. The Czech culture ministry named parts of the complex a cultural monument earlier this month. They plan to turn the munitions shop into a repository on Schindler's life, and it should be completed by 2019.

DIARY OF ANNE (AND OTTO) FRANK

November 14, 2015

The copyright on *The Diary of Anne Frank*, set to expire January 1 in most of Europe, has been extended by at least thirty-five years after the Swiss foundation that holds the copyright claimed Anne's diary actually had a co-author . . . her father, Otto Frank. Otto has long been acknowledged as an editor and compiler of the best-selling work, but by elevating him as an author, Anne Frank Fonds is able to extend its copyright on the work until the end of 2050. Frank left them unread for some time but eventually began transcribing them from Dutch for his Swiss relatives in 1947.

In most of Europe, copyrights expire seventy years after the author's death. Anne died seventy years ago, but Otto didn't pass away until 1980. Anyone in Europe wanting to publish the book will now need to continue asking the foundation for permission and paying it royalties.

The change is not sitting well with many. One lawyer says it implies the foundation has been lying all these years about Anne writing the diary on her own. Others say giving copyright protection to editors undermines authors and calls the foundation's claims that Otto co-authored the diary as spurious.

As the sole member of his family to survive *the Holocaust*, Otto inherited Anne's manuscripts after her death, arranged for the publication of her diary and oversaw its adaptation to the stage and screen. The foundation, which donates proceeds from sales of *The Diary of Anne Frank* to charities, says it is not about the money. Rather, they say, they want to protect Anne's legacy.

MOVIE NIGHT WITH RON AND NANCY

February 26, 2018

As two former actors transitioned to a new career, they never forgot their roots in cinema. Such is the story of former President and First Lady, Ronald and Nancy Reagan. Evening screenings at Camp David, where the bill of fare was 1980s celluloid, is the subject of a new book. The scribe is Mark Weinberg, a former aide to the president. It is published by Simon and Schuster.

Movie Nights with the Reagans: A Memoir is a fascinating yet seldom-told tale of the Aspen Movie Club, the most exclusive gathering of its kind. Many weekend evenings during the Reagan administration, its members appeared at 8:00 p.m. at Aspen Lodge, the presidential residence at Camp David, Maryland, to watch a flick. An evening included toothpicked meatballs and cocktail weaners, popcorn and a private screening room. Guests were staff and personal friends.

Surprisingly, the movies selected were the popular productions of an era, foreign to the type that featured the president or first lady years before. But the topicality of each film allowed the audience an opportunity to discuss

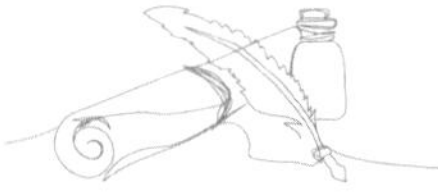

personal and professional issues of the day. Flicks selected included ***Red Dawn***, ***Ferris Bueller's Day Off***, ***Raiders of the Lost Ark***, ***9 to 5***, ***On Golden Pond***, ***The Untouchables*** and their singular favorite, ***Chariots of Fire***.

In all, the executive couple screened almost four hundred films in their eight years in Washington. And none featured a simian named *Bonzo*. In the final analysis, movies at Camp David offered the former actors the same kind of respite that most people seek in a dark theater.

JACKIE O'S NEW BOOK WILL FASCINATE

September 9, 2011

Jacqueline Kennedy: Historic Conversations on Life with John F. Kennedy is due out next week. The work is based on a series of interviews made by Arthur M. Schlesinger Jr. in 1964 and strictly sealed after they were conducted. Here is what literary critics are saying . . . "*Our modern-day Camelot continues to capture our imagination.*" Among recent revelations:

- John Kennedy and his attorney general (brother Robert F. Kennedy) openly shared their contempt over the premise of Vice President Lyndon Johnson's succession as the country's next chief executive. A game plan was presumably in the works by the siblings as early as 1962 to nix this strategy that was set forth by the Democratic National Committee for the election of 1968.

- Jackie initially believed the 1963 assassination of JFK was orchestrated by Johnson. She changed her opinion after LBJ wrote a series of notes to her expressing his personal sorrow and his concern for the former First Lady.

- Jackie and Bobby had a fling that would lead to an alleged affair, initiated by their mutual grief caused by the tragic events on November 22, 1963. It continued until his death in 1968. By a number of accounts, RFK's spouse (Ethel) was sadly aware of the situation.

The new work is set to be published by Hyperion Books on September 14. An introduction has been written by daughter Caroline Kennedy Schlossberg, who gave permission to release these candid interviews and produce a special to air on television. The availability of the Q&A coincides with the fiftieth anniversary of President Kennedy's inauguration.

GOSPEL ACCORDING TO CHARLTON HESTON

March 29, 2017

The actor best remembered for his biblical epics is the subject of a new literary biography. *Charlton Heston: Hollywood's Last Icon* chronicles the life of the Academy Award–winning star of ***Ben-Hur***. His friendship with director Cecil B. DeMille led to significant roles in ***The Greatest Show on Earth*** and ***The Ten Commandments***. Heston, who died in 2008, is credited for playing Moses. Actually, the part was offered after Marlon Brando and Rock Hudson turned down the assignment.

These films secured Heston as a motion picture star for the ages. Then followed ***Planet of the Apes***, sci-fi thrillers ***The Omega Man*** and ***Soylent Green*** and disaster movies such as ***Earthquake*** and ***Airport 1975***.

After serving as a radio gunner on B-25 combat missions during World War II, he made a strong impression in live television dramas. And by 1950, Heston had attracted the attention of movie moguls.

In 1961, Heston was among those protesting Oklahoma City's segregated restaurants. Two years later, studio execs and colleagues failed to talk him out of joining the Reverend Martin Luther King Jr.'s *March on Washington*. Heston was elected president of the Screen Actors Guild six times and opposed the cutting of federal funding for the arts. After the assassinations of King and Robert F. Kennedy, Charlton publicly backed the Gun Control Act of 1968.

Much like Ronald Reagan, Heston drifted from liberalism towards the conservative viewpoint. His late-in-life presidency of the National Rifle Association may have been a questionable decision, given the toll of gun-related deaths. But Heston viewed the right to own firearms in terms of liberty.

On a personal note, I sat in an audience to watch and enjoy Chuck Heston in a production of ***The Caine Mutiny Court-Martial.*** He was riveting, really, a terrific performance.

I expect the life of Charlton Heston will fly off the pages in his new biography.

And, so it goes . . .

Until next time . . . *never forget.*

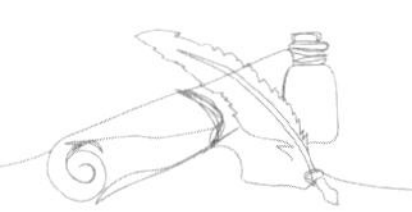

— CHAPTER THREE —

Panning for Gold

When you think of your favorite movie, do you cherish the memory that it evokes in you? It may not be a universal classic, such as ***Gone with the Wind*** or ***Citizen Kane***. However, in your mind, it holds up to any true gem. This chapter breaks out the pan and looks for celluloid nuggets, films that are never discussed by serious critics. But each goes well with popcorn and a big gulp. This was a celebrated twelve-part monthly blog series that highlighted *Forgotten Hollywood* films. All are explored in depth and critiqued.

—Virginia Vandewouwer

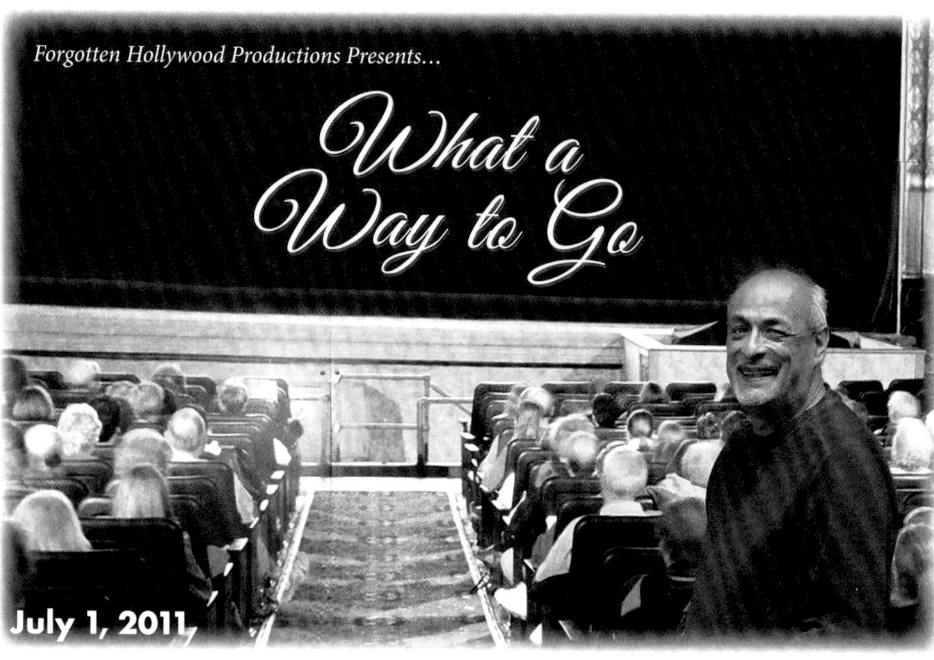

Manny P. here . . .

The script parodies the curse of a frustrated widow (of four husbands) in her search for a thrifty, humble life. She succeeds in inheriting gobs of money by offering seemingly innocent suggestions, which lead to each spouse's demise. The story is told as an amusing episodic flashback with every marriage presented as a homage to a Hollywood genre, including silent film slapstick, European imports and MGM musicals. It is an epic black comedy that was equally doomed with a problematic production history.

Back Story

Twentieth Century Fox yearned for a hit after the debacle of ***Cleopatra***. The studio wanted a big-budget success without cost overruns and overpayment to their stars. They also hoped for a splashy comeback opportunity for Marilyn Monroe. However, the actress tragically died of a drug overdose, leaving a promising script without a lead. Enter Shirley MacLaine, fresh from her triumph in ***The Apartment***.

Casting six male leads also became a major issue. Frank Sinatra wanted Elizabeth Taylor–type cash, Gregory Peck was unavailable and Paul Newman requested top billing, despite appearing in only 25 percent of the film. Robert Mitchum was adroitly chosen to replace Sinatra . . . Paul Newman finally accepted second billing . . . Gene Kelly, Dean Martin, Robert Cummings and Dick Van Dyke followed.

Unfortunately, critics would be less than charitable, citing the length of the motion picture as a main concern. Despite a star-studded effort, ***What a Way to Go*** did not dig Fox out of its budgetary woes.

Positives

Shirley MacLaine capably carried the motion picture. And Paul Newman and Robert Mitchum were surprisingly funny, showing great depth as comedians. Dick Van Dyke was more than able to mix pathos and humor, practically stealing the movie from the other cinematic stars. Add with his co-starring role in ***Mary Poppins***, the television icon solidified his weekly sitcom's popularity. Gene Kelly really shines in this picture. For years, the hoofer was miscast in a variety of dramas, such as ***Inherit the Wind***. Also, he was known as a diva (of sorts). This opportunity was a boost to the latter phase of his career. The musical number featuring Kelly and MacLaine reminds us of his previous work in ***Singing in the Rain*** and ***An American in Paris***.

Edith Head deservedly received an Oscar nod for the seventy-two costumes she placed on MacLaine. Had it not been the year of ***My Fair Lady***, Head surely would have won another statuette for her work.

Negatives

The opening sequence of ***What a Way to Go*** was weak. Dropping a coffin down a flight of stairs was, quite frankly, not funny. I also did not buy the manner in which Paul Newman was dismissed. But these are brief moments in a film loaded with believable slapstick humor.

Dean Martin proved to be a wooden anti-hero. He seemed to lose interest in the project once Sinatra was replaced. Martin's comedic delivery abandoned the singer-turned-actor. If Robert Mitchum and Dean Martin had traded assignments, I believe this picture might have been more satisfying, since Mitchum nurtured his career by playing enjoyable scoundrels. Unfortunately, he was the last actor cast, and it is unlikely this switch was ever considered. Also, Robert Cummings is given little to do as the recipient of each story told. His role as a psychiatrist seemed predictable and totally unworthy of his talent.

Epilogue

What a Way to Go was finally released on DVD in 2004, forty years after its initial release. The wildly cynical approach of the plot suits the mature nature of a baby boom audience that had to endure Watergate, the fall of Soviet Communism and the Wall Street explosion of the 1990s. Aside from ***It's a Mad, Mad, Mad, Mad World***, this is my favorite comedy of the decade.

This is a hilarious flick starring Robert Redford, George Segal and Zero Mostel. The simple premise of the plot . . . a group of bumbling thieves are determined to steal a valuable diamond (a number of times) for a price. The jewel will be returned to an undisclosed African country from where it was originally mined. The film is based upon Donald E. Westlake's novel, which introduces his long-running *Dortmunder* character. The jazz score was written by Quincy Jones.

Back Story

Twentieth Century Fox enjoyed enormous success with the 1969 release of ***Butch Cassidy and the Sundance Kid***. Redford emerged as a leading man in demand. The studio wanted to keep the actor busy on their own lot, despite the fact he was also working on ***Jeremiah Johnson*** and ***The Candidate*** for Warner Brothers. The robust script and great cast may have been pitch-perfect; however, ***The Hot Rock*** was popular only in the United Kingdom when released.

Positives

The picture was shot on location in New York, and the city really shines. Other films that appropriately showcase the unique qualities of Manhattan include ***The Out-of-Towners*** and ***The Taking of Pelham One Two Three***. A particularly funny scene takes place at the site where the World Trade Center was under construction.

Robert Redford plays against type as a quiet crook who suffers from ulcers. His comedic qualities were about to unfold in films like ***The Sting***, ***The Great Waldo Pepper*** and, later, ***Sneakers***. This film might have achieved greater success had it been released just a year later, when movie exhibitors voted Redford *Hollywood's top box-office name*. Fox was acutely aware of Redford's career. The opening scene of *Dortmunder*'s exit from prison was a homage to Butch Cassidy's real release from a Wyoming jail. A similar scene from the 1969 film had been edited from the script by director George Roy Hill.

On the other hand, George Segal was at the height of his career. His previous work on ***The Owl and the Pussycat*** and ***Where's Poppa?*** were well received. His New York accent and manic persona exudes the perfect contrast to Redford's slow burn.

Negatives

Unfortunately, a bit of the humor is lost by the real-life background noise of New York. The 1970s filmmakers were in love with the backdrop that location shooting offered. Dialogue could be the loser in this equation.

Epilogue

The Hot Rock started the movie life of *Dortmunder*. The character would be featured in at least five more motion pictures, including a German entry. This particular gem is worth renting. Film buffs will be quite surprised with how really good the episodic script works on every level. And each of the actors show the incredible depth of their talent.

This is a neo-classic Western starring Gene Hackman, Candice Bergen, James Coburn, Ben Johnson, Dabney Coleman, Jan Michael Vincent and Ian Bannen. It is often a main feature on the Encore Western's Channel.

Back Story

The movie was directed by Richard Brooks, who previously developed the screenplays for ***Key Largo*** and ***Elmer Gantry***. He also marvelously directed ***The Blackboard Jungle***, ***Cat on a Hot Tin Roof***, ***Sweet Bird of Youth*** and ***In Cold Blood***. ***Bite the Bullet*** is his forgotten nugget. The irony of the title . . . it references a toothache suffered by one of the characters, a Mexican ranchero, who covers an exposed nerve in his mouth with a bullet casing.

This movie chronicles a seven-hundred-mile cross-country horse race, based on actual events that took place in 1906. It also offers a parable about the treatment of horses in the Old West and in early cinema. The plot is filled with directed quips and rousing action that are well written and produced. Familiar quips include:

> *"I rather be in hell than in Oklahoma." . . . "Well, each man to his own country."*
>
> *"You sure don't know much" . . . "You're right, but I'm not the one who's lost."*
>
> *"Whiskey for me, beer for my horse."*

Positives

Charles Bronson was originally sought for the lead. Once he turned down the role, Gene Hackman accepted the part. Though he made relatively few Westerns in his career, Hackman is given top support with a colorful cast. Several of the actors really shine, particularly James Coburn, Ben Johnson and an unknown Mario Artaega as the caballero. Johnson and Artaega steal this film every time they are on camera. Candice Bergen also capably handles a very physical role as a contestant in the race.

Brooks takes the time to flesh out each character's story, allowing the audience to have a rooting interest in who should win or lose the race. And unlike Sam Peckinpah Westerns of the 1960s, the violence is not graphic. This picture could have been made decades earlier with Randolph Scott or Joel McCrea in the lead roles. The genius in the script is the way the favorite in the race is written as an insignificant character. Each of the other contestants have reasons why they could lose. Imagined or real, those reasons include bigotry, age and a lack of knowledge of the terrain. The individual shortcomings of each of the entrants make the actual competition quite compelling.

Negatives

Whether the Mexican lives or dies is not disclosed, which is a shame, since one grows to really like this character. Also, issues of a mountainous terrain are not addressed, probably since the movie was over two hours by the time the location is reached.

Dabney Coleman provides a comedic voice as a representative of the contest who has the favorite horse in the race. His part could have been expanded with a villainous edge to add further spice to the race. Coleman is great at playing louses, yet his career in 1975 had not fully blossomed. His role is relatively small and stereotyped as a shortsighted benefactor.

Epilogue

Bite the Bullet captures a glimpse of our nation entering the twentieth century, while still embracing the independent spirit of a previous age. There are references to Teddy Roosevelt and his *Rough Riders* and a love for national imperialism. The promotional material claims the picture is a cinematic throwback to our love of fine Westerns, such as **Shane** and **High Noon**. ***Hidalgo*** later paid homage to this jewel. And Gene Hackman would go on to win his second Oscar for his role in Clint Eastwood's ***Unforgiven*** in 1992, another fine Western.

Critics regard this science fiction drama one of the best of its genre during the 1950's, along with ***Invasion of the Body Snatchers*** and ***The Thing***. Remarkably, it may be the least mentioned. It pioneered the Cold War monster genre, later emulated by a countless number of B movies.

Back Story

The producers of this motion picture decided to cast this film with a talented group of character actors. The screenplay allowed the ensemble cast to shine in tense scenes. Warner Brothers wanted to create horror with a few black comedic elements (the approach initially developed decades earlier by Universal Studios). The movie studio also wanted audiences to believe they were going to see a film noir mystery and waited to shock viewers a full one-third into the flick. However, this is no gangster film. The villains in this piece are overgrown ants . . .

THEM!

Positives

Sandy Descher is not a household name as an actress. Yet this child star was key to the opening of ***THEM!*** Her catatonic look, followed by her screaming the title, set the terrorizing tone for the film.

The casting of James Whitmore as a local New Mexico police officer, Edmund Gwenn as an entomologist and James Arness as an FBI agent was inspired. Whitmore is overwhelmed by the concept of nuclear testing causing an unusual growth of insects.

Gwenn is so credible as an entomologist. As a youngster, I believed he was an expert in the field. Arness is a reliable love interest to the professor's daughter. This piece of science fiction has something for everyone.

Negatives

The demise of one its stars is very unsettling, considering how heroic he is throughout the movie. I do not want to give away who dies. I can tell you it is unbelievably tragic. This is fantasy, but his death was so unnecessary. BOO!

The other negative came as a result of the influence of ***THEM!*** Copycat filmmakers never lived up to the hype of mimicking this fine plot, its cast and the general production values. The genre, though currently popular with filmgoers, has been consistently compromised by creative folks in the industry.

Epilogue

Representatives of Disney Studios decided to hire Fess Parker to play *Davy Crockett* on television after viewing his small role in this film. John Wayne also went to check out ***THEM!*** *The Duke* later recommended James Arness to play *Marshal Matt Dillon* on **Gunsmoke**, crediting his previous cinematic performances. Leonard Nimoy, William Schallert, Dub Taylor and Richard Deacon all had small roles in this classic.

Members of the Academy of Motion Picture Arts and Sciences were impressed. They honored the movie with an Oscar nomination for Best Special Effects. Not bad for a bunch of giant mean-spirited bugs with an attitude . . .

Based on the Davis Grubb 1953 bestseller, this non-fiction thriller was a finalist for the 1955 National Book Award. The novel provides the scribe's account of *Harry Powers*'s story, who was executed in 1932 for murdering two widows and three children in Moundsville, West Virginia.

Back Story

First-time director Charles Laughton helped assemble a fabulous cast: Robert Mitchum, Shelley Winters, Lillian Gish, James Gleason and Peter Graves. Laughton was an Oscar-winning actor who starred in acclaimed motion pictures such as ***The Private Life of Henry VIII***, ***Mutiny on the Bounty*** and ***The Hunchback of Notre Dame***.

Laughton's goal was to create a visually stunning movie based on the European cinematic approaches of German Expressionism of the 1920s and visual metaphors developed by director Fritz Lang, combined with film noir that had been popular for a decade. He developed the elements important in modern thrillers, which inspired Hitchcock's ***Psycho***, ***Wait until Dark***, ***The Boston Strangler***, ***Rosemary's Baby*** and the screen adaptation of Truman Capote's ***In Cold Blood***. But ***The Night of the Hunter*** was not a success with either audiences or critics when initially released. Sadly, Charles Laughton never directed another picture.

Positives

Laughton achieved his directorial goals in his use of biblical themes, which were effectively referenced by his cast. Camera angles were intentionally distorted, and the music score used was haunting. And the screenplay was a fabulous collaboration by Laughton and James Agee.

Robert Mitchum always felt this was his best screen role. He was correct. His menacing approach was alternately playful and frightening. Mitchum exudes confidence in his portrayal, delivering bitter patience while searching for a hidden fortune. Burt Lancaster later mimicked elements of Mitchum's character in ***Elmer Gantry***. The children, portrayed by Billy Chapin and Sally Jane Bruce, produced physically successful performances while playing opposite their adult counterparts. They just about steal the movie from Mitchum, who knew how to command a scene.

Negatives

The Night of the Hunter was a blueprint in the development of modern filmmaking. Quite frankly, the movie was ahead of its time. The complicated camera techniques were second only to what Orson Welles accomplished in ***Citizen Kane***. Audiences were just not prepared for the director's approach, which was the main reason for its lukewarm reception. Looking back, the reaction might have been more of a glimpse at the lack of sophistication by audiences of the day. Or the political climate generated by McCarthyism and the Cold War might have created the desire for a more positive cinematic experience. Charles Laughton should have had a respected resume as a director. Instead, he glumly returned to acting. Filmgoers during Hollywood's Golden Age were the losers for this decision.

Epilogue

Charles Laughton's final acting assignments included roles in ***Witness for the Prosecution*** (an Oscar nomination followed), ***Spartacus*** and ***Advise and Consent***. He was happily married to Elsa Lanchester for thirty-three years. The actor died in 1962.

The American Film Institute and the Library of Congress are among the prestigious organizations that eventually lavished praise on this memorable motion picture. David Lynch, Martin Scorsese, Spike Lee and the Coen Brothers are among today's directors who say they have been influenced by the majesty of ***The Night of the Hunter***. *Harry Powell's* LOVE/HATE tattoos on his knuckles are still considered visually iconic, with creative homage provided by Dan Ackroyd in ***The Blues Brothers*** and referenced in ***The Rocky Horror Picture Show*** and ***The Silence of the Lambs***.

Inspired by the biggest-selling holiday song in modern history, this 1954 Technicolor production, gift wrapped in tinsel, stars Bing Crosby, Danny Kaye, Rosemary Clooney, Vera-Ellen and Dean Jagger. This was the first film to be presented in the wide-screen format, *Vista Vision*, and it was directed by Michael Curtiz, best known for ***The Adventures of Robin Hood*** and ***Casablanca***.

Back Story

Why do I include the top grossing film of 1954 in a series dedicated to forgotten cinematic classics? Over the years, this movie has been shoved aside by television's decision to repeatedly air ***Miracle on 34th Street*** and ***It's a Wonderful Life***. And every year, gobs of new holiday fare grace our movie palaces. As generations pass, ***White Christmas*** has become the ignored classic.

Bing Crosby deserves a better fate. His name is associated with other Christmas carols, including *Do You Hear What I Hear?* and *Peace on Earth/Little Drummer Boy* (sung with David Bowie). Bing WAS Christmas for Americans during Hollywood's Golden Age. And *Count Your Blessings Instead of Sheep* from the film (written by Irving Berlin) was nominated for an Oscar. In fact, Berlin wrote all the tunes for ***White Christmas***. The title-tune actually received a statuette for Best Song in 1942 when it was featured in ***Holiday Inn***.

This delight also features cameos by George Chakiris, Barry Chase and Johnny Grant (the former mayor of Hollywood), and oddly, Carl *Alfalfa* Switzer's photo is used. Originally cast in the film was Fred Astaire, who declined after reading the script. Donald O'Connor replaced Astaire but bowed out due to illness. Danny Kaye was then called, and he accepted the role.

Positives

The teaming of Crosby and Kaye was inspired. This film had a *Road Picture* feel to it. But Danny Kaye is a better dancer and singer, if not funnier, than Bob Hope. Rosemary Clooney performs like an edgy June Allyson. And who does not love her voice when she sings! Vera-Ellen was handed dance routines reminiscent of sequences made famous by Cyd Charisse. Dean Jagger steals the film with a warm authoritative style as a retired general.

The script harkened back to those wonderful moments in Busby Berkeley and Mickey Rooney/Judy Garland motion pictures that set up musical segments on stage. Light drama mixed in with comedy make this a yearly pilgrimage for me (I own a copy of the DVD).

Negatives

Surprisingly, many of the tunes in ***White Christmas*** share little relationship with the holidays, which hurts the production. Two numbers: *Choreography* and *What Can You Do with a General* are weak efforts by the team of Irving Berlin and Bob Fosse. Berlin made the unfortunate decision to dust off former hits from his collection and insert them into this movie. That said, the highlight of the motion picture score comes early with Crosby and Kaye lip-synching *Sisters* and the four main stars singing *Snow*.

Epilogue

A stage adaptation of the musical, Irving Berlin's ***White Christmas***, premiered in San Francisco in 2004 and has been booked in various venues around the United States, including Boston, Buffalo, Los Angeles, Detroit and Louisville. Another version of this production has played to sold-out houses throughout Great Britain.

I endorse taking in as much holiday entertainment as possible. Do not forget to add ***White Christmas*** and ***How the Grinch Stole Christmas*** (the animated television production with Boris Karloff and Thurl Ravenscroft) on your to-watch list.

A movie musical from Samuel Goldwyn, ***Hans Christian Andersen*** is truly a lost gem. It is even forgotten by lovers of Danny Kaye motion pictures and fans of the music of Frank Loesser. Yet, back in 1952, this motion picture was a sensation. It grabbed six Oscar nominations, and generations of kids grew up loving the fables of the Danish storyteller. His heartwarming tales *Thumbelina, The Ugly Duckling* and *Inch Worm* put his village of Copenhagen on the map.

Back Story

Danny Kaye was Sam Goldwyn's golden boy. His movies during the 1940s were among the most lucrative for the studio. With Virginia Mayo, he co-starred in ***Wonder Man***, ***The Kid from Brooklyn***, ***The Secret Life of Walter Mitty*** and ***A Song Is Born***. In 1952, Goldwyn decided a fictional fantasy about the remarkable Dane should only be played by Danny Kaye. This piece of cinema was never intended to be an accurate biography.

Positives

Sam Goldwyn chose Frank Loesser as the composer for ***Hans Christian Andersen***. Fresh from his triumph on Broadway with ***Guys and Dolls***, Loesser was at the top of his game. His lyrics fit the comedic song stylings of Danny Kaye. Moss Hart was a top playwright who was brought in to write the screenplay. His credits include ***You Can't Take It with You*** (which won a Pulitzer Prize), ***The Man Who Came to Dinner***, ***Gentleman's Agreement*** and the 1954 production of ***A Star is Born***. Because he wrote Broadway shows, his magical words suited this particular production.

Negatives

Goldwyn failed to hire known actors to support Danny Kaye, with the exception of Farley Granger and John Qualen. Since Kaye was in most scenes, the script crackled. However, the motion picture does not get due credit by today's critics, mostly because of the uninspired performances by the supporting players. Additionally, the choreography falls flat when compared to the music and lyrics. The ballet sequences get in the way of the plot. By comparison, the operatic scenes during ***A Night at the Opera*** with the Marx Brothers really complement the dichotomy of the comedy, and it remains a bona fide classic.

Epilogue

Danny Kaye was knighted by Queen Margrethe II of Denmark in 1983 for his portrayal of *Hans Christian Andersen*, high praise for the unique comedian. He also received numerous honors, mostly for his unyielding work for UNICEF, including the *Jean Hersholt Humanitarian Award* from the Academy of Motion Picture Arts and Sciences in 1981 and a Kennedy Center Honor. Kaye received the French Legion of Honor (Chevalier de la Légion d'Honneur) in 1986. He was posthumously bestowed the Presidential Medal of Freedom, the highest civilian honor. UNICEF's New York Visitor's Center was renamed to pay tribute to Danny Kaye. He should be remembered for his amazing talent and his unparalleled contributions to humanity. For an instant, he also allowed us to enjoy the simple stories of a Danish cobbler.

One of the finest films ever made with a really lousy title. Starring Walter Matthau, Robert Shaw, Martin Balsam, James Broderick, Jerry Stiller, Hector Elizondo and Tony Roberts, this action-comedy-thriller was the forerunner of the ***Die Hard*** and ***Lethal Weapon*** series of movies; plus, it spawned a 2009 high-tech remake (with a slight change in the title—***The Taking of Pelham 123***), featuring John Travolta and Denzel Washington.

Back Story

Most of the film was produced on location with the cooperation of the New York Metropolitan Transportation Authority and Mayor John Lindsay. An insurance policy was taken out in case someone got a similar idea to hijack a subway train. Only then, the green light was given to produce this motion picture. Critics loved the film for the bureaucratic nature of the heroes, which provided a convincing contrast to trigger-happy villains. Particularly realistic was the banter between Matthau, Stiller and Shaw.

Positives

This project made Walter Matthau a star. He emerged from the shadow of Jack Lemmon and others. His career flourished for the rest of his life. And due to the massive success of ***The Sting*** and ***Jaws***, Robert Shaw became an A-list rugged actor who could elevate the quality of any movie. He was appropriately menacing in ***Pelham***.

The casting was pinpoint perfect. Every character looks like they have spent their entire lives in Manhattan, Brooklyn or Queens. Except for ***The French Connection*** and ***Dog Day Afternoon***, no production made during this time was more effective in the use of location filming.

Negatives

The David Shire–score was critically acclaimed for its raw, in-your-face quality in 1974. By today's standards, it remains really dated. The composer was married to actress Talia Shire, and she openly influenced his work.

Unfortunately, stereotypes of Asians, African Americans, Latinos and Jews are used to facilitate the comedy. It was not necessary, but this type of humor was typical in scripts during this era.

Epilogue

The Writer's Guild of America awarded The ***Taking of Pelham One Two Three*** a well-deserved nomination in 1975. The 2009 remake confirmed that filmmakers were paying attention.

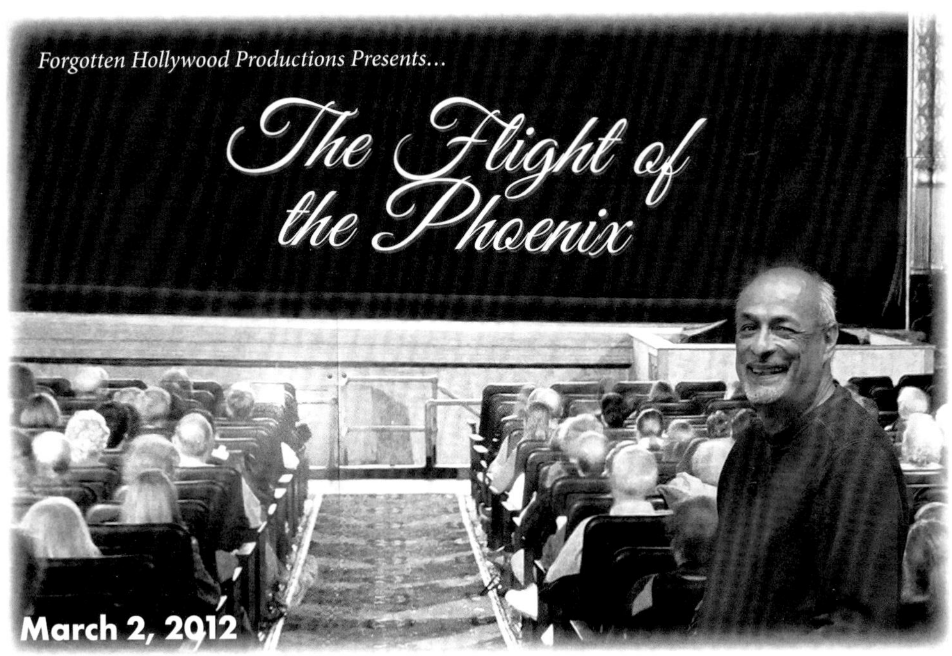

In the tradition of male-dominated motion pictures from the studio era (***The Lost Patrol***, ***She Wore a Yellow Ribbon***, ***Sahara***), this features a stellar cast, a disaster-genre subplot and a bizarre twist in the screenplay's conclusion. When film critics list the fine roles of James Stewart, ***The Flight of the Phoenix*** is often omitted. Richard Attenborough, Peter Finch, Dan Duryea, Hardy Kruger, George Kennedy, Ernest Borgnine and Ian Bannen co-star.

Back Story

The Flight of the Phoenix is based on a 1964 novel by Elleston Trevor. The plot involved the crash landing of a transport plane in the middle of the North African desert. Studios immediately conducted a bidding war for the rights to the book. Twentieth Century Fox developed the vehicle with the intent to create the kind of gritty movie made in the 1950s, involving the collaborative efforts between James Stewart and director Anthony Mann. While audiences enjoyed the exercise, critics found the adventure story unrealistic.

Positives

The ensemble cast was ably directed by Robert Aldrich. His career included strong stark films such as ***Vera Cruz***, ***Kiss Me Deadly***, ***What Ever Happened to Baby Jane?***, ***Hush . . . Hush, Sweet Charlotte*** and, later, ***The Dirty Dozen*** and ***The Longest Yard***. This ideal script was handed to Aldrich in 1965.

The brilliance of making one of the heroes a German engineer in contrast with Americans and British soldiers cannot be denied. Hardy Kruger was up to the task. His character's solution of applying the concept of flight from a toy glider to the rebuilding of a wrecked aircraft was delicious. The relationship between Stewart and Kruger creates an inevitable conflict. The other actors (particularly Richard Attenborough) then react over a cultural war of wills. They ultimately develop into a cohesive team. Without a doubt, Hardy Kruger steals this film.

Negatives

The downing of the plane (a Fairchild C-82A Packet) was problematic. Director Aldrich insisted on multiple takes to get the perfect crash. One of the last takes, which is used in the movie, caused the death of legendary stunt flyer Paul Mantz. The accident haunted James Stewart throughout the filming because he had lost a personal friend.

This motion picture is over two hours long, allowing the director to flesh out each role. If only twenty minutes shorter, ***The Flight of the Phoenix*** might have presented far crisper scenes. Dream sequences created an avenue for women to be cast in the flick, but they really do not advance the plot.

Epilogue

The idea of doing this film intrigued James Stewart, a brigadier general in the United States Air Force. He flew combat missions in 1944 and was appointed operations officer of the 453rd Bomb Group and, subsequently, chief of staff of the Second Combat Wing, Second Air Division of the Eighth Air Force. He completed twenty bombings and remained in the USAF Reserve.

The German public appreciated the role played by Hardy Kruger, which might have helped thaw United States/Germany relations. Bitterness still existed because of postwar trials in Nuremberg that tangentially indicted the entire *Fatherland*; plus, there were constant reminders of the Holocaust in Hollywood scripts involving World War II. Kruger was humble, appropriately suggesting he was just doing his job. This piece of celluloid remains an important contribution to filmmaking as a global experience.

By 1965, Stanley Kramer was an accomplished producer and director. ***Ship of Fools*** is his forgotten classic. A cross-section of international folks aboard an ocean liner in the pre-war era plays out in a drawing-room drama. The undercurrent of a toxic doctrine brainwashing entire countries in Europe, including Italy, Spain and Germany, is at the heart of the plot. It was adapted by Abby Mann from the only major novel written by Katherine Anne Porter.

Back Story

The collaboration of Stanley Kramer and Abby Mann worked well in 1961 when they adapted ***Judgment at Nuremburg***. That motion picture won an Oscar for Best Adapted Screenplay. Mann was the obvious choice to flesh out characters played by Vivien Leigh, Lee Marvin, Jose Ferrer, Simone Signoret, Oskar Werner, George Segal, Elizabeth Ashley and Michael Dunn. The script emerged as a winner.

Katharine Hepburn was originally asked to star but turned it down as she was attending to the declining health of Spencer Tracy. Kramer obliged since he was a close friend of the couple and turned to Vivien Leigh.

Positives

Though the epic motion picture was beaten by ***The Sound of Music*** for Best Picture, the performances of Michael Dunn, Oskar Werner and Simone Signoret made their Oscar races quite compelling. Dunn lost to Martin Balsam in ***A Thousand Clowns***, Signoret lost to Julie Christie in ***Darling*** and Werner was beaten by Lee Marvin (his co-star) for a dual-role in ***Cat Ballou***.

Abby Mann really ignited foolish behavior among strangers as they intermingled in various conversations. Using Michael Dunn, a dwarf, to set up the opening segment was brilliant. His apparent disability is dwarfed by the not-so-obvious psychological disabilities of his fellow passengers. The casual pace of each scene also allows for appropriate character development.

Negatives

The Axis overtones are a little over-the-top. Conversations involving Michael Dunn were believable and poignant. His prophecy of the Nazi *Final Solution* enjoyed the benefit of scripted hindsight. Less honest was Jose Ferrer's uber-fascist propaganda. It beats the viewer up, and his revelation that his character is not German predictably parallels the well-documented psychosis of *Der Fuehrer*.

Like Harper Lee (***To Kill a Mockingbird***), Katherine Anne Porter won major accolades for her only novel in 1962. Its success gave the scribe financial security but deprived her readers from enjoying any future major literary works. She spent the remainder of her career writing short stories. This fact is a real shame.

Epilogue

This was the last film made by Vivien Leigh, a fitting finale. And ***Ship of Fools*** made major stars of George Segal, Lee Marvin and Werner Klemperer; the latter was cast in television's ***Hogan's Heroes***. Michael Dunn garnered a villainous recurring role on ***The Wild Wild West***.

More importantly, ***Ship of Fools*** reminds audiences that a negative political climate can generate globally disastrous consequences. In the capable hands of Stanley Kramer, this point was adroitly made.

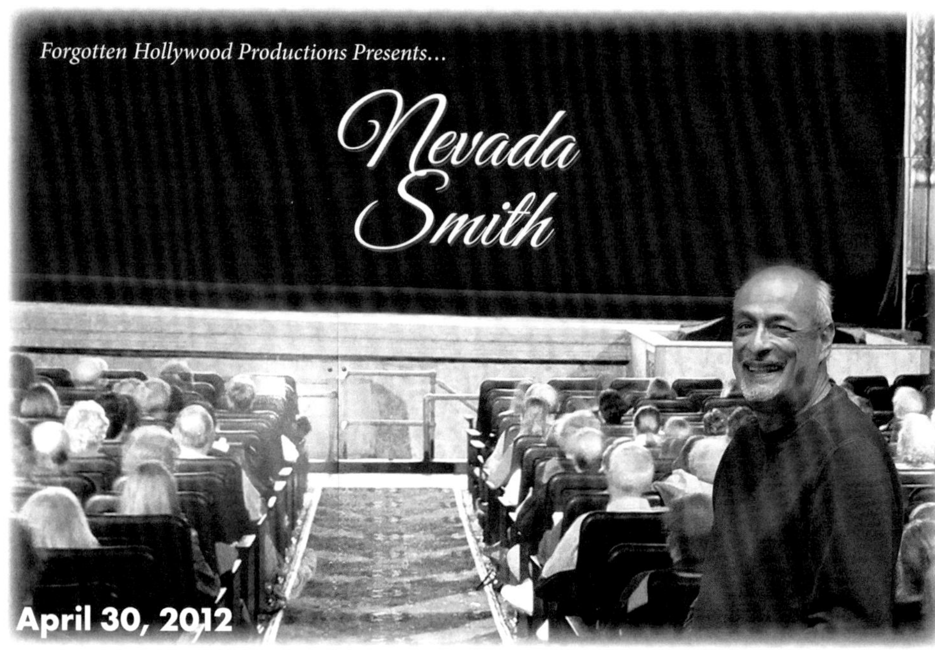

Like ***Bite the Bullet***, this is a forgotten Western. The motion picture was a prequel to ***The Carpetbaggers***, Alan Ladd playing an older version of the main character. The story was based on the Harold Robbins 1961 novel. The plot-line of the movie was drawn from an actual 1960 comic book, *The Rawhide Kid*, inked by Jack Kirby (known for his work with Marvel Comics).

Back Story

Respected director Henry Hathaway had a long career in the silent era and during Hollywood's Golden Age. He discovered Randolph Scott and worked with John Wayne, Marlene Dietrich, Gary Cooper and Marilyn Monroe. Hathaway received his only Oscar nomination in 1935 for ***The Lives of a Bengal Lancer***. Other films in his career include ***The Dark Corner***, ***North to Alaska***, ***The Sons of Katie Elder***, ***True Grit*** and ***Airport***.

Nevada Smith featured a remarkable cast: Steve McQueen, Karl Malden, Arthur Kennedy, Suzanne Pleshette, Brian Keith, Martin Landau, Howard da Silva, Pat Hingle and Raf Vallone. Paramount Pictures brought in Alfred Newman to write the fabulous score.

Positives

On the heels of ***The Great Escape***, ***Love with a Proper Stranger*** and ***The Cincinnati Kid***, ***Nevada Smith*** was released around the same time as ***The Sand Pebbles***. When voted by film fans, Steve McQueen emerged as the most popular actor by the end of 1966.

Nevada Smith was presented in an episodic format. McQueen's character, *Max Sand*, seeks revenge for the murder of his folks. The most compelling scene was the chain-gang segment, and it featured really strong performances from Kennedy, Pleshette, da Silva and Hingle. The evolution of *Max Sand* from a vengeful son to a responsible adult with some measure of peace with his life was crafted quite well in the screenplay.

Negatives

Nevada Smith was made under a cloud of Alan Ladd's apparent suicide in 1964. The coroner ruled his death an accident due to alcohol and drugs, though he had previously tried a number of times to kill himself. Alan Ladd played an older *Nevada Smith* (*Max Sand*) in ***The Carpetbaggers*** but died prior to its release.

More time could have been spent in the development of characters played by Landau, Keith and Malden, since they were such respected actors. Due to the length of the film, this was just not possible. I assume great performances were left on the cutting-room floor.

Epilogue

Harold Robbins is the fifth most successful author of all time. He wrote over twenty-five amazing novels, selling over 750 million copies in thirty-two languages. In 1966, Henry Hathaway was at the autumn of his career. He is remembered for steady work for almost half a century. On the other hand, Iron Eyes Cody, Strother Martin and a young Loni Anderson have cameo parts in this film. None received screen credit.

Steve McQueen became the highest paid actor when cast in ***The Towering Inferno***, and he remains a popular star. His estate limits licensing his image to avoid commercial saturation experienced by other deceased celebrities.

Consequently, ***Nevada Smith*** is an appropriate contribution to the modern American Western, thanks to the collaborative efforts of Robbins, Hathaway and McQueen.

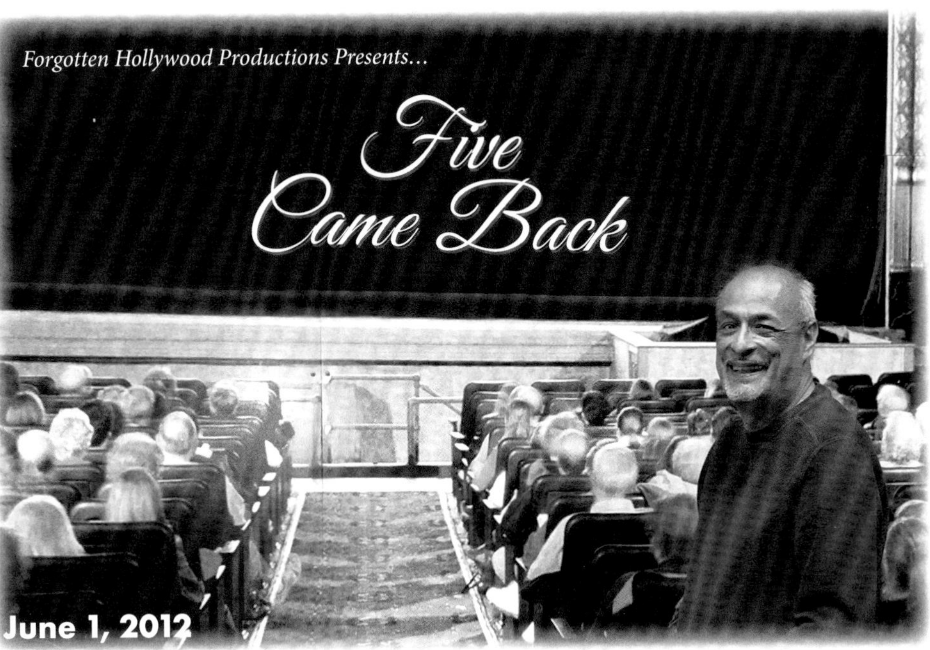

The last forgotten classic gem in my twelve-part series is also the oldest production. ***Five Came Back*** was released in the golden year of 1939. RKO Studios may have been part of *Poverty Row*, but actors such as Katharine Hepburn and Cary Grant made fine films at this lot.

Back Story

This B movie was a pioneering flick in the disaster genre. The biggest moneymakers in cinema were unabashedly influenced by this motion picture. Essentially an ensemble cast, the film featured great character actors in starring roles, including Chester Morris, Wendy Barrie, Patric Knowles, John Carradine, Allen Jenkins, Joseph Calleia, C. Aubrey Smith and, remarkably, Lucille Ball.

The script was co-written by the future acclaimed and maligned screenplay scribe Dalton Trumbo. Director John Farrow is best known for his work on ***Wake Island*** and ***Hondo*** and as the screenwriter for ***Around the World in Eighty Days***. His wife was actress Maureen O'Sullivan and his daughter is Mia Farrow.

Positives

The cast is magnificent . . . Lucille Ball, John Carradine, Patric Knowles and, especially, Joseph Calleia. As an anarchist, Calleia is a prototype of the anti-hero later popular in the 1950s. Patric Knowles, usually cast in heroic roles (***The Adventures of Robin Hood***, ***The Wolfman***, ***The Charge of the Light Brigade***), played against type, which showcased his acting ability. This guaranteed a long career for the credible co-star.

The title of the film is also quite glib. The audience can easily figure out who will survive this plane crash. However, the melodramatic demise of certain characters guarantees to keep you at the edge of your seat. The words on the scripted page are really a strength.

Negatives

Making an anarchist an anti-hero would come back to haunt Dalton Trumbo. Anarchists were known throughout American history in the disruption of our free society. In 1901, President William McKinley was assassinated by an anarchist. The government's creation of the Federal Bureau of Investigation was in response to anarchist bombings in our nation's capital. The anarchist character in ***Five Came Back*** was cited by the House Un-American Activities Committee as evidence that Trumbo's politics lay in the American Communist Party.

The paranoia of our country did not allow the anti-hero in scripts to thrive. Other movies faced the same fate as they were pulled from theatres. The 1948 ***We Were Strangers*** comes to mind as an unfortunate example. The billing of Joseph Calleia was pitiful. He steals this film from his peers. Sixth billing is an insult to his performance and his character development in the script.

Epilogue

The real treat of ***Five Came Back*** is the historic early work of the great Lucille Ball. Despite an uneven cinematic career, elements of her comedic ability are in full display in 1939. ***I Love Lucy*** on celluloid!

The High and the Mighty, ***The Flight of the Phoenix*** and the **Airport** series of films owe a debt of gratitude to Dalton Trumbo's script, John Farrow's direction and the fine ensemble cast that appeared in ***Five Came Back***. Farrow remade the film in 1956, calling it ***Back to Eternity***. This original motion picture should be considered in the pantheon of great releases during that magic year of 1939.

Until next time . . . *never forget.*

— CHAPTER FOUR —

Shop and Compare

We often watch movies and think to ourselves, *"What would it have been like to have a different actor or a different character in that part?"* This occurs while reading books. You become aware of the vast possibilities. We find ourselves comparing aspects of a movie around the water cooler or while bending an elbow at our local pub with friends and strangers. This chapter takes well-known movies and their stars and compares the similarities and differences. After reading this section, you may want to re-examine some of these films and develop new and different points of view. At any rate, this should be a lot of fun!

~ Virginia Vandewouwer

SHOWSTOPPERS

December 18, 2017

Manny P. here . . .

The opening scene in ***La La Land*** is an absolute showstopper in the tradition of cinematic musicals. This made me ponder about the finest showstopping ensemble moments in iconic productions. Here are some personal favorites:

- *Who Will Buy?*/**Oliver!** – What starts as a simple moment involving a woman selling flowers becomes a massive piece that includes hundreds of singers, dancers and extras. All are performing at the pleasure of the title character, played by Mark Lester. A quintessential showstopping scene!

- *Tradition*/***Fiddler on the Roof*** – This is the finest opening number until ***La La Land***, and it introduces the entire troupe, including *Tevye*, portrayed by Chaim Topol (*left*). This wonderful musical was directed by Norman Jewison. It concludes with an intimate violin solo by the great Isaac Stern. The premise of the plot unfolds in the first five minutes.

- *Tonight*/***West Side Story*** – The entire cast needs no choreography for this number. All of the main characters simply sing variations on the theme, and it blends like a thousand-piece jigsaw puzzle. *America* and *Gee, Officer Krupke* are fine honorable mentions.

- *Luck Be a Lady*/***Guys and Dolls*** – Frank Sinatra had the recorded hit tune. But Marlon Brando anchors a memorable moment in the movie that takes place in a sewer. The backdrop is sensational. It is amazing what one pair of dice can spark.

- *Shipoopi*/***The Music Man*** – This is the only number that primarily features Buddy Hackett. The choreography replicates work done by Busby Berkeley. To be fair, this is one musical that has several showstoppers, such as *Ya Got Trouble (part 2)/Seventy-Six Trombones*.

- *I'm Getting Married in the Morning*/***My Fair Lady*** – Stanley Holloway as *Alfred P. Doolittle* in the one big number late in the production. Showstoppers traditionally showcase a co-star, and this guilty pleasure is no exception.

- *Cell Block Tango*/***Chicago*** – This recent entry pays homage to the choreography inspired by Bob Fosse. The scene is told in episodic moments that simply begins with a leaky faucet. It first appeared in the 1975 Broadway show that featured Chita Rivera.

WHAT'S IN A NAME?

August 27, 2018

William Shakespeare once surmised in ***Romeo and Juliet . . .*** *"A rose by any other name would smell as sweet."* Character names in cinema are one of the many delights when a scribe places pen to paper. Here are three iconic examples of screenplay creations, with names that resonate in motion pictures . . . and beyond.

- *Eric Von Zipper* – The *Beach Party* series of films was a vehicle for Frankie Avalon and Annette Funicello and an acquired taste from the mind of Samuel Z. Arkoff at American International Pictures. These flicks feature scantily dressed all-American young adults and collections of character actors put in dumb situations, including Buster Keaton, Don Rickles, Boris Karloff, Bob Cummings, Morey Amsterdam, Buddy Hackett, Keenan Wynn, Paul Lynde and Mickey Rooney.

  Most successful of the cameos was Harvey Lembeck, a looney guy on screen; never mind that he was immensely talented. He portrayed the head of a motorcycle gang, who was the antithesis of the surfer heroes. The *Von Zipper* character was a parody of Marlon Brando's role in ***The Wild One***. Lembeck made these beach movies palatable.

- *Pussy Galore* – *James Bond* films pushed the hedonistic envelope. The villain's moll in ***Goldfinger*** had a name that might cause one to blush when uttered. Honor Blackman assumed the role with confidence. Her appearance coincided with The Beatles *British Invasion* and an end of youthful innocence after the assassination of President John F. Kennedy.

  Amazingly, *Galore* first was mentioned in the 1959 novel written by Ian Fleming. Easily, the most memorable *Bond Girl* name, *Galore* was almost cut from ***Goldfinger*** by censors.

- *Liberty Valance* – John Ford had a passion for the grandeur of frontier life. In ***The Man Who Shot Liberty Valance***, the producer and director adapted the screenplay from a short story, with one major stroke . . . the characters are given splashy names, such as *Ransom Stoddard, Tom Doniphon, Dutton Peabody, Link Appleyard* and *Cassius Starbuckle.*

  Liberty Valance is the illustrious center of this sagebrush saga, the villain played by Lee Marvin. His character inspired a 1962 hit tune performed by Gene Pitney. It was written by Burt Bacharach and Hal David.

Honorable mentions: *Eulalie Mackechnie Shinn* (Hermione Gingold in ***The Music Man***) and *Ratso Rizzo* (Dustin Hoffman in ***Midnight Cowboy***).

MISTAKEN IDENTITY

February 17, 2016

Famous screen characters in cinema are considered culturally iconic. What if characterizations lead to a series of films that have little to do with the initial fare? The urban legend lives on through generations of moviegoers. Consider three examples during Hollywood's Golden Age.

- ***Frankenstein*** – *Baron Frankenstein* was the creator of the tall creature that terrorized Eastern European hamlets and, in one instance, the American home of Abbott and Costello. His son, also named *Frankenstein,* would revive the fiend.

Other mad scientists kept the franchise alive for almost two decades. But *Frankenstein* and his offspring were not played by Boris Karloff, Bela Lugosi, Lon Chaney Jr., Glenn Strange or Peter Boyle; they were portrayed by Colin Clive, Basil Rathbone and Gene Wilder! By the way, the genetically man-made monster was actually named *Adam*.

- ***The Thin Man*** – *Nick Charles,* the posh detective, was fleshed out in the writings of Dashiell Hammett. The first in the series of flicks paired William Powell with Myrna Loy (*Nora Charles*). The initial movie was directed by W. S. Van Dyke in 1934 and earned Powell an Oscar nod. *Nick Charles* was not *The Thin Man*. He is actually the character the detective is initially hired to find. In cinema, he also became the first victim in the series. The actor caught by Nick and Nora at the end of the mystery was the ubiquitous Porter Hall. Each subsequent sequel had *The Thin Man* in the title, just to sell movie tickets.

- ***The Pink Panther*** – *Inspector Clouseau* was the bumbling detective forever in search of *The Pink Panther*. Peter Sellers perfected the role of the cagey law-enforcement boob in a number of movies. It is just *The Pink Panther* was not a jewel thief, a British royal or, even, an animated character; rather, it was the nickname of a really gaudy diamond. The erudite criminal known as *The Phantom* was elegantly presented by David Niven.

THE RESEMBLANCE IS STRIKING

January 10, 2018

The common wisdom is today's actors do not match up to stars of Hollywood's Golden Age. When I make comparisons, modern headliners offer favorable similarities. Here are my Top Ten:

1. Tom Hanks/James Stewart – This is one comparison frequently mentioned. With age, Hanks has developed an edge, much as Stewart did in his later career. Who could not see Hanks befriending an invisible rabbit? Stable marriages additionally enhance their popularity.

2. Daniel Day-Lewis/Paul Muni – Muni meticulously prepared for roles as he became invisible on screen. He also stepped away from his career at various times. Day-Lewis is a respected actor and adopted this method-approach that Muni perfected.

3. Ralph Fiennes/Laurence Olivier – Both are comfortable in starring parts, as well as character roles in support of the storyline. Fiennes has the style, grace and talent of his predecessor. One more thing . . . the pair could excel in villainy with aplomb.

4. Kevin Costner/Henry Fonda – They were realistic on the prairie and within the confines of the Oval Office. Comedic and dramatic opportunities are no issue for Costner, nor for Fonda. The fabric of America suits these screen icons. Either wears plain-spoken heroism well.

5. Gene Hackman/Spencer Tracy – You accept each of their characters, and this makes them the best in the business. Clark Gable once called Spence *"an actor's actor."* Hackman could be described as such. Both were two-time Oscar-winners, and both should have won gobs more.

6. Al Pacino/James Cagney – Ferocity best describes the approach of these two giants of cinema. They portrayed criminals you want to root for. There exists this fatalism in their eyes that transcends the body of their work, making them kindred spirits.

7. Michael Keaton/Jack Lemmon – They are at their best equally handling comedy and drama with total ease. Tragic turns have wonderfully funny moments. Each gives the audience a full spectrum of emotions with deceptive range.

8. Jeff Bridges/Clint Eastwood – Bridges can deliver a performance without uttering a word. John Wayne's bravado was too chatty; Gary Cooper had too much of an aw-shucks attitude. Eastwood's silence sets a scene with such command. So this comparison is more appropriate.

9. Robert De Niro/Edward G. Robinson – It is natural to compare De Niro to Humphrey Bogart. However, De Niro is a fine comedian, and his approach better resembles Robinson. Additionally, the two have been pretty remarkable gangsters.

10. George Clooney/Cary Grant – Both are incredibly good looking. However, this belies their undeniable talent. They are willing to play against type. Plus, Clooney's and Grant's on-screen personas markedly differ from their real-life personalities.

Your thoughts?

THE LANGUAGE OF CINEMA

December 30, 2017

Hollywood's Golden Age has a language all its own. I find myself using this unique form of communication in everyday life. Often, I get looks of confusion. But at the end of the day, it serves my purpose. And it sure beats the insane notion of texting emojis as a means of conversation.

Writer Damon Runyon was taken by the romance of real-life gangsterism in popular culture. The crimes of John Dillinger, Bonnie and Clyde, Al Capone, among others, fascinated common folks in the throes of the Great Depression. The criminal plots in cinema made stars of James Cagney, Edward G. Robinson, Humphrey Bogart and Paul Muni. Plus, Warner Brothers was THE studio that squarely tackled societal ills.

Runyon-esque was born from the pen of Damon Runyon, who forged a polite society of gangsters with a language that was peculiar and kind. ***Lady for a Day*** and ***Guys and Dolls*** were among celluloid adaptations contritely utilizing this basis of conversation to advance a narrative. The productions humanized the criminal, if not their crimes. Runyon, who died in 1946, would never live long enough to experience the phenomenon of ***The Godfather*** trilogy, the modern glamorization of a crime family. It is the *Runyon* in me that makes me courteous to a fault, even while directly dressing down an individual. There is little reason to curse in my lexiconic sphere.

But I digress. I find that using the language of cinema helps get me through a day filled with success and setback, wonder and banality, laughter and tears.

Here are quotes I often use:

- *"Another banner day at the Bailey Building and Loan."*

  A potential accusation of embezzlement is the last straw for *George Bailey* in ***It's a Wonderful Life***. It is urban legend that James Stewart uttered this beauty while contemplating suicide after an unexplained disappearance of cash. I often make the comment when things are not going my way or if I am caught in an embarrassing act. The actual quote: *"Another red-letter day for the Baileys!"*

- *"I'm shocked, shocked, to find that gambling is going on in here."*

  Everybody has friends who predictably let you down. When they do, it is not shocking; it is annoying. The Claude Rains's quote feigns contempt. Truth be told, it is simple sarcasm in a movie filled with quotable snark—***Casablanca***.

- *"Even a man who is pure in heart and says his prayers at night may become a wolf when the wolf bane blooms and the autumn moon is bright."*

  A human being is fallible. This theme is articulated a number of times by characters played by Evelyn Ankers, by Maria Ouspenskaya and, again, by Claude Rains in ***The Wolfman***. Consider it a worthy aside to mutter to yourself during an inevitable moment of weakness.

Thank you Strother Martin for a paraphrase of a comment in ***Cool Hand Luke***. I leave you here with this reminder:

"What we do not have here is a failure to communicate."

FIVE IGNORED OSCAR-WORTHY ROLE

October 29, 2015

I am always reading Facebook opinions about performances by actors that were snubbed by the Academy of Motion Picture Arts and Sciences. I have my own opinion about this. Most of the time, Oscar gets it right, at least in terms of a nomination. In five instances, I completely scratch my head:

- Lon Chaney Jr./***Of Mice and Men*** – Not only was this a breakthrough role, it also allowed the actor to step out of the formidable shadow of his father, the greatest dramatic screen star of the silent era. He brings John Steinbeck's *Lenny* to life. The only explanation is that the film was released in 1939. . . . Even Frank Morgan and Margaret Hamilton in ***The Wizard of Oz*** and Bela Lugosi in ***Son of Frankenstein*** were passed over as well.

- William Bendix/***Lifeboat*** – Here was a talented actor of drama and comedy. He shows both in this Alfred Hitchcock thriller. His performance still tugs at my heart. That said, he was ignored by the Academy.

- Edward G. Robinson/***Double Indemnity*** – He was always good in every role. He was never better in support of Barbara Stanwyck and Fred MacMurray. Surprisingly, Robinson never received one nomination for a statuette in his entire career!

- Humphrey Bogart/***The Treasure of the Sierra Madre*** – This was a career-defining role. It should have earned the actor at least a nod. Urban legend suggests that he was a nominee. But the only attention he received from the Academy was for ***Casablanca***, ***The African Queen*** and ***The Caine Mutiny***.

- George C. Scott/***Dr. Strangelove*** – The iconic actor steals the film from such scene-stealers as Peter Sellers, Slim Pickens and Sterling Hayden. This film proves Scott could do comedy.

Honorable Mentions: Myrna Loy/***The Best Years of Our Lives*** and Robert Preston/***The Music Man***. Loy was surprisingly snubbed for a competitive Oscar her entire career. Preston earned a well-deserved Tony Award for his role as *Professor Harold Hill*.

MOVIES SELDOM GET IT RIGHT

January 9, 2015

The controversy surrounding Lyndon B. Johnson's role over civil rights as depicted in ***Selma*** is just the latest flap regarding artistic license, an argument that goes back to Hollywood's Golden Age. The more celebrated recent furor involves ***Lincoln*** (Connecticut lawmakers were in a major uproar for incorrectly depicting their state's representatives of the day voting against the Thirteenth Amendment); ***Zero Dark Thirty*** (suggesting intelligence gathered through torture helped lead to Osama bin Laden's capture, and this led to a public outcry that was spearheaded by Senators Diane Feinstein and John McCain); and ***JFK*** (many still take as fact conspiracy theories floated by Oliver Stone).

I write in my *Forgotten Hollywood* book series that this often occurs by screenwriters not bound to the truth. It is the job of historians and critics to point out the corrections when movie moguls get the facts wrong in a production. The argument of filmmakers remains that they are simply trying to entertain. A character in the movie ***The Man Who Shot Liberty Valance*** succinctly sums up how history was portrayed in the Old West by real newspaper reporters. The John Ford–Western boldly pokes fun at the tall tales created and the historical implications from the narrative:

> *When legend becomes fact, print the legend!*

> The most celebrated legend by Hollywood was created from the script of the 1939 drama, **Drums along the Mohawk**. As I surmise in my *Forgotten Hollywood* chapter on *Ward Bond*:

> *Bond plays Adam Helmer, a Revolutionary War hero. Helmer, a frontiersman, is actually credited in warning the people of German Flatts, New York, of an impending raid by Indians and Tories (British sympathizers). Due to his efforts, only two men were killed in the attack. Unfortunately, the true depiction in the novel and the subsequent film version differs, giving credit to Gil Martin, a settler in the Mohawk Valley. This inaccurate discrepancy is the highlight in the movie. The heroic assignment was made by Darryl F. Zanuck to showcase the actual star of the film, Henry Fonda.*

My book series is quick to point out these missteps because that is my literary job as a film and Americana historian. I do not agree with those folks who claim a movie is less great because it gets the facts wrong.

The bottom line . . . As a Screen Actors Guild member, my awards ballot will be based on acting style, production qualities and effective use of narrative storytelling, not on whether the facts behind the motion picture are correct. My suggestion to a theatre-going audience: Visit the snack counter, buy a tub of popcorn and a soft drink and then . . . *enjoy the legend!*

MORTAL MONSTERS OF THE SILVER SCREEN

October 21, 2017

The history of horror has roots prior to the studio era of Hollywood. Silent movies are filled with cinematic classics (***The Cabinet of Dr. Caligari***, ***The Phantom of the Opera*** and ***The Hunchback of Notre Dame*** come to mind) and made genuine stars out of actors, such as Lon Chaney and Conrad Veidt.

Universal Studios provided vivid films of the genre, including ***Dracula***, ***Frankenstein***, ***The Invisible Man***, ***The Mummy***, ***The Wolfman***, among others. ***King Kong*** became an instant classic in 1933 for RKO. Paramount Pictures produced a definitive version of ***Dr. Jekyll and Mr. Hyde***.

October is a perfect month to examine the psyche of nefarious behavior. I offer three iconic examples of scripted characters so vile and absent of any redeeming qualities. They are the best visualization during Hollywood's Golden Age of hideous human beings that explode on screen.

Let us first consider *Lonesome Rhodes* from ***A Face in the Crowd*** and *Jack Ripper* from ***Dr. Strangelove***. But crime for crime's sake is not part of their internal makeup. *Cody Jarrett* from ***White Heat*** is a worthy honorable mention in my written examination. The ignition of a massively fatal detonation that would kill law enforcement officers chasing him is quite over the top. However, Jarrett reacts in murderous ways; he does not initiate the instinct.

Here are my TOP THREE candidates of humanity in gruesome turmoil during Hollywood Golden Age . . .

- *Tommy Udo/**Kiss of Death*** – Richard Widmark's screen debut earned him an Oscar nod. Like *Cody Jarrett,* he is a malignant gangster. Unlike *Jarrett, Udo* will attack characters that get in his way for the sheer joy of the process. The prescient scene earning *Udo* a place on the list . . . shackling a squealer's wheelchair-bound mom and then pushing her down a staircase to her death. Hard to watch. Yet this horrific incident compels viewing each time the scene appears on the screen.

- *Reverend Harry Powell/**The Night of the Hunter*** – Bob Mitchum's signature role, it led to him being cast in such movies as ***Cape Fear***. Directed by Charles Laughton, the film is ahead of its time in presenting horror in human form. *Powell* is like a female black widow spider and uses gullibility and revivalism to conduct murder just for the chance to abscond with cash. This flick influenced later work, including ***Elmer Gantry*** (for its cynicism), ***To Kill a Mockingbird*** (for its atmosphere) and ***Psycho*** (for sheer horror). Shelly Winters is the visual victim played in a backdrop of triangulation, based on the production sets of ***The Cabinet of Dr. Caligari***. Lilian Gish plays the heroine that puts religion on its purest path. Audiences stayed away in 1955. They find this an unabashed classic in 2017.

- *Norman Bates/**Psycho*** – Alfred Hitchcock spent a lifetime searching for the perfect human monster. Anthony Perkins personifies Hitch's screen villainy and would be typecast for the rest of his career. Psychologists debate reasons why *Norman* would act so efficiently as a killing machine, mental instability at the core of any discussion. The modern horror was born in 1960 with the shower scene. In fact, actual serial killers bare striking resemblances to the apparent normalcy of *Norman Bates*. Hitchcock struck a chilling chord that resonates to this day. Even a new documentary analyzes the entire shower scene . . . need I say more?

Sleep well, tonight . . . and set your moral compass!

FORGOTTEN VICTIMS IN FLIGHT

April 20, 2016

Over the years, a common reason famous people have died in airline crashes is because of monetary access to travel like a bird. That said, early aviators, such as Amelia Earhart, may have been doomed by unrealistic goals. The Kennedy curse did not begin with the lone guns of Lee Harvey Oswald and Sirhan Sirhan. Joe Kennedy Jr. and Kathleen Kennedy spent their last moments of life on a winged craft way back in the 1940s. War was an obvious reason why Carole Lombard and Big Band leader Glenn Miller died tragically when their aircrafts disappeared or crashed. Bad weather contributed to the demise of Buddy Holly, Ritchie Valens and the Big Bopper in the 1950s and Otis Redding and The Bar-Kays in the 1960s. More recently, we have lost Jim Croce, John Denver and composer James Horner.

Here are five cinematic legends who perished on planes, rarely referenced today . . .

- Knute Rockne – The legendary football coach at Notre Dame, Rockne was a bona fide star in his field of endeavor. His story was immortalized in a production that starred Pat O'Brien as the iconic coach. The Warner Brothers film ***Knute Rockne, All American*** co-starred Ronald Reagan (in one of his finest moments on screen), Gale Page and Donald Crisp.

  Rockne died in the crash of an airplane—TWA Flight 599—in Kansas on March 31, 1931, while enroute to participate in the production of the film ***The Spirit of Notre Dame***. The unexpected, dramatic death of Rockne startled the nation that triggered a national outpouring of grief, comparable to the passing of presidents. The funeral itself was broadcast live on network radio across the United States and in Europe, as well as to parts of South America and Asia.

- Will Rogers – A folksy poet, who set the modern standard for rural comedy, in truth, was a savvy entertainer that became a nationwide cross-culture phenomenon during the silent era of cinema. Inheriting the mantle from Mark Twain, this common man was a cowboy, vaudeville performer, humorist, newspaper columnist, social commentator and stage and motion picture actor (making over twenty films in the sound era).

  Rogers was an advocate for the aviation industry after noticing advancements in Europe. He befriended Charles Lindbergh, the most famous aviator of the era. In 1935, the famed pilot, Wiley Post, became interested in surveying a mail-and-passenger air route from the West Coast to Russia. Rogers visited Wiley often at an airport in Southern California, and he asked Post to fly him through Alaska in search of new material for his newspaper column. On August 15, they left Fairbanks, Alaska. They were a few miles from Point Barrow in bad weather and landed in a lagoon to ask directions. On take-off, the engine failed at low altitude, and the aircraft plunged into the lagoon with a sheared-off right wing, and the plane ending up inverted in the shallow water. Both men died instantly.

- Leslie Howard – A major movie star, who facilitated the careers of Humphrey Bogart and Wendy Hiller, he was cast as *Ashley Wilkes* in ***Gone with the Wind***. He also starred in ***Pygmalion*** (written by George Bernard Shaw), ***Of Human Bondage*** and ***The Petrified Forest***.

  Howard was active in anti-German propaganda and was reputedly involved with British or Allied Intelligence. This may have led to his death on June 1, 1943, when an airliner on which he was a passenger was shot down over the Bay of Biscay, sparking conspiracy theories over the tragedy. One hypothesis . . . His plane was targeted because Adolf Hitler believed that British Prime Minister Winston Churchill was a passenger.

- Mike Todd – The famed producer of ***Around the World in Eighty Days***, Mike Todd was one the many husbands of Elizabeth Taylor. Their friends included husband-and-wife Eddie Fisher and Debbie Reynolds.

  On March 22, 1958, Todd's private plane *Lucky Liz* crashed near Grants, New Mexico. The plane suffered engine failure while being flown overloaded in icy conditions at an altitude that was too high for only one engine working under the heavy load. The craft went out of control and crashed, killing all four on board. Five days before, Todd flew on the plane to Albuquerque to promote a showing of his film. Taylor had been too ill to accompany him on the trip.

- Sonja Henie – Like Knute Rockne, Sonja Henie was a Norwegian sports superstar. She was a three-time Olympic champion in figure skating. Henie's connections with Adolf Hitler and other high-ranking German officials made her the subject of controversy during the advent of World War II. Controversy appeared first when Henie greeted Hitler with a Nazi salute at an exhibition in Berlin right before the 1936 Winter Olympics, and she was strongly denounced by the Norwegian press. After the occupation of Norway, German troops saw Hitler's autographed photo prominently displayed on the piano in the Henie family home.

  Hollywood studio chief Darryl Zanuck signed her to a long-term contract at Twentieth Century Fox, which made her one of the highest-paid actresses of the time. She appeared with Glenn Miller (a tragic victim of an airline mishap over the English Channel) in the insanely popular musical, ***Sun Valley Serenade***. Henie was diagnosed with leukemia in the mid-1960s. She died of the disease in 1969 during a flight from Paris to Oslo.

An honorable mention goes to Paul Mantz, a pilot who perished as he performed a stunt crash during the filming of ***The Flight of the Phoenix*** in 1965. The actual footage was used in the final print of the film, and the entire production was dedicated to the doomed pilot.

GOLDEN AGE PRESIDENTS UP FOR OSCAR

February 18, 2014

The Academy Awards are next month, and since yesterday was President's Day, I thought it might be fun to explore Hollywood's Golden Age to see who earned Oscar nods for playing a chief executive. Remember, last year was the initial instance of an actor winning a statuette as a commander in chief, Daniel Day Lewis in the title role of **Lincoln**. Bill Murray also received consideration as *FDR* in **Hyde Park on Hudson**.

Recent accolades include Frank Langella's turn in 2008 in ***Frost/Nixon***, a 1997 nomination for Anthony Hopkins as *John Quincy Adams* in ***Amistad*** and James Whitmore in a one-man tour de force in 1975 as *Truman* in ***Give 'em Hell, Harry!*** Paul Giamatti additionally earned an Emmy for his performance as *John Adams*. We can add Tony recognition in 1972 for William Daniels (also as *John Adams*) in ***1776***.

Henry Fonda was aced out of any chance for Oscar consideration when he played *Honest Abe* during Hollywood's greatest year in 1939. Fonda played unnamed presidents in ***Fail-Safe*** and ***Meteor*** and the son of Theodore Roosevelt in ***The Longest Day***.

Only three actors offered Oscar-worthy consideration during the studio era. Raymond Massey was one of a dozen actors who have portrayed Abraham Lincoln (including Frank McGlynn during the Silent Era) and Massey was the first recognized by the film academy. Four years later, Alexander Knox appeared in the title role in ***Wilson***, produced by Twentieth Century Fox. Plus, Peter Sellers captured a nomination in 1964 as a fictional president, one of his three parts in ***Dr. Strangelove***.

Wilson was a sweeping 1944 bio-pic that Darryl F. Zanuck wanted to bring to the screen. Woodrow Wilson's story included a wife who died while he was in office, the Great War and an eventual stroke by the lead character. The story had all the makings of a bona fide classic. But Zanuck hated the completed production and instructed all who worked at Fox to ignore the five nominations presented by the Academy or risk termination. His decree worked . . . Knox lost to Bing Crosby in ***Going My Way***.

By the way, two actors I have written about in *Forgotten Hollywood Forgotten History* have been presidents in movies: Lionel Barrymore as *Andrew Jackson* in ***Lone Star*** that starred Clark Gable and Ave Gardner and Van Heflin in ***Tennessee Johnson***, when the actor headlined as the chief executive who succeeded Lincoln in the White House. Barrymore also appeared in the latter film as Andrew Johnson's nemesis, *Thaddeus Stevens*.

One thespian who should have received award consideration was Ralph Bellamy, also playing *FDR* in ***Sunrise at Campobello***. The adapted stage play takes place just as Roosevelt contracted polio. It ends after Franklin places in nomination New York Governor Al Smith as the Democratic standard-bearer for president during the 1920 campaign. Smith would go on to lose the election to Warren Harding, a chief executive who has NEVER been portrayed on celluloid.

OSCARS HONORS FILM'S PAST

February 19, 2012

This year's Academy Awards ceremony will feature motion pictures paying homage to cinema's fascinating legacy. Many of the top nominees offer interesting back-stories that I am happy to share with you.

- ***Hugo*** – Martin Scorsese is committed to movie restoration. His latest production takes us back to the origins of film during the silent era. Georges Méliès created innovative magic on screen during the first decade of the twentieth century.

A Méliès renaissance took place just after the advent of sound in cinema. France's Motion Picture Academy eventually restored much of the director's work feared lost, which is why Scorsese wanted to tell this compelling story.

- ***Midnight in Paris*** – Here is a Woody Allen comedic fantasy taking us back to a time during the City of Lights' *Lost Generation* of the 1920s. Among the artistic-elite featured: Cole Porter, Gertrude Stein, Salvador Dali, F. Scott Fitzgerald, Pablo Picasso, Ernest Hemingway and Josephine Baker. The words, music and visual art created by these avant-garde intellectuals had a distinct impact on the origins of the studio era in cinema, including the use of art deco, jazz and scripts based on ***A Farewell to Arms***, ***For Whom the Bell Tolls*** and ***The Great Gatsby***.

- ***The Artist*** – The transition of the silent era to talkies had a profound effect on the Hollywood community. It helped maintained stardom for Greta Garbo and Joan Crawford and created opportunities for Broadway actors, such as Humphrey Bogart, Spencer Tracy and James Cagney. This fateful decision also ruined careers. The most notable was John Gilbert, whose thin voice did not translate well to sound. Overnight, Gilbert became an alcoholic and prematurely died. This moment in Hollywood is well-chronicled on celluloid, including in ***The Jazz Singer***, three versions of ***A Star Is Born***, ***Singing in the Rain*** and, now, ***The Artist***.

- ***My Week with Marilyn*** – Postwar English cinema blossomed through the concerted efforts of Alec Guinness, Alistair Sim and Laurence Olivier. Legendary studios such as Pinewood and Hammer focused on British comedy, drama and horror of the 1950s and 1960s.

  This delightful movie provides a snapshot during a week when Marilyn Monroe desperately traveled to the United Kingdom in her search for consideration as a serious actor, while Olivier reached for surefire stardom. Neither succeeded, but the historic pairing in ***The Prince and the Showgirl*** had a lasting impression on both stars, as well as on Vivien Leigh and Arthur Miller, Olivier's and Monroe's respective spouses at the time.

There is little doubt Hollywood's reverence to its past will continue.

Until next time . . . *never forget.*

— CHAPTER FIVE —

Standing Room Only

From coast to coast and throughout middle America, tiny stage theatres and movie palaces sprung up to provide towns with dusty and paved roads live and cinematic performances from the late nineteenth century and into the early twentieth century.

As the silent era was concluding, movie moguls traveled across the country to Broadway in order to find great voices to complement this new genre of film making. Among those destined for stardom: Clark Gable, Humphrey Bogart and Spencer Tracy. From this time frame came the emergence of movie theater palaces, these bijous resembling many of the stages in Manhattan.

From Flo Ziegfeld to Andrew Lloyd Webber; from the balcony to standing room only, we present Broadway in its rich splendor.

On a personal note, my brother and I were privileged to be in the audience of the longest-running play on Broadway, ***The Fantasticks***, and it WAS really fantastic!

—Virginia Vandewouwer

A FANTASTICKS RUN

March 20, 2017

Manny P. here . . .

The off-Broadway phenomenon, ***The Fantasticks***, will end its record-breaking run this spring, bringing down the curtain on a show (featuring confetti and a cardboard moon) that started when Dwight D. Eisenhower was president. The musical, which features *Try to Remember*, closes June 4, having played a total of 21,552 performances in Manhattan.

For nearly forty-two years, this show originally ran at the 150-seat Sullivan Street Playhouse in Greenwich Village, finally closing in 2002 after 17,162 performances, the victim of destruction after 9/11. It reopened four years later at The Theater Center, an off-Broadway complex in the heart of Times Square, where it will end after a run of almost forty-four hundred shows. Scores of actors have appeared in ***The Fantasticks***, from the opening cast that included Jerry Orbach to Ricardo Montalban, Kristin Chenoweth and Oscar-winner F. Murray Abraham.

The tale is a mock version of *Romeo and Juliet*. It has since become the nation's longest-running musical. By comparison, ***The Phantom of the Opera*** is Broadway's longest-running show at twelve thousand. Its only rival is ***The Mousetrap*** in London, the longest-running show in the world, having passed twenty-six thousand performances. (I have enjoyed all three productions.)

In 2015, producers also declared the show would close that summer. But, two donors kept the stalwart, low-tech show open. This time, they are serious. A new production is scheduled to start previews June 17 in the same theater.

So, let us bid adieu to ***The Fantasticks***!

GRAUMAN'S CHINESE THEATRE TURNS NINETY

May 18, 2017

A symbol of Hollywood's Golden Age, Grauman's Chinese Theatre is turning ninety. Today known as the TCL Chinese Theatre, the landmark movie palace first opened on May 18, 1927, and it has been hosting movies, actors and fans ever since. Films such as ***King Kong***, ***The Wizard of Oz*** and ***Star Wars*** had their premieres at this glamorous locale.

Sid Grauman's masterpiece cinema house stands on a bustling corner of Hollywood Boulevard, next door to the Dolby Theatre, where the Oscars are now presented, and across from the historic Roosevelt Hotel, where the first Oscars' ceremony was held in 1929. Hollywood's take of a Chinese temple, it boasts a pagoda-shaped roof, ornate marble carvings and a cement forecourt filled with celebrity footprints. The theater still hosts dozens of premieres each year, and its iconic footprint forecourt draws an estimated five million tourists annually from around the world. Ticket prices have risen, however. It cost seventy-five cents to see a movie in 1927. An IMAX 3-D screening today runs twenty-two dollars.

A showman and entrepreneur, Grauman started building the Chinese Theatre in 1926, the same year he and other Hollywood titans established the Academy of Motion Picture Arts and Sciences. He imagined an elegant and otherworldly cinema palace that would transport visitors to ancient China, with its serene gardens and regal temples.

Silent film star Norma Talmadge came to see Sid at his new building along Hollywood Boulevard when she accidentally stepped in wet cement out front. Inspiration took hold . . . Grauman believed celebrity footprints would be a fun way to promote his new theater. He welcomed friends and business partners, Mary Pickford and Douglas Fairbanks, to purposely put their hands and feet in wet cement, and the tradition was born. More than three hundred actors, directors and producers have followed suit. ***Alien: Covenant*** director Ridley Scott added his prints recently.

There are a couple of time capsules buried beneath the forecourt. The first was planted in 1942 to mark the release of ***Mrs. Miniver***, which won six Oscars. Beneath Greer Garson's prints is a capsule containing a copy of the script and a thirty-five-millimeter print of the film. A second capsule commemorates the theater's fiftieth anniversary. Buried in 1977, it holds a theater ticket, a sixteen-millimeter print of a Chinese film and a program from opening night in 1927.

The city of Los Angeles declared the splendid theater a historic-cultural monument in 1968. It underwent the biggest renovation in its history in 2013 to create stadium seating and add a state-of-the-art IMAX screen—the only one in the world with an old-fashioned curtain that opens just before the feature presentation.

The company plans to expand the brand around the world, with a San Diego location set to open later this year. But for countless tourists and celebrities, past and present, the Chinese Theatre will always stay on Hollywood Boulevard, representing the golden age of cinema.

THE SHOW MUST GO ON

March 14, 2015

Fifty fans of classic cinema had the opportunity to watch Orson Welles's 1941 groundbreaking film, ***Citizen Kane***, partly based on the late William Randolph Hearst, at the media tycoon's own private theater at Hearst Castle, a concession the magnate would probably not have made.

The screening Friday with a price tag of one thousand dollars was part of the San Luis Obispo Film Festival. This included an exclusive tour of the estate, which is now a state park, and a reception on the mansion's patio overlooking the Pacific Ocean. It will benefit the nonprofit, *Friends of Hearst Castle*, a preservation group.

Welles's cinema classic was shown before in the Hearst Castle's visitor center in 2010. But this is the first time the movie was screened in the opulent, fifty-seat theater at the hilltop estate. Great-grandson Stephen Hearst, the vice president and general manager of Hearst Corp.'s Western Properties, gave his blessing to the festival to screen the film both times.

William Randolph Hearst sought to derail the movie, which portrayed the rise and fall of an obsessively controlling media mogul. The film went on to win an Oscar in 1942 for Best Original Screenplay and is now considered one of the greatest American films. The film, a searing critique of a newspaper magnate, has many similarities to Hearst's life.

But Stephen Hearst said the screening, which was hosted by TCM's Ben Mankiewicz, the grandson of Herman Mankiewicz, who co-wrote the ***Citizen Kane*** screenplay, was an opportunity to draw the distinctions between William Randolph Hearst's life and Welles's fiction.

On my Facebook page, I mentioned that this is like the Richard Nixon Library having a *Watergate* exhibit . . . which it does, by the way!

OY VEY

July 3, 2018

An updated off-Broadway production of ***Fiddler on the Roof***, directed by Oscar and Tony winner Joel Grey, will be performed in Yiddish for the first time in the United States. A preview starts this evening for the show and using the language its characters would have spoken.

Based on short stories by Sholom Aleichem originally penned in Yiddish, ***Fiddler*** is set in 1905 in a Jewish village in czarist Russia. A Yiddish version of the production translated by actor and writer Shraga Friedman as *Fidler afn Dakh* was performed in Israel in 1966 but was never staged in the United States until now.

Yiddish, which is based on dialects used in Hebrew and other languages and is written with the Hebrew alphabet, was once spoken by millions of Eastern European Jews but fell victim both to the Holocaust and a desire for assimilation. The new production exemplifies how decades of work to preserve Yiddish by organizations, including the *Folksbiene*—Yiddish for *World Stage*—have paid off.

Immigrants to the United States built a thriving Yiddish theater scene, and it launched the career of famed acting teacher Stella Adler and thespians such as Edward G. Robinson. The *Folksbiene* was founded in 1915 and was once one of a dozen Yiddish theater companies on Manhattan's Lower East Side. It presents examples from the Yiddish theater canon, new productions and adaptations of Yiddish literary works such as ***Yentl***.

Joel Grey's papa was Mickey Katz, a musician and actor who performed Yiddish comedy and songs. Grey actually does not speak much Yiddish but has been learning while rehearsing. The eighty-six-year-old is best remembered for his award-winning role as the host in ***Cabaret***, a musical that improbably turned the rise of Hitler into popular entertainment.

Fiddler on the Roof opened on Broadway in 1964, starred Zero Mostel as *Tevye* and ran for eight years. It has been a favorite of schools and community theater groups ever since and has been revived on Broadway four times. Its songs, including *If I Were a Rich Man* and *Sunrise, Sunset*, are familiar even to people who have never seen the show.

This updated culturally accurate version should have critics shouting . . . *L'Chaim!*

FOUNDING FATHER GOES HOME

June 10, 2018

The blockbuster musical ***Hamilton*** is finally traveling to the nation's capital, and its citizenry is preparing for the visit. Lin-Manuel Miranda's historical musical about the life of Alexander Hamilton is starting a three-month run at the Kennedy Center.

Ironically, Hamilton did not spend much of his professional career in Washington. The United States capital was in Philadelphia while he served as the nation's first treasury secretary, and the federal government did not move to Washington until 1800, four years before his death.

The myriad museums of modern Washington have been preparing specialized exhibits. The Postal Museum has already launched an exhibit—*Alexander Hamilton: Soldier, Secretary, Icon*—and it includes mail, portraits and postage stamps reflective of his life. A highlight of the exhibit are the two flintlock pistols made of walnut, brass and gold that were used in the July 11, 1804, duel with Vice President Aaron Burr, resulting in Hamilton's demise. These pistols are on loan from the private collection of J. P. Morgan Chase and Co.

The Library of Congress is unveiling its own Hamilton display, drawing on its collection of over twelve thousand of Hamilton's papers and documents. Miranda based his musical on a 2004 biography, *Alexander Hamilton* by Ron Chernow, which drew from the LOC material. Also, there is material chronicling a historic meal between Hamilton and Thomas Jefferson.

The Library of Congress is supplementing the physical exhibit by making a vast number of Hamilton-related papers accessible online. These include the *Reynolds Pamphlet*, his one-hundred-page public response to his involvement in the first American political sex scandal.

With a song in its heart, the District of Columbia is mad about the boy.

BIG APPLE TO RECOGNIZE SONDHEIM

October 11, 2011

Stephen Sondheim is the most prolific Broadway composer of our lifetime. His credits include ***West Side Story*** and ***Gypsy*** (as lyricist) and creating ***A Funny Thing Happened on the Way to the Forum***, ***Follies***, ***A Little Night Music***, ***Into the Woods*** and ***Sweeney Todd***. In cinema, he contributed tunes for ***Reds*** and ***Dick Tracy***.

Sondheim has won multiple Tony and Grammy awards, an Oscar and a Pulitzer Prize. To honor his eightieth birthday, the Henry Miller Theatre was renamed the *Stephen Sondheim Theatre* in 2010. On November 1, New York will bestow the city's highest honor to the composer for career achievement in the arts. He receives the *Handel Medallion* at Alice Tully Hall in Manhattan.

Congratulations to a living legend . . . Stephen Sondheim!

Until next time . . . *never forget.*

— CHAPTER SIX —

Filibuster

Political theatre is captivating because we find ourselves immersed in the public debate of real issues that generate winners and losers. Issues can affect the livelihood of people across the nation.

Golden Age Hollywood recognized the drama and created memorable productions, including ***Mr. Smith Goes to Washington***, ***Citizen Kane***, ***A Face in the Crowd***, ***Born Yesterday***, ***The Best Man*** and ***Advise and Consent***.

In today's political climate, we find ourselves strangely captivated with sometimes unbelievable headlines, followed by incredulous stories. And ironically, cinema tells us when we are repeating history, for better or for worse. We begin this chapter with a filibuster of sorts . . .

—Virginia Vandewouwer

MR. MURPHY GOES TO WASHINGTON

June 17, 2016

Manny P. here . . .

The *filibuster* is a powerful parliamentary device in the United States Senate. Rules permit a senator, or series of senators, to speak for as long as he or she wishes and on any topic he or she chooses, unless three-fifths of the senators duly chosen and sworn (usually sixty out of one hundred senators) bring debate to a close by invoking cloture. Most defenders call the filibuster "*the soul of the senate.*"

On Wednesday, Senator Chris Murphy of Connecticut, with the aid of other colleagues, held the floor of the Senate for fourteen hours and fifty minutes. Murphy was fighting for a vote on two measures related to the issue of gun control:

- *Make it illegal for people on the FBI's various suspected terrorism watch lists and no-fly lists to buy guns*
- *Expand universal background checks*

Murphy's filibuster was motivated by the Orlando massacre over the weekend and the Sandy Hook tragedy that took place in his home state in 2012. Due to his arduous effort, Senate Republicans agreed to put the bills to a vote on Monday.

Since 1900, fourteen filibusters have been initiated in the Senate, which have lasted at least eight hours over a variety of issues, including civil rights, health care, tax cuts and an increase in our national debt. However, the most famous filibuster may have been the one *Jefferson Smith* delivered in 1939. He is the fictional character portrayed by James Stewart in the Frank Capra classic, ***Mr. Smith Goes to Washington***.

In the film, a junior senator (not unlike Senator Murphy) fights for a national boy's camp at fictional *Willet Creek*, instead of a dam-building graft scheme included in an appropriations bill. The senator talks non-stop for almost twenty-four hours, reaffirming the American ideal of freedom and disclosing the true motives of the scheme. *Smith*'s effort derails the vote.

Oscar-voters were shocked when Stewart (or Clark Gable in ***Gone with the Wind***) was denied a Best Actor statuette, with the award going to Robert Donat for ***Goodbye, Mr. Chips***. One speculates that Stewart received an apology Academy Award the following year for his performance in ***The Philadelphia Story*** (denying the Oscar to a more-deserving Henry Fonda for his role in ***The Grapes of Wrath***).

No matter the political party, America loves the filibuster.

SEVEN DAYS IN MAY

May 11, 2017

A Pentagon insider working with intelligence initiates surveillance on the president of the United States. The result is an attempted coup by the military at the highest levels because the executive branch is cozy with the Soviet Union. The head of the Joint Chiefs of Staff fails and is forced to resign; in essence, he is dispatched.

Seven Days in May was loosely based on actual facts and reflected the political climate of the day. In 1961, President John F. Kennedy accepted the resignation of a vociferous anti-Communist, General Edwin Walker, who attempted to indoctrinate troops under his watch with personal radical views. He also described former President Harry Truman, former First Lady Eleanor Roosevelt, former Secretary of State Dean Acheson and other public figures as Russian sympathizers.

The production was directed by John Frankenheimer, and it starred Burt Lancaster, Kirk Douglas, Fredric March, Edmond O'Brien and Ava Gardner. The screenplay was adroitly adapted by Rod Serling, based on the book by Fletcher Knebel and Charles W. Bailey II.

President Kennedy had read *Seven Days in May* shortly after its publication and believed the described scenario could actually occur in the United States. According to Frankenheimer, he received encouragement and assistance from JFK through Press Secretary Pierre Salinger, who conveyed the president's desire that it be produced. The exterior of the White House was even made available. But the Pentagon was vehemently against the completion of this movie.

The motion picture was released three months after the assassination of President Kennedy in February 1964 and opened to wonderful reviews. Critics called it a thrilling piece of fiction.

THE FISCAL CLIFF CONNECTION

November 29, 2012

Congressional Republicans are taking in a movie. They are getting a lesson in the art of compromise by watching Steven Spielberg's ***Lincoln***. In this latest cinematic work, *President Abraham Lincoln* (played by Daniel Day Lewis) and *Secretary of State William H. Seward* (portrayed by David Strathairn) conspire with the rest of the Cabinet to initiate a plan that encourages the House of Representatives to ratify the *Thirteenth Amendment* to end slavery.

To understand the premise of compromise during nineteenth century politics, please examine the 1860 Republican convention, which pitted the nationally revered Seward against the dark horse Lincoln. After the GOP made a stunning selection, it was assured of winning the election since the Democratic Party was fractured with candidates from the North and South. Just as President Obama selected his primary opponent, Hillary Clinton, as his new secretary of state, Lincoln turned to Seward and offered him the esteemed position. He accepted with the caveat that if he disagreed with the president, Seward's point of view would be considered.

In 1865, Lincoln was re-elected on the promise of ending the Civil War. But he disagreed with Seward as to when this might exactly happen. The president believed Congress should first put an end to slavery by federal law, while Seward believed the *Emancipation Proclamation* was a de facto executive order by Lincoln, his responsibility as commander in chief. Plus, the secretary of state thought it to be a waste of political capital to try to pass an iffy law in a separate branch of government. He was convinced Lincoln and the Republicans would lose.

Based on Doris Kearns Goodwin's book, *Team of Rivals*, the film documents the effort by Lincoln and Seward to pass the *Thirteenth Amendment*. They resort to patronage, bribery, patriotic rhetoric and the nuanced (if gritty) art of politics, so the sixteenth president's legacy would be assured as he approached his second term of office.

While I do not suggest today's Congress make their votes solely based on the seedy promises of insider jobs, pork barrel spending, money and/or influence, this cinematic effort celebrates our Founding Fathers' design that government works best through compromise and the noble concept of *We the People* as a representative effort to tackle and solve our nation's ills.

May I also endorse, here and now, a David Strathairn nomination for a Best Supporting Actor Oscar for his role as *Seward*. His distinguished career now includes a most appropriate feather in his proverbial cap. I hope the voting members of the Academy of Motion Picture Arts and Sciences are listening. Of course, I am willing to compromise and lend my support to Tommy Lee Jones for his performance as *Senator Thaddeus Stevens*.

WAG THE DOG

April 14, 2018

A spin doctor and a Hollywood producer fabricate a war to distract citizens from a presidential sex scandal. Something from the pages of today's headlines? Actually, I reference a 1997 production that starred Dustin Hoffman, Willie Nelson, Robert De Niro, Anne Heche, Denis Leary, Kirsten Dunst and Woody Harrelson.

Directed by Barry Levinson and nominated for two Oscars, ***Wag the Dog*** chronicles the directive of a fictional conflict in Albania, hoping the media will concentrate on this instead of an Oval Office transgression involving an unnamed president and an underage girl. This artificial hostility, complete with a patriotic country theme song and fake footage, is designed to rally the vox populi. The contrived hoax is initially successful with the president quickly gaining ground in the polls.

Critic Roger Ebert offered this analysis:

> *The work is a satire that contains just enough realistic ballast to be teasingly plausible; like Dr. Strangelove, it makes you laugh and then it makes you wonder.*

A FACE IN THE CROWD

May 3, 2016

A megalo-maniacal media type transforms the way pockets of our country absorb a twenty-four-hour news cycle, modern advertising, television-viewing habits and, even, our political system. I am not referring to the 2016 presidential race. Sixteen years after the celebrated ***Citizen Kane*** and two decades before the scathing ***Network***, there was ***A Face in the Crowd***.

Based on a collection of short stories compiled in 1953, ***A Face in the Crowd*** was smartly written by Budd Schulberg. Elia Kazan took on the controversial director's assignment. And the cast included Patricia Neal, Walter Matthau, Anthony Franciosa and in their screen debuts, Andy Griffith and Lee Remick. To underscore the era of television culture in America, Kazan incorporated cameos by media personalities of the day: Earl Wilson, Sam Levinson, Mike Wallace, John Cameron Swayze and Walter Winchell. Schulberg and Kazan had previously collaborated on the Oscar-winning ***On the Waterfront***, which deservedly won eight statuettes.

Griffith, in a role starkly different from the amiable *Sheriff Andy Taylor* persona, was quite ferocious in a down-home kind of way. Screenwriter Schulberg (channeling his inner David Mamet) based a significant part of the *Lonesome Rhodes* character's facade on Will Rogers, adding a distinctively un-Rogers-like level of amorality and cruelty. Schulberg later explained that he interviewed Will Rogers Jr. during his candidacy for Congress. The younger Rogers reportedly told Schulberg that his father socialized with the very establishment types he mocked in his public pronouncements, adding that his father was actually a political reactionary in private life, not the populist he claimed to be.

Aspects of the *Lonesome Rhodes* character was also likely inspired by 1940s and 1950s CBS radio-television star Arthur Godfrey. The scene where *Rhodes* spoofs his sponsor in Memphis echoes Godfrey's reputation for kidding his own advertisers. Godfrey claimed he would not advertise products he did not believe in and routinely ridiculed both the sponsors' stodgy ad copy and, occasionally, company executives. The more Godfrey did this, the more sales increased. At one point in the film, *Rhodes* states he is missing a broadcast and requests that Godfrey fill in for him.

The year was 1957 when ***A Face in the Crowd*** was released, during the height of the Cold War. Very real narcissists, who manipulated our fears and put a red scare into homes from the radio and in newspaper columns, were the dominant spin-masters. Walter Winchell and Hedda Hopper ruined the careers of actors, directors and screenwriters with an anti-Communist diatribe that permeated society.

To understand media, politics and today's influence of television, ***A Face in the Crowd*** is a must-see motion picture. It is celluloid that birthed the screenplays of later generations, such as ***Network***, ***Broadcast News*** and last season's ***Trumbo***. After viewing the latter film, Kirk Douglas (just one face in today's crowd) wrote:

> *At ninety-eight years old, I have learned one lesson from history: It very often repeats itself. I hope that Trumbo, a fine film, will remind all of us that the Blacklist was a terrible time in our country, but that we must learn from it so that it will never happen again.*

THE OLDEST OBSESSION

November 21, 2017

A scoundrel conveys his wry message with confident revivalist overtones. His recitation on morality is embraced as he traverses small town America, where religion is celebrated in everyday life. He achieves the pinnacle of his chosen profession, only to be taken down as his sordid past comes to light. Yet he shall survive to fight another day. I am referencing the 1960 classic, ***Elmer Gantry***.

The film is based on a satirical novel written by Sinclair Lewis in 1926, which presents aspects of religious activity in middle-America in fundamentalist and evangelist circles and the nature of the 1920s public at-large. The yarn's anti-hero is initially attracted by liquor, easy bankrolls and libertine women. After various forays into evangelism, he becomes a successful Methodist minister, despite his behavioral hypocrisy and serial sexual escapades.

After publication in 1927, *Elmer Gantry* created a public furor. The book was banned in Boston and other towns and denounced from pulpits across the United States. A cleric suggested that Lewis should be imprisoned for five years, and there were threats of physical violence against the writer. Evangelist Billy Sunday once called Lewis *"Satan's cohort."*

This explosive movie earned Burt Lancaster and Shirley Jones well-deserved Academy Awards. The film also co-starred Jean Simmons, Arthur Kennedy, Dean Jagger and Patti Page. The character of *Sharon Falconer* was based on the career of Canadian-born, radio evangelist Aimee Semple McPherson, who formed the Pentecostal Christian denomination known as International Church of the Foursquare Gospel in 1927.

The female characters in this tale are clearly victimized and react at the pleasure of the male protagonist. The fire-and-brimstone overtones add to *Elmer's* ferocity in his quest for providing wholesale deliverance for an exacting price, his sordid behavior, notwithstanding. The movie ends in an ironic twist with the sudden, if convenient, repentance of *Gantry*. Quoting *1 Corinthians 13:11* in an impromptu revival, he is circumspect as he moves on. Incidentally, this production begs for a screenplay sequel that was never penned.

Today's toxic nationalism is suggested through analysis from the cinema of the 1960s and candid writings of insightful scribes of the 1920s, including F. Scott Fitzgerald, H. G. Wells, Ernest Hemingway and, of course, Sinclair Lewis. Remember this as you vote for candidates campaigning for entrance into the nation's body politic. Vetting is recommended.

INDISCRETION

October 27, 2016

This is a rags-to-riches story of an individual who made a career in business and decides to enter politics. He offers a populist message that resonates with select constituents, and the businessman is on track to win his election. His campaign is derailed when an indiscreet affair is revealed. Despite the revelation, the candidate feels he is sure to win. Instead, he loses.

The above cautionary tale was a scene in a screenplay written in 1939 for a production that was released in 1941. ***Citizen Kane*** was penned by Orson Welles and Herman Mankiewicz, and the pair earned an Oscar for Best Original Screenplay for their efforts.

The quasi-biographical film examines the life and legacy of *Charles Foster Kane*, played by Welles, a character resembling the American newspaper magnate William Randolph Hearst, Chicago tycoons Samuel Insull and Harold McCormick and aspects of Welles's own life. Mankiewicz based the original outline on the life of Hearst, whom he knew socially and came to hate after he was exiled from Hearst's circle.

Kane's career in the publishing world is born of idealistic social service but gradually evolves into a ruthless pursuit of power. *Kane*'s marriage disintegrates as he begins an affair with amateur singer *Susan Alexander* while he is running for governor of New York. Both his wife and his political opponent discover the affair, and the public scandal ends his political career. The character of his opponent, political boss *Jim W. Gettys*, is based on Charles F. Murphy, a leader in New York City's infamous *Tammany Hall* political machine. The character of *Susan Alexander*, based on actress Marion Davies (the mistress of Hearst), was a major reason the newspaper publisher tried to destroy the production. Hearing about ***Citizen Kane*** enraged Hearst so much he banned any advertising, reviewing or even mentioning it in his newspaper chain. He had his journalists actually libel Welles.

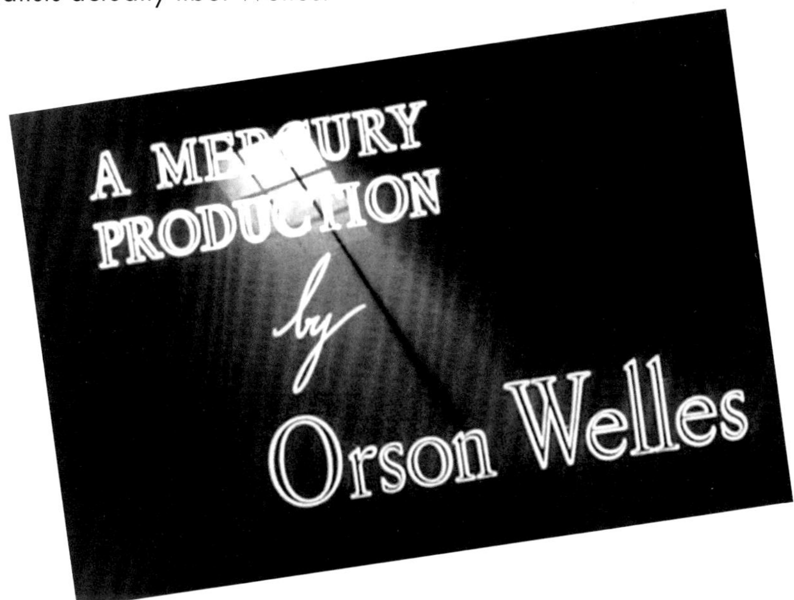

Here is an interesting aside . . . The *News on the March* newsreel scene presents *Kane* keeping company with Adolf Hitler and other dictators, while he smugly assures the public there will be no war. This reflects the political divide between intervention and isolationism that was being waged in the United States; the motion picture was released six months before the attack on Pearl Harbor while President Franklin D. Roosevelt was laboring to win public opinion in support of the Allies prior to World War II. In the rhetoric of ***Citizen Kane***, the destiny of isolationism is realized in metaphor of *Kane*'s own fate—eventually dying wealthy, lonely and surrounded by his collection of artifacts.

An epilogue . . . Anyone who claims 2016 is the strangest year in politics only has to return to 1941 when ***Citizen Kane*** was released, the year when Roosevelt earned a third term as our president, defeating in a landslide a maverick businessman Wendell Willkie, the Republican dark-horse candidate. He crusaded against FDR's perceived failure to end the Great Depression and his supposed eagerness for entry into war. Roosevelt carried thirty-eight states; Willkie won only ten states. So much for a businessman in politics.

DO THE HUSTLE

July 14, 2017

Politicos meet with foreign operatives to offer contributions that encourage the peddling of influence. I am referring to the very-real Abscam sting operation that took place in the late 1970s and early 1980s.

The FBI, aided by the Justice Department, videotaped politicians accepting bribes from a fictitious Arab company in return for certain favors. Over thirty political figures were investigated; among those, six members of the United States House of Representatives and one senator were convicted. One congressman did not accept any bribes. John Murtha of Pennsylvania would remain a distinguished member of Congress for the remainder of his career.

The Abscam operation is dramatized in the 2013 movie production ***American Hustle***, directed by David O. Russell. This is described as a fictionalization, rather than a straight, adaptation. The film featured Christian Bale, Amy Adams, Bradley Cooper, Jennifer Lawrence and Jeremy Renner. It received ten Oscar nominations, including Best Picture, Best Director, Best Original Screenplay, and all four acting categories. It received zero Academy Awards.

When the investigation became public in the early 1980s, an ethical controversy focused on the use of the sting technique. Ultimately, all Abscam convictions were upheld on appeal. But some judges criticized the tactics used and lapses in FBI and DOJ supervision. A few voters supported the operation; others argued that Abscam was an entrapment scenario. Among the concerns expressed were the undercover agents' involvement in the illegal activity, the possibility of entrapping individuals, the prospect of damaging reputations of innocent civilians and the opportunity to undermine legitimate rights to privacy. Congressional concerns over the nature of sting operations still persist to this day.

I know of one president who might express his concerns about this process of investigation . . . but I digress.

BREAKING THE SILENCE

December 6, 2017

A mega-producer engages with a beautiful blond actress for an afternoon meeting. It turns out to be a ruse. The executive unzips his pants and forces the budding star onto a couch. She rebukes the encounter and storms out of the office. The year was 1943.

Judy Holliday helped pave the way to this current moment in history by standing up to sexist, entitled bullies. She was not the first. However, her story will be told in a new production entitled ***Smart Blonde***; a reference to Holliday's IQ of 172. Screenwriter Willy Holtzman acquired the rights to share her personal life from her son, Jonathan Oppenheim.

No director is attached. Yet, given the subject matter, it seems fitting for a woman to helm the project. It would not feel right if only men collaborated on a tale about a woman standing up for herself and fighting sexual harassment, no matter the professional cost.

Holliday won an Oscar in 1951 for ***Born Yesterday***, an adaptation of the Broadway play. She also appeared in ***Adam's Rib***, ***Bells are Ringing*** and ***It Should Happen to You***.

An early champion was Katharine Hepburn. Holiday spoke before the House Un-American Activities Committee, testifying about her Communist connections in 1952. She died of breast cancer, two weeks before her forty-fourth birthday in 1965.

I was inspired to write this blog by today's reveal by *Time* magazine that the 2017 *Persons of the Year* are *The Silence Breakers*, individuals who have globally shared collective experiences of sexual harassment and assault. *Time* got this selection right in my humble estimation.

THE CONSTANT GARDENER

November 4, 2017

A simple-minded rube gleans what he knows of the world from television and becomes a lightning rod within political circles with access to the White House. This was the impetus of the next-to-last production made by Peter Sellers . . . ***Being There***. This 1979 movie is worth a visit due to a poignant relevance to today's sovereign climate.

Hal Ashby directed, and he displays similar acuity as in his previous work, ***Harold and Maude***. ***Being There*** is political satire, hilarious and subtle. The supporting cast is formidable, including Jack Warden, Shirley MacLaine, Melvyn Douglas and Richard Dysart. This script is smart and based on the novel by Polish-born scribe Jerzy Kosinski.

During filming, Sellers refused most interviews and kept his distance from the other actors. His performance was universally lauded by critics and is considered to be the crowning triumph of Sellers's remarkable career. Though he lost an Academy Award to Dustin Hoffman, Peter did receive a New York Film Critics Circle Award, a Golden Globe and a BAFTA. Douglas earned a second Oscar of his distinguished career for his performance (the first was in 1963 for his role in ***Hud***).

The premise of the production is on target: A naive gardener unwittingly becomes a much-sought-after political pundit and a commentator on the vagaries of our modern free society. Television, as a medium that deals almost exclusively in image and surface, remains an easy avenue for an individual to advance so meteorically to celebrity. An audience that embraces his fame actually believe this character can literally walk on water. Ultimately, his followers surmise the small screen has inaugurated artificial displays of divinity, a Gospel celebrating faux-patriotism. Plus, Russians contribute to the whirlwind of government ascension.

Per chance . . . does any of this sound familiar?

SAROO

June 22, 2018

A child is traumatically separated from his family and winds up in a foster-family system. Eventually, he is adopted. Two decades later, he embarks on a heartfelt journey to find his actual family. The search is problematic, but it brings a tear to your eye when the reunion occurs. This is the narrative from one of the finest movies from the last decade.

Lion is the 2016 production that features fine performances from Nicole Kidman, Dev Patel, Rooney Mara and the remarkable Sunny Pawar (who portrays the boy *Saroo*). The movie was appropriately nominated for six Academy Awards.

The motion picture was made on location in Khandwa and Calcutta, India, and Tasmania and Melbourne, Australia. The plight of this lost youngster, who resembles *Oliver Twist*, presents a sparse narrative, creates a visually stunning presentation that tugs at your heartstrings and rings incredibly true, considering recent immigration policies.

I have watched the film a number of times. This cinematic experience is expert Hollywood (or Bollywood) craftsmanship.

TWO-BIT THIMBLE RIGGER

July 17, 2018

A con artist blows into town to warn citizens about the TROUBLE invading the community, due to modernization that might corrupt the youngsters of any hamlet. Along the way, this *two-bit thimble rigger* bamboozles the mayor and his spouse, the school board, a librarian, parents and children. This is the underlying story of ***The Music Man***.

In the early 1960s, a number of anti-heroes were the subject of important cinema that spoke to the gullibility of small-town and big-city America. What emerged from Hollywood were films such as ***A Face in the Crowd***, ***Elmer Gantry*** and, of course, ***The Music Man***. These narratives border on satire, with characters working themselves into a fervent frenzy.

The Music Man was written by Meredith Wilson, and his purposeful theme was to lampoon the modest values of any collective. For the record, *Professor Harold Hill* is oft described as a *bang beat, bell-ringin', big haul, great go neck-or-nothin', rip-roarin', ever'time-a-bull's-eye salesman;* as a *fast-talking, self-centered, woman-chasing traveling man*; and a *road agent, highwayman* and a *pickpocket*. In one instance, the Iowa townspeople are labeled as *neck-bowed Hawkeyes*. When apprised of their gullible foolishness, the town fathers suggest tar and feathers as an appropriate punishment for this so-called *spellbinder*.

The real crime is that Robert Preston (*Professor Hill*) was snubbed by the film academy for his larger-than-life performance. Others in the perfectly cast musical include Buddy Hackett, Shirley Jones, Ron Howard, Paul Ford, Hermione Gingold, Pert Kelton and a superb barbershop quartet, The Buffalo Bills.

The book of *Revelations* speaks of fire and brimstone that might befall our planet. Just after the turn of the twentieth century, our young industrialized society was shaken to its core by an arrival of Halley's comet. And in the late 1930s, the entire Eastern seaboard was terrified by a Martian invasion, which was descriptively penned by H. G. Wells in *War of the Worlds*. The radio broadcast presented by *Mercury Theatre on the Air* employed techniques similar to those in *The March of Time* newsreel. The result was frightening in its presentation and in its aftermath.

The difference between oft-told parables and the current political climate is redemptive happy endings, designed to keep audiences satisfied. Let us hope that we as a culture will be just as lucky during these turbulent times. Rejecting false prophets is a great start.

TAKING THE LAW INTO YOUR OWN HANDS

July 9, 2016

During Hollywood's Golden Age, several movie productions addressed the issue of citizens taking the law into their own hands with tragic consequences. In mid-1930s, Fritz Lang directed ***Fury***, the movie that made Spencer Tracy a bona fide star. Accused of kidnapping a child, Tracy's character becomes the vile target of mob rule determined on burning down the jailhouse. He survives to exact revenge on those unruly folks with his unique brand of justice. The film sends a powerful message on how an innocent person can become a cynical beast as a result of his near-death experience.

The ***Ox-Bow Incident*** was a pet-project Western of filmmaker William A. Wellman, which focused on a lynch-mob bent on sagebrush justice. The victims of this unruly posse beg for their day in court.

However, the three so-called murderers and horse-thieves, led by actors Dana Andrews and Anthony Quinn, are unceremoniously hanged. Moments after the tragic incident, the real criminals are discovered, and further, the man they are accused of killing is very much alive. The mob must spend each waking hour of the rest of their born days owning up to their horrific actions. The movie is grim and quite graphic for its time.

The culture of mob violence has existed since the beginning of time. We are a civilized people who should defiantly shy away from this hypocritical practice of collective impromptu justice. This archaic solution to any perceived crime belongs in the dust bin of history.

ACE IN THE HOLE

April 2, 2018

On Easter Sunday, I celebrated my one-year anniversary at KNX 1070 News Radio in Southern California as a weekend traffic anchor. The afternoon turned out to be remarkable.

With thirty minutes left in my shift, I received a telephone call from a traffic tipster. He relayed information about a major incident along the Glendale Freeway. Drivers were getting out of their cars to look over the right shoulder wall onto the Los Angeles River. What they saw was a massive first-response presence in what turned out to be a missing-person situation. It affected traffic flow, so I reported the details about a lost boy on the air.

With the aid of the next traffic reporter (Logan Davis), we were able to ascertain that a huge news story was unfolding. I passed the information on to our KNX news desk. With my shift over, after twice reporting the incident, I went home. It became our lead story for the rest of the evening and during our *morning drive* cast. This story was reported over the CBS network, and it ran over the Associated Press national wire.

The incident reminded me of two movies that had similar themes in the 1950s. ***Ace in the Hole*** was directed by Billy Wilder and starred Kirk Douglas. It tells the tale of a man trapped by a cave-in, and the incident becomes a huge news story, making the reporter famous across the nation. The newsman's approach to the incident is ruthless and eventually proves fatal. This was Wilder's next production after ***Sunset Boulevard***. Though not a popular motion picture when released, it has garnered critical acclaim over the years.

The climax of ***Them!***, a science fiction thriller involving large radioactive ants and starring James Arness, James Whitmore and Edmund Gwenn, was more to the point. A couple of kids are lost in a maze of tunnels that are adjacent to the Los Angeles River and saved from an unspeakable fate at the last minute by our stars. Learning about a labyrinth of man-made caves from the flick, I surmised the real effort might have proved problematic for numbers of volunteers who spent their Easter looking for the aforementioned missing youth.

The fortunate news: The kid was found Monday morning, alive and in stable condition. He was transported to the hospital and eventually reunited with his parents. The victim was discovered in a sewage drain pipe, with a search-and-rescue team taking twelve hours for recovery.

As part of KNX 10-70 team-coverage, I felt incredibly blessed to tangentially contribute in the positive outcome of the saved teen. Kudos to Jan Stevens, Bob Brill, Pete Demetriou, Cooper Rummell and the rest of the KNX crew for a combined effort in this worthwhile assignment. Working for such a fabled community resource makes me proud.

Until next time . . . *never forget.*

Seventh-Inning Stretch

As they say, baseball is as American as apple pie, peanuts, popcorn and Crackerjacks. It has a way of bringing a diverse crowd together, and each inning provides compelling scenarios. The players are a colorful bunch of characters with names like *Dizzy*, *Yogi* and *Rube*. They cuss and spit and chew their cud. All the while, we root for our favorite team; in our case, they are the boys of summer, *dem bums*, those lovable Dodgers! Their tradition stretches over a century with stops in Brooklyn and Chavez Ravine, nestled in the heart of Downtown Los Angeles. By the way, if you need to get up and stretch . . . go ahead! We are at the midway point of our literary journey.

Take me out to the ballgame . . .

—Virginia Vandewouwer

OUR NATIONAL ANTHEM

July 4, 2017

Manny P. here . . .

Francis Scott Key, apparently better at lyrics than a melody, put his description of the battle of Fort McHenry to an old English tune that had a lot less to do with patriotism than it did with booze and women. This year marks the one hundredth season that it was played for the first time at a World Series game—an event that helped cement it in our collective consciousness to become our national anthem. The *Star-Spangled Banner*'s history is rooted in our national pastime.

On September 5, 1918, newspapers were dominated by reports of World War I, including the latest American dead. The World Series was in Chicago with the Cubs hosting Babe Ruth and the Boston Red Sox. The games were played at Comiskey Park, home of the White Sox, instead of their new locale at Wrigley Field (called Weegham Park at the time). But in a city jittery over the war, the game that day attracted fewer than twenty thousand fans, the smallest World Series crowd in years. In the seventh inning, the band from the navy training station, north of Chicago, started to play the *Star-Spangled Banner*.

The head of the navy band at the time was the well-known conductor and composer, John Philip Sousa. He was not at the game, but he had recently arranged the version that is still played today. The 1918 World Series was the first time the band could test the newer version. Players took off their caps as they faced a flag that fluttered atop a pole in right field as the twelve-piece band started to play. A couple of fans began to sing. Then others joined in. And when the last notes hit, a great volume of cheering rolled across the stadium. Not everybody thought what happened was a huge deal. Sports writer Ring Lardner wrote about it, but only as a punch line at the end of his column.

It was not until 1931 that Congress and President Herbert Hoover officially designated the ditty as our national anthem. During World War II, Major League teams began playing it each day.

And today, it is played at almost every American sporting event, from Little League and the Super Bowl to medal ceremonies at the Olympics. Happy Independence Day!

DEM BUMS

October 29, 2017

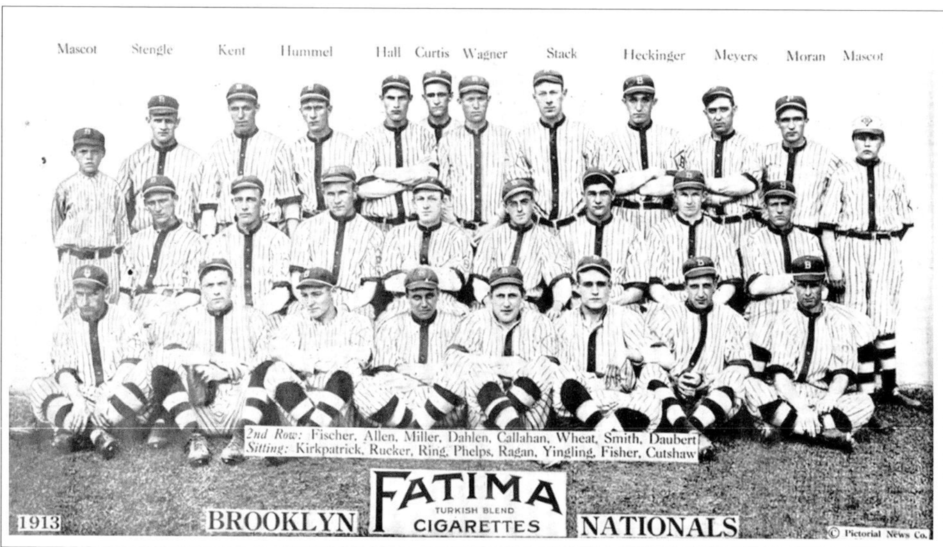

Prior to their move to Los Angeles, the Dodgers were the daffy team that played at Ebbets Field in Brooklyn.

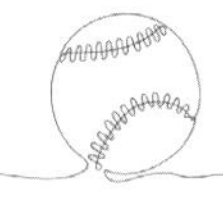

They were active in the Major Leagues from 1883 until 1957, winning only one World Series in 1955. The signing of Jackie Robinson in 1947 to play in Brooklyn secured the team's influential legacy.

After the so-called wilderness decades of the 1920s and 1930s, the Dodgers were rebuilt into a contending club, first by general manager Larry MacPhail and then by the legendary Branch Rickey. They finally won National League pennants in 1941, 1947, 1949, 1952 and 1953, only to lose to the New York Yankees in all five of the subsequent World Series. The spring ritual that provided hope, followed by immense disappointment, became an annual theme to their long-suffering fans. *Wait 'til next year* was the unofficial Dodgers slogan.

To add insult to injury . . . in 1951, Brooklyn led the National League by a prodigious thirteen and a half games in mid-August over their arch rivals, the Giants. However, they caught the *boys of summer*, which forced a three-game playoff. It came down to the final contest. Brooklyn seemed poised to secure the pennant, holding a 4-2 lead in the bottom of the ninth inning. Bobby Thomson would crush a stunning three-run walk-off homer from the Dodgers' Ralph Branca to secure the National League Championship for New York. To this day, Thomson's home run is known as *the shot heard round the world.*

One final indignity . . . the year after *Dem Bums* took it all, Yankees pitcher Don Larsen pitched the only perfect game in World Series history and the only post-season no-hitter over the next fifty-four years. The Dodgers lost in seven games in 1956.

The Dodgers remained in the Flatbush neighborhood of Brooklyn for just one more season before they ventured to the West Coast. Ebbets Field was one of several historic Major League ballparks demolished in the 1960s. Today, apartment housing replaces the famed ballpark.

The Dodgers have played in nineteen World Series, nine in Brooklyn and ten in Los Angeles. Currently, the Dodgers are searching for their seventh World Series championship. They are tied with the Houston Astros, a team that has never won a World Series and competing in only their second Fall Classic.

Like historian Doris Kearns Goodwin, I root for the Dodgers and have waited almost thirty years for their next World Series victory.

VIN SCULLY'S FINAL WEEK

September 19, 2016

Vin Scully is heading into his final week behind the microphone at Dodger Stadium before concluding his career on October 2 in San Francisco, where the Los Angeles Dodgers end the regular season against the rival Giants. His sixty-seven years with the Dodgers make Scully the longest-tenured broadcaster with a single team in professional sports.

Scully discovered his love of baseball walking home from grade school. He passed a Chinese laundromat and saw the score from game two of the 1936 World Series. His aspirations came true at the age of twenty-two when he was hired by a CBS radio affiliate in Washington, DC. The next year, he joined Red Barber and Connie Desmond in the Brooklyn Dodgers radio and television booths.

In 1953, at age twenty-five, Scully became the youngest person to broadcast a World Series game, a mark that still stands. Through the years, Scully has entranced generations of baseball fans with his dulcet tones as he spins stories about the game and its players while working alone on the air. In 1958, he accompanied the Dodgers when the franchise relocated to Los Angeles from Ebbets Field. Fans had trouble recognizing the players during the team's first four years at Los Angeles Memorial Coliseum. He credits the birth of the transistor radio as the greatest single break of his career. That radio-listening habit carried over when the team moved to Dodger Stadium. Fans at the games held radios to their ears, and those not present listened from home or their car, allowing Scully to connect to generations of families with his words.

The Dodgers plan to honor their second-longest tenured employee (behind former manager Tom Lasorda), beginning Tuesday night with a Scully bobblehead giveaway. Friday is an appreciation day for Scully, with a pre-game ceremony featuring speakers associated with his career. Commissioner Rob Manfred will offer a fifty-thousand-dollar donation from Major League Baseball to the Jackie Robinson Foundation in Scully's name, with Dodgers manager Dave Roberts toting the oversized check. After the speeches, both teams will line up on each side of home plate, remove their caps and listen to John Williams conduct the Los Angeles Philharmonic in the National Anthem behind the mound. And a post-game fireworks show is set to the top calls of Scully's career. The first fifty thousand fans at Saturday's game against Colorado will receive a limited-edition solid bronze coin. On the front is an image of Vin with his signature introduction:

"It's time for Dodger baseball!"

Previously, at the start of each series, the umpires have turned to face Scully's booth and tipped their caps to him. To his surprise and delight, players and managers have come to him. Throughout the season, they have made the long trek from the visiting clubhouse in right field to his fifth-floor broadcast booth in the press box named for him, bringing gifts. In San Francisco, the Giants will honor Scully at his final game. Two Bay Area television stations will carry an inning of his broadcast, as stations in other cities have done this season.

Now eighty-eight, Scully was adamant about not having an extended farewell. For the last time at home on Sunday, Vin will open his broadcast with the same reassuring greeting:

"Hi, everybody, and a very pleasant good afternoon to you wherever you may be."

FOUR TO BASEBALL HALL OF FAME IN 1955

January 7, 2015

With the current selection by the Baseball Writers Association of America of four retired Major League ballplayers to its Hall of Fame—Randy Johnson, Craig Biggio, John Smoltz and Pedro Martinez—in July joins fabulous company. Let us look back at the last time this happened—1955.

One of the larger classes was inducted on July 25, 1955, as the Hall of Fame welcomed BBWAA inductees Joe DiMaggio, Gabby Hartnett, Ted Lyons and Dazzy Vance and Veterans Committee picks Frank *Home Run* Baker and Ray Schalk. At the biggest induction ceremony since 1939, the crowd fav was easily DiMaggio, according to the *New York Times*.

Hollywood's connection to one of these inductees is quite obvious. DiMaggio was briefly married to Marilyn Monroe. Considered one of the all-time great ballplayers, the *Yankee Clipper* had a half-dozen red roses delivered three times a week to her crypt for twenty years.

When there is an influx of qualified candidates, as there were for many years after the hall was opened, voters tend to spread their votes out. DiMaggio's 88.8 percent is not an aberration of the time, and a player of his caliber would probably receive over 95 percent if voted on in today's era (as did Cal Ripken Jr., Tony Gwynn, Rickey Henderson, etc.).

Not making the cut that year . . . Hank Greenberg (who was inducted in 1956), Joe Cronin, Hack Wilson, Red Ruffing, Max Carey and Zack Wheat. All these gentlemen were eventually selected to represent these hallowed grounds.

UCLA HONORS JACKIE ROBINSON

November 26, 2014

UCLA will retire number forty-two across all of its sports in honor of Jackie Robinson. This was announced by Director of Athletics Dan Guerrero.

All three UCLA student-athletes who currently wear number forty-two—senior women's soccer defender Ally Courtnall, sophomore women's softball utility player Jelly Felix and freshman football linebacker Kenny Young—will each be able to finish out his or her Bruin career donning the iconic number.

With UCLA football players wearing number forty-two on their helmets and Robinson's iconic number forty-two painted onto the Rose Bowl field, UCLA made the announcement during the break between the first and second quarters of its annual crosstown rivalry football game with USC. In conjunction with UCLA, the city of Pasadena and the Rose Bowl Operating Committee, the Rose Bowl subsequently unveiled Jackie Robinson's iconic number near the east scoreboard and will make it a permanent fixture in the historic stadium this offseason.

Additionally, UCLA will also permanently display Robinson's iconic number forty-two inside each of its athletic competition venues. The retirement of Robinson's number forty-two follows UCLA's announcement of a series of twenty-two athletic and recreation facilities across campus that will be named the Jackie Robinson Athletics and Recreation Complex. Campus recognition of the complex will be an in-ground number forty-two at each entry point to UCLA's training centers, competition sites, fields and stadiums as a reminder of Robinson's courage in the face of adversity.

Seventy-five years ago, Jackie Robinson claimed a place at UCLA. From 1939 to 1941, he starred in four sports. In football, Robinson played both offense and defense, returned punts, caught and threw passes, kicked extra points and, in the process, earned honorable mention *All-American* accolades. In basketball, he twice led the Pacific Coast Conference in scoring. In track, he won the NCAA championship in the broad jump. And in baseball, he began his legendary journey as a highly regarded shortstop for the Bruins.

Six years later, Jackie Robinson claimed a place in history. Wearing number forty-two for the Brooklyn Dodgers on April 15, 1947, Robinson shattered the color barrier in Major League Baseball. Despite racial abuse, jeers from fans and fellow players, death threats and profound harassment, he endured it all with grace and dignity—not to mention exceptional play—earning Rookie of the Year honors and a National League Most Valuable Player award. He helped the Dodgers win the 1955 World Series. A career .311 hitter, Robinson played in six Fall Classics, six consecutive All-Star games and was inducted into the Baseball Hall of Fame in 1962, during his first year of eligibility.

Fighting tirelessly for civil rights and integration in professional sports after his time at the ballpark, Robinson best summed up his legacy with a typically understated yet poignant quote:

"A life is not important except in the impact it has on other lives."

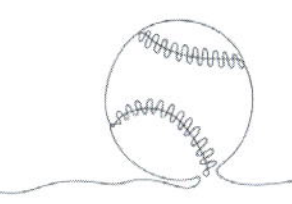

HAMMERIN' HANK CELEBRATES EIGHTY YEARS

February 9, 2014

At a private party celebrating his birthday, friends, former teammates and luminaries paid tribute to Henry Aaron, who turned eighty on Wednesday. His tribute continued when he spoke as part of the *Living Portrait Series* at the Smithsonian American Art Museum. In addition, a painting of the baseball great, done by Ross Rossin of Atlanta, will be unveiled at the National Portrait Gallery.

Attorney General Eric Holder motioned toward a window and paid Aaron a huge compliment, saying President Obama's path was made easier. Former slugger Reggie Jackson compared Henry to Jackie Robinson, who broke baseball's color barrier in 1947. Frank Robinson spoke of the thrill of entering the Baseball Hall of Fame with Hank in 1982. Other speakers included Hall of Famers Jim Rice, Rickey Henderson and Ozzie Smith, who grew up in Aaron's hometown of Mobile, Alabama. Former teammate Robin Yount said he was his mother's second-favorite player—behind Aaron! Bud Selig, the commissioner of Major League Baseball, spoke of his friendship with Henry, which dates back to 1958. Selig also talked of his long-overdue acceptance in a career often overshadowed by Mickey Mantle and Willie Mays. As the event ended, Aaron and his wife of forty years beamed as the crowd sang *Happy Birthday to You*.

Forty years ago, Henry Aaron surpassed the hallowed record of Babe Ruth on his way to 755 career home runs while combating racism with a quiet dignity. After Hank's retirement from the Major Leagues, his legacy continues to grow . . .

JOSH GIBSON READY FOR LIMELIGHT

March 21, 2017

An opera about Negro Leagues baseball great Josh Gibson, whose home run stroke rivaled Babe Ruth's, will have its world premiere in Pittsburgh next month. ***The Summer King***, presented by the Pittsburgh Opera, premieres April 29. Gibson's life story also figured in ***Fences***, the film starring Denzel Washington that was originally a play by Pittsburgh native August Wilson.

Gibson was one of the first three Negro Leagues players to be inducted into the National Baseball Hall of Fame, which lists his career batting average as .350. He was twice named Negro National League batting champ and led the league in home runs three times. Gibson played for two Pittsburgh teams: *The Homestead Grays* and *The Crawfords*. Gibson passed at thirty-five from a brain aneurysm a few months before Jackie Robinson integrated baseball in 1947.

The Pittsburgh Opera partnered on ***The Summer King*** with the Josh Gibson Foundation, which is run by Gibson's great-grandson Sean. While ***Fences*** brought attention to his great-grandfather, the opera will tell a more complete story. A ballpark named for Gibson is located in Pittsburgh's Hill District, not far from the August Wilson House, the late playwright's childhood home. The museum will host a block party on April 29, starting at noon, a few hours prior to the opera premiere, to mark Wilson's birthday.

Nearly all fourteen principal roles in ***The Summer King*** are played by African Americans, a rarity in operas (***Porgy and Bess*** notwithstanding). Renowned mezzo-soprano Denyce Graves plays Gibson's lover and bass-baritone Alfred Walker will play Josh Gibson.

The Michigan Opera Theatre in Detroit plans to stage ***The Summer King*** in March 2018.

A FALL CLASSIC FOR THE AGES

October 25, 2016

At long last, either the Chicago Cubs or the Cleveland Indians will win the World Series. The two teams with the longest current dry spells in baseball will finally meet and for the first time in post season.

The Indians have not won it all since 1948, two seasons before Vin Scully debuted in his first game of a sixty-seven-year Major Leagues announcing career and a year after Jackie Robinson broke the color barrier, both with the Brooklyn Dodgers. The *tribe* did play against the Florida Marlins in 1997, only to lose in seven games.

The Cubbies have not even been to a Fall Classic since 1945, two months after the end of World War II. And of course, Wrigley Field has not seen its home team emerge as a champion since 1908 when a Roosevelt was president . . . Theodore Roosevelt! Hall-of-Famers Ernie Banks, Billy Williams, Ferguson Jenkins, Ron Santo and Ryne Sandberg never played in a single MLB World Series game for their entire combined careers.

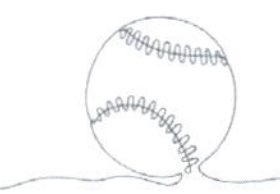

For perspective . . .

In 1908 . . . The Academy Awards would not exist for another nineteen years. D. W. Griffith became a director. And Bette Davis, James Stewart, Rex Harrison, Carole Lombard, Fred MacMurray, Ethel Merman, Milton Berle, Buddy Ebsen, Don Ameche, Burgess Meredith and Van Heflin were born. ALL are deceased.

In March 1945 . . . The Academy Awards were held, and ***Going My Way*** was the Best Picture of the year. Bing Crosby won Best Actor, and the Best Actress statuette was awarded to Ingrid Bergman for ***Gaslight***. Other notable movies include ***Laura***, ***Double Indemnity***, ***A Guy Named Joe***, ***Mr. Skeffington***, ***Meet Me in St. Louis***, ***Thirty Seconds Over Tokyo*** and ***Lifeboat***.

In March 1948 . . . The Best Picture was ***Gentleman's Agreement***. Ronald Colman took home the Best Actor Oscar for ***A Double Life***, and Loretta Young pulled the biggest upset in Academy Awards history and was named Best Actress for her role in ***The Farmer's Daughter***. Other important nominees include ***Forever Amber***, ***Mourning Becomes Electra***, ***Miracle on 34th Street***, ***The Ghost and Mrs. Muir***, ***The Egg and I***, ***The Bishop's Wife*** and ***Song of the South***.

This is for sure . . . One team will emerge as champion; the other will continue its curse. Somewhere above, Ernie Banks is exclaiming: *"Let's play seven!"*

Until next time . . . *never forget.*

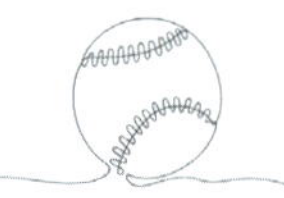

— CHAPTER EIGHT —

Ripped from the Headlines

Sensationalized stories go back to the days of William Randolph Hearst. Yellow-journalism articles sold newspapers.

Hollywood has always been able to find itself in the middle of steamy gossip that ended up in print, and a curious public ate it up! We have collected a bevy of fascinating and, in certain instances, lurid tales that will intrigue you . . . and may even shock you. Dare I say these stories are ripped from the headlines and features notable names, such as Rock Hudson, Natalie Wood, Harrison Ford, Marlon Brando and Charlie Chaplin. Let us hope we have piqued your interest!

—Virginia Vandewouwer

SOMETHING FISHY

August 7, 2018

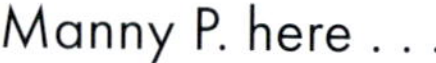

Manny P. here . . .

The son of Stephen King has turned detective in efforts to solve a cold-case murder. And it has a connection to the Steven Spielberg classic ***Jaws***. Joe Hill fleshed out this theory after watching the flick on the big screen in 2015.

The comic book and horror writer had recently been reading about the *Lady of the Dunes*, an unknown woman found brutally murdered in the sandy dunes of Provincetown, Massachusetts, in late July 1974 while ***Jaws*** was being filmed, one hundred miles away in Martha's Vineyard. A female extra in ***Jaws*** resembles the figure presented in a composite sketch of the victim.

Fifty-three minutes into the movie, a woman with a blue bandana over her auburn hair is seen briefly waiting to board a ferry in a non-frightening scene. The *Lady of the Dunes* was believed to be in her mid-twenties to thirties when she was murdered in late June or early July. The naked woman's hands were removed, preventing fingerprint identification. Her head, which suffered a fatal blow, rested on jeans and a blue bandana. Hill gets goosebumps when he watches the scene.

The theory is making the rounds on the internet. One added complication . . . The casting director for the film died in 2009. Local investigators are pondering Hill's speculative analysis.

CSI ITALY . . . UNEARTHING MONA LISA

April 6, 2011

An Italian research team is traveling to Florence to dig up the remains of a Renaissance woman who they believe posed for Leonardo da Vinci for the *Mona Lisa* portrait. This project aims to locate the remains of Lisa Gherardini, the wife of a silk merchant. Art lovers have long linked Gherardini to the iconic painting.

Giorgio Vasari, a sixteenth-century biographer, wrote that da Vinci painted a portrait using Gherardini, who was born in 1479. A few years ago, an amateur Italian historian said he had found a death certificate showing that she died in 1542, with her burial spot specifically in central Florence.

The project follows a popular trend that uses crime scene investigator–like methods in art history and has drawn (no pun intended) their share of criticism based on the inconclusive nature of the research. Some scholars have suggested that such scientific techniques add little when it comes to appreciating or understanding a work of art. If successful, the research might unveil targeted characteristics of Gherardini's face matching those in the painting, answering whether she could be the actual model in question.

The first step is ground-penetration radar to search for the bones compatible with Gherardini's. The group will also look for traces of possible diseases or bone structure to match what we know about her life. If such bones are identified, the researchers will conduct carbon dating and extract DNA, which will be compared to DNA extracted from the bones of Gherardini's children, some of whom are also buried in Florence.

Finally, if skull fragments are found, depending on how well-preserved they are, the research group might attempt a facial reconstruction. This step will be crucial in determining whether Gherardini was indeed the subject with the famous smile for Leonardo da Vinci.

His birthplace is in question, and there are zero findings of a birth certificate. What gives? No, I am not talking about President Obama. The big mystery gripping all of Great Britain is questions surrounding Charlie Chaplin.

Secret papers released on Friday by the National Archives in London suggest Chaplin may not have been born a Brit on the day generally accepted as his birthday. After scouring the many files at Somerset House for his birth certificate, including checks for his supposed alias *Israel Thornstein*, British Intelligence concludes that the iconic star may not have been born in the United Kingdom. Investigations in France and Russia have also drawn similar conclusions. It seems no evidence exists as to where Charlie Chaplin was born. Rumors that he was a child of gypsies have proved similarly unfounded. This hypothesis has been fact checked. . . . Really?

What is known . . . The United States banned the actor from entering the country in 1952. J. Edgar Hoover considered Chaplin a threat to democracy. The American government has long surmised after careful investigation that the silent screen star was a Communist. He was finally allowed to appear, decades later, at the Academy Awards to accept an honorary Oscar.

Because of the many mysteries surrounding Chaplin during his lifetime, he was finally knighted after a twenty-year delay in March 1975. He took his many secrets to the grave when he died in Switzerland in 1977. Meanwhile, a current FBI-style search, which has transfixed two continents, will continue . . .

Allied intelligence wants to close this cold case file in 2012. So far, it is not meant to be.

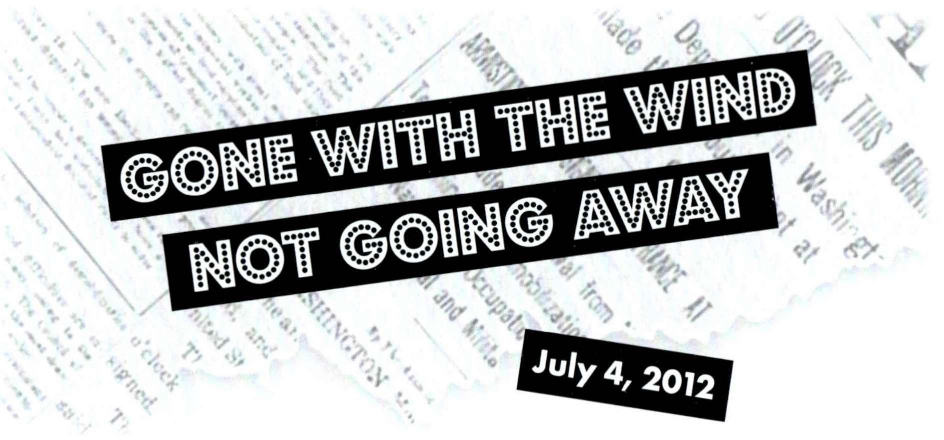

Calm down, folks. . . . No one in the federal government is planning to ban ***Gone with the Wind*** from purchase or from future theatrical screenings.

A *New York Post* columnist last week started the fuss by suggesting the classic flick and its themes were suspect in its romanticizing of the Confederate war against the States. He concluded by asking his readers to consider (as he surmised):

> *The offensively sympathetic celluloid portrayal of slavery and enshrining the falsehood that the Civil War was not fought over slavery—in the wake of the Charleston church slaughter.*

The reason for the panic . . . Extremist social media sites have suggested that the *Post* writer was a flaming socialist fanatic. They also piggybacked the charge with an inflammatory photo of a book-burning scene from the film—***Fahrenheit 451***. Fair-and-balanced websites decided to pick up the story. Since then, ***Gone with the Wind*** has skyrocketed in popularity.

Warner Brothers, which has distributed ***Gone with the Wind*** since 1996 (it has sold more theater tickets than any other film, ever), is a politically progressive company, sensitive and socially responsible enough about outdated racial attitudes to have placed disclaimers on some older films and cartoons. Still it is a company with stockholders, and there is no way it is going to completely withdraw a film as lucrative as ***Gone with the Wind*** from circulation.

Truth be told . . . Columnist Lou Lumenick stopped far short of calling for ANY censorship, even for the more blatantly racist ***The Birth of a Nation***. However, his soul-searching words caused a run on ***Gone with the Wind*** Blu-ray purchases, surpassing sales of the highly popular ***Fifty Shades of Gray*** and ***American Sniper*** on Amazon.

One can argue the merits of the Best Picture of 1939. But I assure you, this movie will not be banished to a museum for viewing. It seems Americans do give a damn about this epic feature!

The son of the founder of *The Hollywood Reporter* has apologized for decisions exacted by his dad at the beginning of the Cold War. In a story circulated by the trade publication, Willie Wilkerson has expressed remorse on the eve of the sixty-fifth anniversary of his father's role in the 1947 Hollywood blacklist that ruined the livelihood of writers, actors and directors accused of having Communist ties.

The elder William R. Wilkerson printed the official list of names targeted by the House Committee on Un-American Activities (HUAC) in its 1947 hearings. Among the notable careers disrupted or ravaged by this announcement: E. Y. Harburg, Howard Koch, Ring Lardner Jr., Edward Dmytryk and Dalton Trumbo.

AMERICANS.....
DON'T PATRONIZE REDS!!!!

YOU CAN DRIVE THE REDS OUT OF TELEVISION, RADIO AND HOLLYWOOD.....
THIS TRACT WILL TELL YOU HOW.

WHY WE MUST DRIVE THEM OUT:

1) The REDS have made our Screen, Radio and TV Moscow's most effective Fifth Column in America . . . 2) The REDS of Hollywood and Broadway have always been the chief financial support of Communist propaganda in America . . . 3) OUR OWN FILMS, made by RED Producers, Directors, Writers and STARS, are being used by Moscow in ASIA, Africa, the Balkans and throughout Europe to create hatred of America . . . 4) RIGHT NOW films are being made to craftily glorify MARXISM, UNESCO and ONE-WORLDISM . . . **and via your TV Set they are being piped into your Living Room—and are poisoning the minds of your children under your very eyes ! ! !**

So REMEMBER — If you patronize a Film made by RED Producers, Writers, Stars and STUDIOS you are aiding and abetting COMMUNISM . . . every time you permit REDS to come into your Living Room VIA YOUR TV SET you are helping MOSCOW and the INTERNATIONALISTS to destroy America ! ! !

Wilkerson initiated the blacklist as a targeted response against the moguls who presumably denied him the opportunity to establish a film studio in the late 1920s. He then created *The Hollywood Reporter*. Just after World War II, Wilkerson authorized negative editorial stories aimed at Communist sympathizers with their influence on the motion picture industry. The publication ignited the practice of naming names.

During his tenure as editor in chief of *The Hollywood Reporter*, Wilkerson was also known for opening nightclubs along the Sunset Strip, co-financing the construction of the Flamingo Hotel in Las Vegas with Bugsy Siegel and discovering Lana Turner at the Top Hat Cafe, located on Sunset Boulevard. Wilkerson brought the aspiring talent to Zeppo Marx, who was a theatrical agent after he retired from acting (Zeppo was one of the Marx Brothers). The *Lana Turner-Schwabs Drug Store* legend was fabricated by the MGM publicity department.

The details of *The Hollywood Reporter*'s role in the blacklist era are chronicled for the first time in a lengthy article published on Monday. The younger Wickerson surmised his dad might have apologized for curtailing so many careers had he lived long enough. He died in 1962, two years after the blacklist was broken by Kirk Douglas, who hired Trumbo to supervise the script for ***Spartacus*** and, most importantly, offered the writer screen credit.

William Wilkerson's son has released the following statement:

> *On behalf of my family, and particularly my late father, I wish to convey my sincerest apologies and deepest regrets to those victimized by this unfortunate incident.*

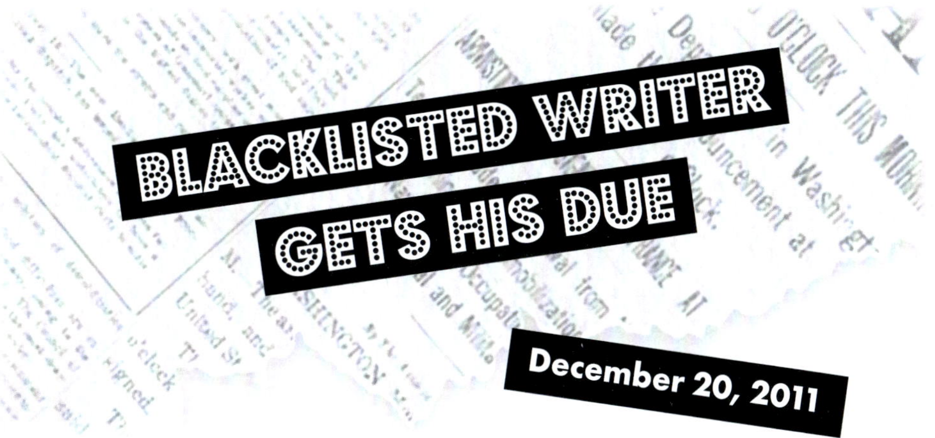

I want to personally congratulate Lawrence O'Donnell, host of MSNBC's *Last Word*, for his story on a segment about a recent decision made by the Writers Guild of America. Due to the unyielding efforts of the children of Dalton Trumbo and Ian McLellan Hunter, the screenwriter (Trumbo) was belatedly added to the credits of the 1953 Paramount comedy ***Roman Holiday***. The film starred Gregory Peck, Audrey Hepburn and Eddie Albert.

Christopher Trumbo was a playwright who spent his adult life studying the details of the *Hollywood Ten* and the blacklist during the McCarthy Era. Chris died in January of 2011. Tim Hunter, a television director, joined his lifelong friend in helping get Trumbo's dad the credit he richly deserved.

Dalton Trumbo was a successful screenwriter, and his credits included ***Five Came Back***, ***A Guy Named Joe***, ***Our Vines Have Tender Grapes***, ***Kitty Foyle*** and ***Thirty Seconds Over Tokyo***. After a conviction by the House Un-American Activities Committee (HUAC) for the scribe's involvement in the Communist Party, he was blacklisted from movie studios for a decade. During the 1950s, Trumbo sold scripts without receiving screen credit. Among these films . . . ***The Brave One***, which won the Oscar for Best Screenplay of 1956. Robert Rich was given the Academy Award, a person who did not exist.

Trumbo officially returned to writing for the movies when Kirk Douglas insisted that Trumbo be given screen credit for his work on ***Spartacus*** in 1960, and this helped break the blacklist. A year before his death, he was given his statuette for ***The Brave One*** by the Academy of Motion Picture Arts and Sciences. In 1993, Dalton Trumbo was posthumously awarded his Oscar for co-writing ***Roman Holiday***.

In a statement issued last week by the WGA West President Chris Keyser, the guild issued an apology to the Trumbo family. He hoped the gesture of inclusion of the screenwriter credit to the Paramount film might ease the pain that can never be erased. Also, this serves as a reminder to do the right thing and avoid the impulse of censorship for political reasons.

Lawrence O'Donnell is well-known for his long association with ***The West Wing***, acting as executive story editor, co-producer, consultant and executive producer throughout various episodes from 1999 to 2006. He won an Emmy for his work in 2001, capturing a statuette for Outstanding Drama Series. Again, politics and Hollywood make strange bedfellows.

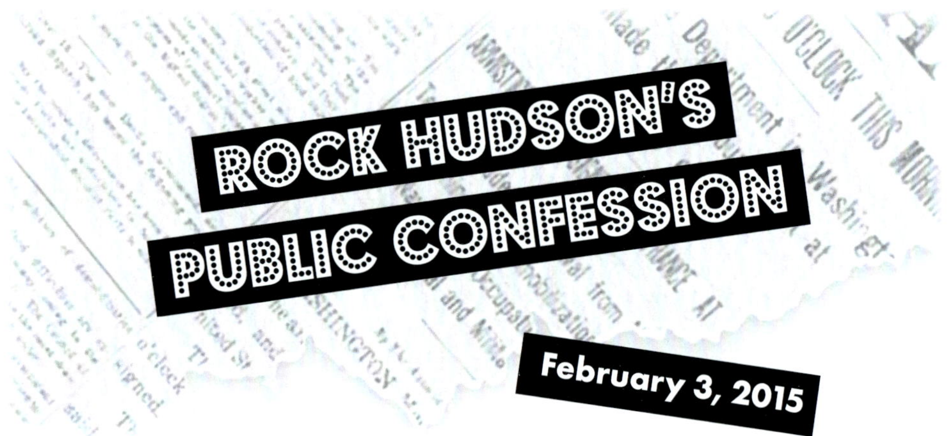

Reports have surfaced that nine weeks before his death by complications from AIDS on October 2, 1985, Rock Hudson was in France trying to get treatment not available in the United States. But Nancy Reagan refused his request for the White House to help.

When Hudson collapsed on July 21, 1985, shortly after arriving in Paris, he was admitted to the American Hospital. He wanted to see Dr. Dominique Dormant, the French army doctor who had been working on experimental AIDS treatment HPA-23 and who had secretly treated the actor months after his diagnosis. Dormant, however, could not get Hudson transferred to the military hospital. Over the next ten days, as the public first became aware that Hudson was gay and had AIDS, the medical team made a number of desperate attempts to get help, including sending a telegram to the White House.

Hudson was a friend of then-president Ronald Reagan from their acting days. The July 24 telegram pleaded with the White House to request that the commanding officer reconsider admitting the star to the military hospital. The Reagan staffer who received the telegram spoke with Nancy Reagan. He recommended she refer the issue to the United States Embassy in France. The Reagans were very conscious of not making exceptions for people just because they were friends or because they were celebrities. She agreed and, though her husband called Hudson to wish him well, the official response was that Nancy Reagan did not feel this was something the White House should get into. Dormant was eventually able to treat Hudson, but his condition was too advanced.

Today, the former First Lady simply does not recall the incident in question. It is generally regarded that the publicity generated by Rock Hudson and Magic Johnson has led to medical advancements in the battle against HIV/AIDS.

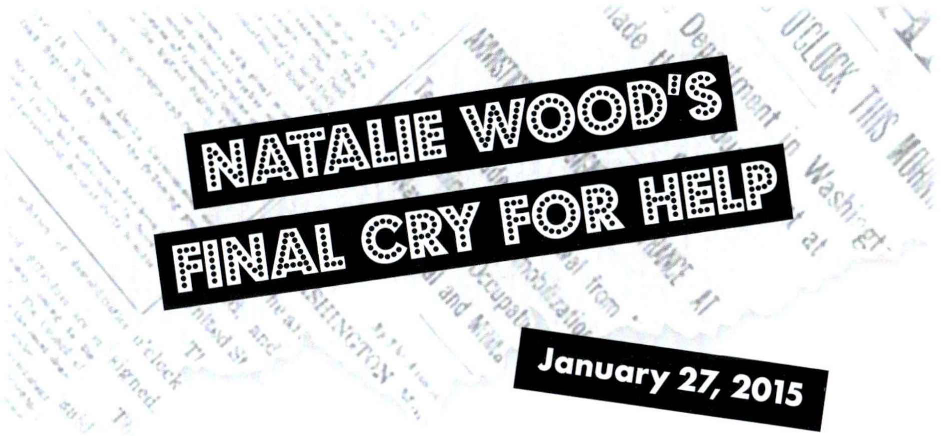

Natalie Wood was screaming for help as she drowned, according to a witness whose account has never been disclosed. Retired stockbroker Marilyn Wayne has provided credible eyewitness testimony that the star was shouting desperate cries for aid but was ignored.

Relatedly, the Los Angeles police last week said that substantial new evidence has led them to reopen their investigation into the Wood's drowning off Catalina Island thirty years ago this week. Her death was ruled accidental at the time. A police source has described Robert Wagner, now eighty-one, as a person of interest in the updated case.

They were onboard their yacht *Splendour* with her alleged love interest Oscar-winner Christopher Walken on that fateful evening. Wagner has always maintained Wood accidently slipped and drowned as she drunkenly tried to tie up a dinghy against the boat. Natalie's sister has claimed that the actress was so scared of water, she never would have ventured off alone to Avalon late into the evening.

With this new witness coming forward, the questions homicide detectives are exploring: Did Wagner or Walken hear the cries of distress? Did they attempt to save Wood from drowning after she fell into the ocean? Investigators plan to hold a news conference. They are asking for individuals to come forward with information about the case and to contact sheriff's officials or an anonymous tip line that has been set up.

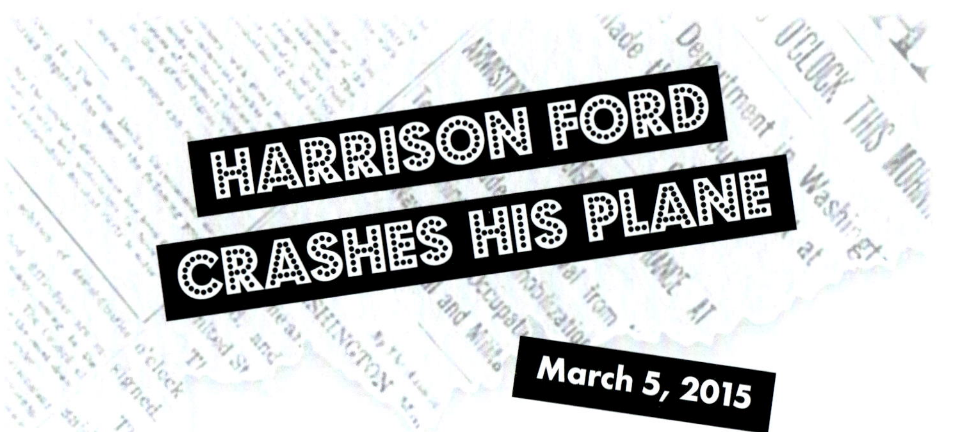

Harrison Ford crash-landed his vintage airplane at a Los Angeles golf course this afternoon. He suffered moderate injuries and was taken to a hospital. The actor's single-engine plane went down at about 2:30 p.m. in the Venice area. The pilot was breathing and conscious when he was taken to a hospital, where he was listed in fair to moderate condition.

The seventy-two-year-old ***Star Wars*** and ***Indiana Jones*** actor is an aviation enthusiast, who often flies out of the Santa Monica Airport near Penmar Golf Course. The plane is mostly intact after the wreck, and Harrison was the only person aboard. Nobody on the ground was hurt, but people rushed to the scene.

The actor is cast to portray swashbuckling, space-age, soldier of fortune *Han Solo* in his fourth ***Star Wars*** movie. The original ***Star Wars*** in 1977 made Ford an overnight star, and he remains an A-list actor. He has played whip-slinging archaeologist *Indiana Jones* in four movies of the series.

Ford got his pilot's license in the late 1980s and has served as a spokesman for various airline groups. He stepped down as chairman of a youth program for Experimental Aircraft Association in 2009.

Our best wishes to the intrepid Harrison Ford.

Governor Rick Perry formally presented the Texas Legislative Medal of Honor posthumously to Major Audie L. Murphy today in a public ceremony in Farmersville, Texas. The award was accepted by Murphy's sister, Mrs. Nadine Murphy-Lockey.

Murphy was America's most decorated World War II combat soldier, earning an astounding thirty-three decorations, medals and citations, including the United States Medal of Honor, the Distinguished Service Cross, a Silver Star, a Bronze Star, a Legion of Merit and a Purple Heart. Throughout his career in the service, he received every valor decoration the military awarded at that time.

After the war, Audie Murphy appeared in over fifty films, spanning a twenty-one-year career, most notably playing himself in the 1955 autobiographical war film ***To Hell and Back*** (based on his 1949 memoirs), which set a box-office record for Universal Studios. It was not broken until ***Jaws*** was released in 1975. In an effort to draw attention to the problems of returning Korean War and Vietnam War veterans, Murphy

spoke out candidly about his own problems with post-traumatic stress disorder. It was known during Murphy's lifetime as *battle fatigue* and *shell shock*, terminology dating back to World War I.

On May 28, 1971, Murphy was killed when his private plane crashed into Brush Mountain near Catawba, Virginia, in conditions of rain, clouds, fog and zero visibility. As a result of legislation introduced by the United States Congress five months after his death, the Audie L. Murphy Memorial Veterans Hospital in San Antonio was dedicated in 1973. It is currently part of the South Texas Veteran's Health Care System.

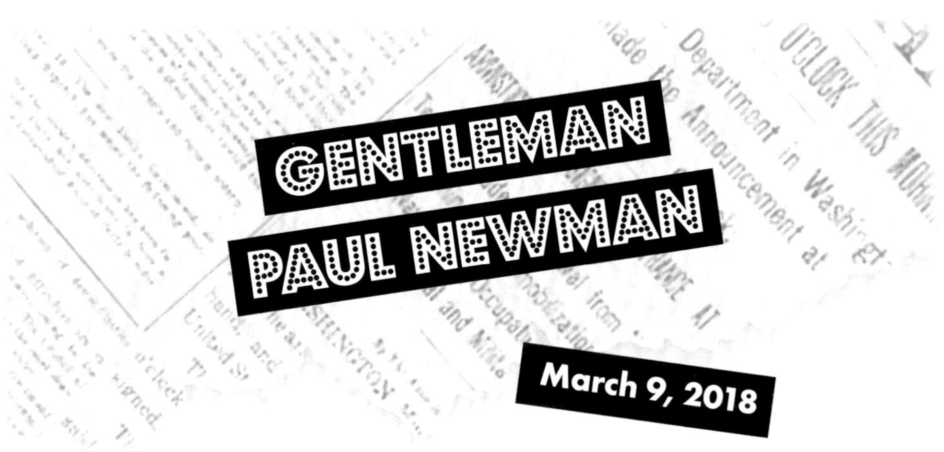

Susan Sarandon, who is promoting her new movie, ***Bombshell: The Hedy Lamarr Story***, told *BBC 5 Live* that she once got equitable income with her male counterparts because Paul Newman helped bridge the pay inequality between male and female wages. Over his career, he was known for his political activism. The incident was similar to last year's Michelle Williams/Mark Wahlberg cash issue during the reshoot of ***All the Money in the World***.

The Hollywood starlet was featured in the 1998 film ***Twilight*** with Newman and Gene Hackman when she discovered that both were offered a greater income. Sarandon suggested that her former co-star gave her a portion of his salary when finding out they were getting more loot. Sarandon, who received equal billing alongside her male co-stars, alluded Newman and Hackman benefited from a favored nations clause, the agreement whereby producers ensure actors are given the same terms as their fellow stars. Susan was afforded no such offer.

The actress, who just received an Emmy nomination for her role as *Bette Davis* in ***Feud: Bette and Joan***, additionally told the radio station that unwanted exchanges between starlet and producer need to vanish. She added that Harvey Weinstein's behavior in the industry was despicable, but the casting couch will remain in the film world, much to the chagrin of her peers.

Sarandon's revelations on International Women's Day are part of the ongoing dialogue about the pay gap in Hollywood between men and women and movements to curtail institutionalized sexism in the industry. Studio Era stars, such as Paul Newman, remain unscathed in these controversies. He exudes class, even in memory.

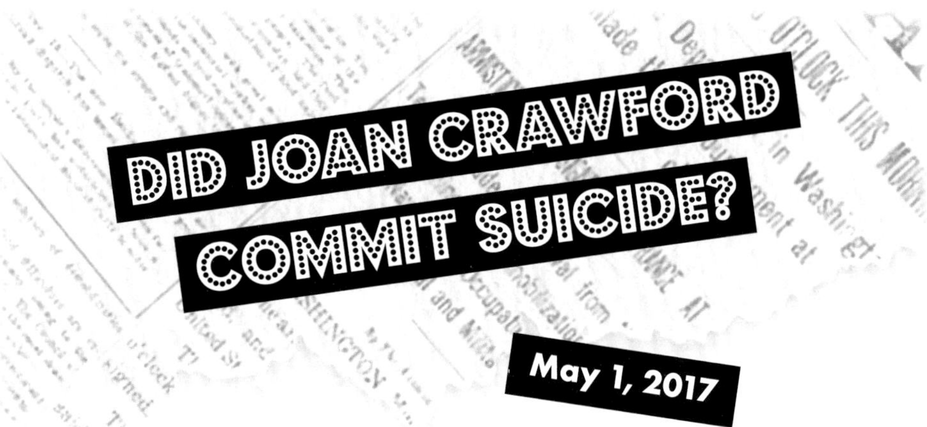

DID JOAN CRAWFORD COMMIT SUICIDE?

May 1, 2017

Joan Crawford is one of the most iconic movie actors to have ever graced the silver screen. Despite her fame and critical acclaim, she died alone inside her Manhattan apartment. The final episode of the brilliant FX anthology ***Feud: Bette and Joan*** gave viewers a glimpse into Crawford's final weeks, pointing out how solitary it was for the woman, who at one time was the toast of Tinseltown.

Crawford made a decision to end her movie career after fifty years when her looks began to change with age and the offers started to dry up. She was found deceased inside her apartment on May 10, 1977, at the age of sixty-nine, seventy or, maybe, seventy-two. Out of respect, the lowest of these ages was officially published. Now, Crawford's death is shrouded in mystery.

Crawford's loneliness was amplified after her four adopted kids opted out of a Mother's Day visit. Plus, she was aware daughter Christina was penning a scathing account about growing up with the woman, who millions loved and adored.

The best indication Crawford was planning for the end . . . she gave away her beloved shih tzu to friends to care for, despite the fact she had not let the pooch out of her apartment for close to a year. She was dead forty-eight hours later. The actual date of her passing also had added significance: it was her twenty-second wedding anniversary with her fourth husband, Alfred Steele.

Soon after Crawford's death, multiple friends came forward, convinced the star's death was a suicide from an overdose of sleeping pills, with the strongest claim coming from Joan's own daughter Cynthia. Upon learning her mom's cause of death had been listed as acute coronary occlusion, she pointed out her mother had been suffering from cancer and had absolutely no history of heart problems.

Meanwhile, the medical examiner did not conduct an autopsy. The coroner eventually stated if he had been aware that she had taken her own life, he would have performed a thorough examination of the actress's corpse. The cause of her death may never really be known.

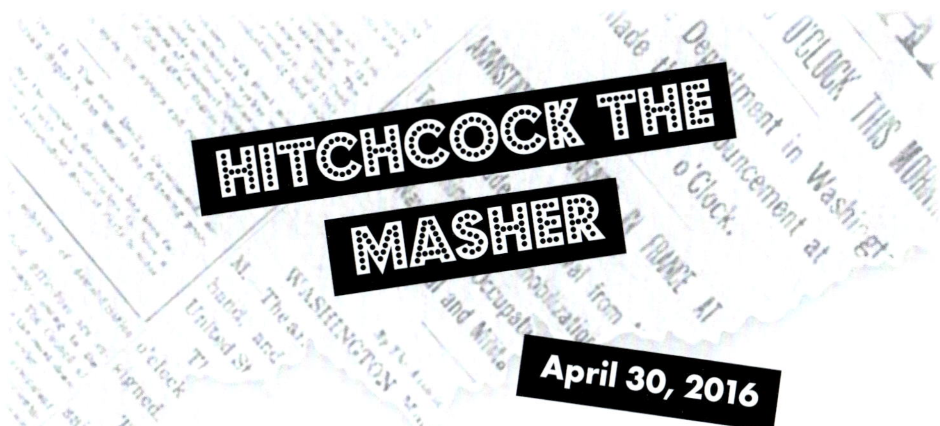

Actress Tippi Hedren recently shared with a crowd that she endured bizarre harassment (sexual and otherwise) at the hands of director Alfred Hitchcock during and after the productions of ***The Birds*** and ***Marnie***. Then a thirty-two-year-old model, Hedren had no acting experience when Hitchcock spotted her one morning in 1962 appearing in a diet drink commercial on the ***Today Show***. She recounted the story with Ben Mankiewicz during a conversation at the *TCM Classic Film Festival*. After an elaborate, twenty-five-thousand-dollar screen test that he personally directed, Hitch signed Hedren to a five-year personal contract that turned out to be a nightmare.

Though ***The Birds*** is considered to be Hitch's last masterpiece, playing the main character caught in an avian holocaust was a harrowing experience for Hedren. She was originally told mechanical birds would be used in a scene where her character is attacked by crows and seagulls in a house. In fact, real birds—not all of them declawed—were thrown at her for a week while the cameras rolled. Her doctor told Hitchcock that she was so traumatized she needed a week off. When the director said it was not possible, Tippi quoted the physician: "*What are you trying to do . . . kill her?*" She spent a week recovering at home in bed.

Rod Taylor, playing her romantic interest in ***The Birds***, was given instruction to not touch the girl—meaning Tippi. And the possessive Hitchcock gave the same order to Sean Connery, her co-star in Hedren's second and last movie with Hitchcock, ***Marnie***.

A studio executive at Paramount Pictures suggested actress Lee Remick to Hitchcock for the title role. Eva Marie Saint, the star of ***North by Northwest***, unsuccessfully pursued the role. Hitch also considered two other actresses, who like Tippi Hedren, were under his personal contract—Vera Miles and Claire Griswold, wife of director Sydney Pollack. Instead, Hitch opted to use Hedren.

It was during the making of ***Marnie*** that Hitchcock's demands for Hedren to have lunch with him in the studio commissary escalated to meals in his office and, finally, to intimate champagne toasts after each day's shooting was completed. She became uncomfortable with his suggestive behavior. After expressing her discomfort to the director, Hitchcock would never use her in another film and refused all requests to loan her out for other movies while she was under contract, derailing her then-promising career.

She finally returned to the big screen in 1967 with a supporting role in Charlie Chaplin's last movie, ***A Countess from Hong Kong***, starring Marlon Brando and Sophia Loren. The movie was made at the same studio where Hitchcock had his headquarters. By then, he refused to acknowledge her existence. And that was that!

Hollywood and American history crossed paths as Hurricane Sandy pounded the Eastern Seaboard. One of the casualties of this weather event was the *HMS Bounty*, a replica used in the filming of ***Mutiny of the Bounty*** in 1961. The ship was built for MGM, and it appeared in several feature-length movies and dozens of television shows and documentaries. Recently, the *Bounty* was used in ***Pirates of the Caribbean: Dead Man's Chest***, starring Johnny Depp.

Mutiny on the Bounty starred Marlon Brando and Trevor Howard and was based on the novel by Charles Nordhoff and James Norman Hall. The film retells the 1789 real-life mutiny aboard the *Bounty*, led by master's mate *Fletcher Christian* against the ship's captain, *William Bligh*. This was a big-budget remake; the first one was produced in 1935. The original epic was directed by Lewis Milestone and starred Clark Gable, Charles Laughton and Franchot Tone.

After filming and a worldwide promotional tour, MGM berthed the ship in St. Petersburg as a permanent tourist attraction, where she stayed until the mid-1980s. In 1986, Ted Turner acquired the MGM film library and the *Bounty* with it. He used it to promote his enterprises, and he loaned it to the production company that filmed ***Treasure Island*** with Charlton Heston in 1989.

Turner donated the vessel in 1993 to the Fall River Chamber Foundation, which established the Tall Ship Bounty Foundation to operate the ship as an educational venture. In February of 2001, it was purchased from the foundation by HMS Bounty Organization LLC, and it was used as a vehicle for teaching the nearly lost arts of square-rigged sailing and seamanship.

The *HMS Bounty* sank along the high seas off the coast of North Carolina on Monday morning. The Coast Guard reports fourteen crew members were air-lifted from the sailing facility. The search for the ship's captain continues, and one person died, Claudene Christian. She is no relation to the legendary Fletcher Christian. The 180-foot schooner now lies at the bottom of the Atlantic. It is a ghastly conclusion to a mighty structure with a historic pedigree.

In other news, the birthplace of Frank Sinatra and the childhood home of Grace Kelly (Hoboken, New Jersey) has experienced total devastation from the superstorm with widespread flooding. Elia Kazan's 1954 film ***On the Waterfront*** was shot along what is now the damaged beachfront community. Normalcy is not expected to occur in the area until next spring.

Thoughts and prayers go out to the Christian family and the spouse of the captain, who valiantly attempted to sail out of harm's way of Hurricane Sandy. It will be remembered as a perfect storm.

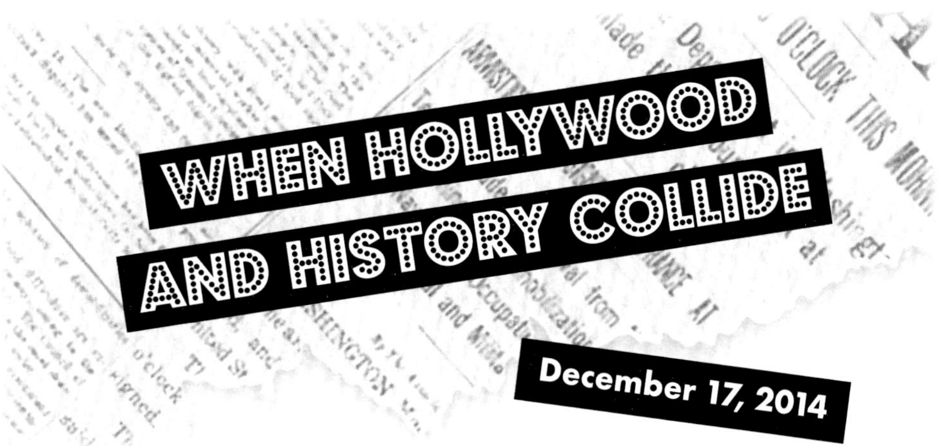

The year 2014 will be remembered for its holiday season as Sony Pictures pulled the plug on a film release, due to cyber and personal threats on our freedom to make satirical comment. The cyber threats were quite real, laying waste to Sony Pictures Entertainment as it was internet hacked. First-run movies and employees' private emails were illegally distributed to the public. The implied 9/11 style security threats on movie theaters remains conjecture as of this writing.

Under the threat of terrorist attacks and with the nation's largest multiplex chains pulling the film from its screens, Sony Pictures took the unprecedented step of pulling the December 25 release of ***The Interview***. Sony cancelled the motion picture release in light of the decision by the majority of exhibitors not to show the film. AMC Entertainment, Regal Cinemas and Cinemark Theatres—the three top theater chains in North America—announced they were postponing any showings of the comedy about a television host tasked by the CIA to assassinate North Korea leader Kim Jong Un. The cancellation was a startling blow to the Hollywood studio, shaken by leaks and intimidation over the last several weeks by an anonymous group calling itself *Guardians of Peace*.

Sony Pictures, which distributes much of Columbia Pictures classic film library, had acquired Lorimar Studios, previously on the MGM lot in Culver City. Many in the industry saw this brazen movie-lot acquisition as an expansive purchase, like vultures picking at the dead bones of a formally mighty creature. With recent email revelations from the moguls who run Sony regarding negative personal opinions about President Obama and actors, such as Angelina Jolie and Leonardo DiCaprio, little capital sympathy exists for the studio from insiders in Hollywood.

Yet the bigger picture is clear. Sony's announcement is met with widespread distress across Hollywood and throughout many other realms that followed on what amounted to one of the most significant hacking attacks on a corporation. With a modest budget of forty million dollars, ***The Interview*** was predicted to earn around thirty million in its opening weekend. Should the film not be released theatrically, Sony would also lose tens of millions in marketing costs already incurred. The Asian market had previously cancelled the release of the flick, another massive monetary blow to the movie studio.

Cinematic political satire has a long and rich tradition. French and Italian filmmakers have never shied away from such drama. ***Duck Soup***, ***The Great Dictator***, ***To Be or Not to Be***, ***Dr. Strangelove*** and ***Fail Safe*** are noteworthy examples of American classic cinema that has tackled the notion about rogue countries doing unsettling things against common people.

Our freedoms have been compromised in a startling way. Newt Gingrich tweeted: *"America had lost its first battle in the war of cyber terrorism."* A former senior national security official in the George W. Bush administration commented that Sony made the wrong decision. SAG Award nominee Steve Carell called it: *"A sad day for creative expression."* Jimmy Kimmel also surmised that Sony's decision *"validates terrorist actions and sets a terrifying precedent."* These are not over-statements in my estimation.

The truth . . . America's long running military conflict remains intact. The Korean War began in 1950, and it never really concluded. It has been seen as both a civil war and a proxy conflict in the Cold War between the United States and the Soviet Union. While not directly committing forces, Soviets have provided strategic planning, weapons and material aid to North Korean and Chinese armies. The United States keeps a military presence in the area as an effort to uphold the armistice between South and North Korea.

In the final analysis, the ultimate joy of making movies remains viable on all levels of global culture and society. Let us hope this art form will always be a courageous option of individual expression. The Sony Pictures decision to buckle from bully threats should be the exception, not the rule. I hope I never fear the opportunity to express my opinion over this or any other controversial issue. *Just sayin'* . . .

Today, I stand with the Belgium's citizenry in the wake of this morning's bombing attacks. I am proud that members of my extended family are Belgian.

After three devices devastated Brussels, killing at least twenty-six and injuring more than one hundred people, the country has turned to an iconic children's comic strip to show solidarity with the Belgian capital. *The Adventures of Tintin*, written by Belgian cartoonist Georges Remi under the pen name Hergé, has long been a symbol of Brussels and a national hero in Belgium. Now, *Tintin* has become an emblem of solidarity for the city rocked by a terrorist attack that has claimed the lives of innocent citizens.

The books have sold in the tens of millions, but only in Belgium has the fearless reporter and his dog *Milou* been ingrained in the DNA of most youngsters since the 1950s. Creator Hergé died in 1983 and is considered a national treasure in his native Belgium. The character is at the center of art galleries, museums, murals and themed restaurants, drawing tourists from around the world. The *Tintin* cartoon books have been translated into seventy-plus languages, from Chinese to Armenian and English to Spanish.

On Tuesday morning, *Tintin*, the intrepid young investigative journalist who solves fantastical mysteries, was not on another adventure. Instead, he and his pup were crying for the people of Brussels. Internet followers are lending their languages in a display of outrage, defiance and concern to the cacophony of voices following the Brussels attacks. Folks from around the world have posted pictures of *Tintin* on social media with captions such as: *I am Belgium* and *Sadness*.

My personal sentiment . . . *JeSuisBruxelles*.

Until next time . . . *never forget*.

— CHAPTER NINE —

Across the Pond

With our passports in hand, we set sail across the Atlantic. This voyage will prove to be enlightening, for our destination is jolly old England. Great Britain is dripping with history and culture that stretches back centuries. The British are known for their literature, their architecture and their royals, all of which you can enjoy with a spot of tea.

Moreover, we cannot forget to mention the marvelous actors and filmmakers that we have been fortunate enough to inherit from the Brits. Included in the mix, you will also find a lovable bear, all stuffed with fluff, and his adorable cohorts. As Shakespeare might say . . . "*What is past is prologue.*"

~ Virginia Vandewouwer

A BRITISH FAIRY TALE

May 19, 2018

Manny P. here . . .

It has occurred before; notably, when actress Grace Kelly became Princess Grace of Monaco. The tradition continues when England's Prince Harry and actress Meghan Markle will wed in an Anglican service with American flavor . . . mixing prayers, classical music, a gospel choir and soul sounds. Kensington Palace has released the order of service for this ceremony in fifteenth-century St. George's Chapel at Windsor Castle.

This service is led by the dean of Windsor, David Conner. Archbishop of Canterbury Justin Welby will solemnize the marriage, and head of the United States Episcopal Church, Michael Bruce Curry, will deliver a sermon. Markle, who attended a Roman Catholic school, has been baptized into the Church of England (Queen Elizabeth II is the supreme governor) as she prepares to join the royal family.

All are waiting to see what Markle wears and the designer she has chosen for her wedding gown. Prince Charles, Harry's father, will walk her down the aisle, after Markle's dad became too sick to attend. Meghan's mum will be sitting close by. And in the gallery will be some of Harry's buddies from his ten years of military service—an experience that included tours of duty in Afghanistan—and pals from the many charities he supports.

The couple consulted Prince Charles about the orchestral music played before the service. Selections include works by Johann Sebastian Bach, Edward Elgar, Gabriel Fauré and Franz Schubert. The chapel choir will perform a motet by sixteenth-century composer Thomas Tallis. A London-based gospel ensemble, *Kingdom Choir*, will sing Ben E. King's *Stand by Me*. Jane Fellowes, the sister of Princess Diana, will read from the biblical *Song of Solomon*.

The ceremony is based on *Common Worship*—a most modern of Church of England service options—and includes prayers and hymns, as well as readings and musical selections chosen by the couple and their families. The Church of England does not allow couples to write their own wedding vows—they have to stick to the script. Meghan and Harry will vow:

> *To have and to hold, for better, for worse, for richer, for poorer, in sickness and in health, to love and to cherish, till death us do part.*

In front of six hundred wedding guests, including Oprah Winfrey, George Clooney, Elton John, Spice Girl Victoria Beckham, sports stars David Beckham and Serena Williams and actor Idris Elba, Meghan and Harry will exchange rings to:

> *Those whom God has joined together let no one put asunder.*

After guests deliver *God Save the Queen*, Britain's national anthem, the newlyweds will exit the chapel to strains of an allegro from *Symphony No. 1* by eighteenth-century composer William Boyce and the gospel sounds of *Amen/This Little Light of Mine*.

After the ceremony, the newlyweds will ride in a horse-drawn carriage through the streets of Windsor, flanked by a British military procession with officers on horseback. Then they are off to a couple of gala receptions. The first is hosted in the afternoon by the queen—with finger foods, wine and champagne. A second smaller reception is being thrown by Charles. To kick off the festivities, the queen honored her grandson with a new title, *Duke of Sussex*, making the thirty-six-year-old Markle *Duchess of Sussex*.

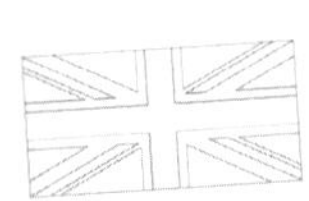

The wedding marks a new chapter in the sovereign history of the monarchy . . . an American woman with biracial roots added to its upper ranks. Harry's status as an English royal and Markle's entertainment-industry presence on the television series ***Suits*** has turned Saturday's wedding into a global event. This is Hollywood royalty colliding with a storied British monarchy.

Even though she is divorced, Meghan Markle is no Wallis Simpson!

A PROVINCIAL READING LIST

May 28, 2014

For decades, British students have grown up reading the American classics *To Kill a Mockingbird, Of Mice and Men* and *The Crucible*. Now, if students want to read those books, it will be on their own time. Harper Lee, John Steinbeck and Arthur Miller are out—perhaps replaced by the likes of Charles Dickens, Jane Austen and George Eliot.

British Education Secretary Michael Gove decided the English literature list for a national exam needs to be more provincial, so he is swapping American texts in the curriculum for British ones. The new books have not yet been announced, but Secretary Gove's decision has prompted an outcry.

Many authors and academics note a number of the thematic parallels between the Education Department's actions and the themes of the books getting the ax. *The Crucible* uses the Salem witch hunts as a metaphor for McCarthyism; *To Kill a Mockingbird* teaches lessons about tolerance and diversity.

In a statement, the United Kingdom Department of Education insists no books have been banned. The statement notes the curriculum sets out minimum requirements and that teachers are free to add any other texts to the syllabus. The changes, first reported in the *Sunday Times*, focus specifically on a standardized test known as the General Certificate of Secondary Education. A new GSCE syllabus for English Lit is scheduled to be published this week.

BRITISH BOOKS ARE BENCHED

July 15, 2014

London has become a literary playground. The National Literacy Trust, along with public art promoter Wild in Art, has commissioned and placed fifty benches around town that are painted to look like pages and scenes from famous books. For the whole summer, each is dedicated to an iconic London-related author or character.

The seating areas honoring books, authors and characters include the characters *Sherlock Holmes, James Bond, Hercules Poirot, Peter Pan, William Shakespeare* and *Bridget Jones*. The benches are on display until mid-September and then will be auctioned at Southbank Centre in October.

Established in 1993, the National Literacy Trust is an independent charity dedicated to raising literacy levels in the United Kingdom. The official patron is Her Royal Highness, The Duchess of Cornwall. They work to improve reading, writing, speaking and listening skills in the United Kingdom's most disadvantaged areas via community projects and support for schools.

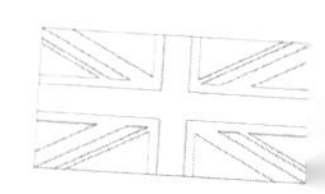

AN AUTHOR OF NOTE

July 18, 2017

Exactly two hundred years after Jane Austen died, a new ten-pound note featuring an image of one of England's most revered authors has been unveiled—right where she was buried. At the unveiling of the new tenner at Winchester Cathedral, Bank of England Governor Mark Carney said: *"It highlights a universal appeal of Austen's work."*

Austen, whose novels included *Pride and Prejudice*, *Emma* and *Sense and Sensibility*, is widely considered a perceptive chronicler of English country life during the Georgian era. Combining wit, romance and social commentary, her books have been adapted a number of times in movies and television.

The new note, due to go into circulation on September 14, is the bank's latest effort to make its notes more secure by using plastic, not paper.

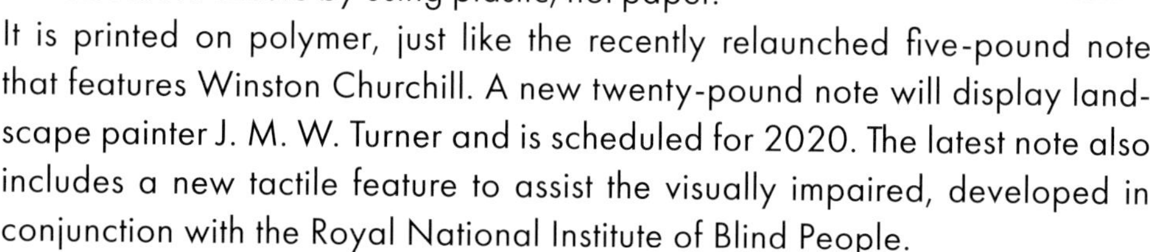

It is printed on polymer, just like the recently relaunched five-pound note that features Winston Churchill. A new twenty-pound note will display landscape painter J. M. W. Turner and is scheduled for 2020. The latest note also includes a new tactile feature to assist the visually impaired, developed in conjunction with the Royal National Institute of Blind People.

Apart from Queen Elizabeth II, whose portrait is on all United Kingdom currency, Austen is only the third woman to appear on the modern-day British banknote, after medical innovator Florence Nightingale and social reformer Elizabeth Fry. Austen was chosen during a campaign for more female representation.

Those holding the current ten-pound note, which features Charles Darwin, have only until spring 2018 before they are withdrawn.

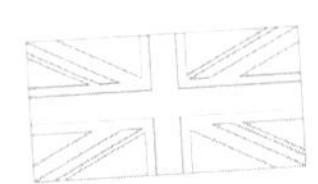

BIG BEN THEORY

August 14, 2017

A fixture of London landscape and soundscape, *Big Ben*, is falling silent for four years. The bell will cease its regular tolling, while extensive repairs are made to the famous clock tower looming over the Palace of Westminster, home to the British Parliament. However, politicians will review plans to silence *Big Ben* during repairs after having decided against a lengthy muting of the beloved bell.

The massive bell will mark its last hour at noon on August 21 and then will pause for four years while the *Elizabeth Tower*, which houses *Big Ben*, is restored. Quieting *Big Ben*'s mighty bongs will help preserve the hearing of workers involved in the project. An updated restoration of the Parliament buildings is likely to begin in the early 2020s.

The great bell has chimed nearly every hour for the past 150 years. It has had previous breaks in service for maintenance and conservation in 2007, 1983-1985 and 1976. The thirteen-ton bell, forged in the 1850s, is accompanied by chimes that ring out every quarter hour.

The clock has a Victorian-era mechanism that triggers the bell and chimes. Its four faces are expected to get refurbished. The clock will keep time with the help of an electric motor, while its mechanism is being repaired.

The bongs of *Big Ben* became associated with Britain by those around the world during wartime BBC news broadcasts. It is still heard live each day on radio through a microphone in the belfry. The BBC will use a recording during the renovation works.

Big Ben will still bong for annual national events, such as New Year's Eve and Remembrance Sunday.

AGATHA CHRISTIE ESTATE GOES AMERICAN

March 1, 2012

Majority ownership from the estate of the most prolific writer from the United Kingdom has been purchased by Acorn Media Group, a Maryland-based company. Agatha Christie Limited has sold the rights to the characters created by the literary sleuth, including *Miss Jane Marple* and *Hercule Poirot*, plus great works, such as *And Then There Were None*, *Murder Most Foul*, *Witness for the Prosecution*, *Death on the Nile*, *Evil under the Sun*, *The Mousetrap* and *Murder on the Orient Express*.

Agatha Christie's books have sold more than two billion copies. They still continue to sell amazingly well long after the author's death in 1976. According to the Guinness Book of World Records, she is considered the best-selling novelist of all time. Her estate claims that her works rank third, behind those of William Shakespeare and *The Bible*, as the most widely published books. According to Index Translationum, Christie is the most translated individual author, with only the collective corporate entities of Walt Disney Productions surpassing her.

The upside to the negotiated agreement . . . Hollywood studios and Broadway producers may find it easier to acquire use of the writer's work on this side of the pond. Notable thespians as Charles Laughton, C. Aubrey Smith, Tyrone Power, Margaret Rutherford, Albert Finney, Ingrid Bergman, Sean Connery, Lauren Bacall, Bette Davis and Peter Ustinov have played characters based on the scribe's pen to paper.

Ironically, while Agatha Christie was alive, she never lived more than a couple of miles from her birthplace. Her last known residence was in Wallingford, Oxfordshire, England.

LONGEST RUNNING SHOW IN ENGLAND

April 22, 2017

The longest running stage play is Agatha Christie's ***The Mousetrap*** in London, with its world premiere on October 6, 1952. However, Queen Elizabeth II is Britain's oldest and longest-reigning monarch, having become the official figurehead on February 6, 1952. She is also the world's longest-reigning living monarch, since the death of Thailand's King Bhumibol Adulyadej, last year. The reign of the Queen remains longer than the stage play!

England marked the Queen's ninety-first birthday on Friday with a number of gun salutes. She enjoyed her day with a visit to the races. Elizabeth II,

who owns and breeds thoroughbred horses, was seen chatting with jockeys at Newbury Race Course, not far from Windsor Castle. She visited the racecourse with daughter Princess Anne and sat in the royal box.

There were also official celebrations in London, where a troop of the Royal Horse Artillery rode horse-and-gun carriages past Buckingham Palace before staging a forty-one-gun salute in Hyde Park at noon. Outside the palace, a band of guardsmen in scarlet tunics and bearskin hats played *Happy Birthday to You* during the Changing of the Guard ceremony.

And at the centuries-old Tower of London, there was a second salute with sixty-two guns. *Long live the Queen!*

CHA-CHING AND TIGGER TOO

July 10, 2018

The original hand-drawn map of *Winnie-the-Pooh's Hundred Acre Woods* has sold at auction for over four thousand pounds, a record price for any literary illustration. E. H. Shepard's drawing sold at Sotheby's in London for almost three times its presale estimate. It was last sold in 1970 for seventeen hundred pounds.

Shepard's 1926 sketch features beloved characters, including *Pooh* and *Christopher Robin*, and landmarks such as *Bee Tree* and *Eeyore's Gloomy Place*. Shepard's illustration cemented the popularity of A. A. Milne's bear and his woodland buddies. In 2014, an ink drawing of the characters playing the game *Poohsticks* sold for a then-record three hundred thousand pounds.

The map and four other Shepard *Winnie-the-Pooh* illustrations sold for a total of just under a million pounds at Tuesday's auction.

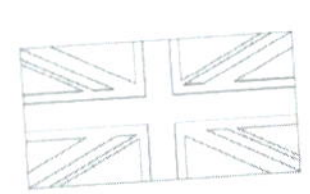

BRITISH FILM POLL PICKS VERTIGO AS BEST

August 2, 2012

The British Film Institute has made their choices for the greatest films of all time. These selections are compiled and updated every decade and printed in the official magazine, *Sight and Sound*. There were over eight hundred critics, programmers, academics and distributors who participated in this international survey.

Vertigo narrowly trumped ***Citizen Kane*** as cinema's finest contribution. This marks a first time that Alfred Hitchcock has bested Orson Welles in this kind of classic film analysis. Other provincial entries in the Top Ten include 1927's ***Sunrise***, ***2001: A Space Odyssey*** and ***The Searchers***. Contributions abroad by Jean Renoir and Federico Fellini were also mentioned.

Personally, I am astounded by the selection of number one. After recently watching ***Citizen Kane***, I was again mesmerized by its intelligent craftsmanship. The cinematography is stunning. ***Vertigo*** is a faux Euro experience. The camera work is over-the-top and in-your-face, often getting in the way of an already convoluted plot line. The British film maker was better suited in delivering nonstop action in ***North by Northwest***, riveting drama in ***Rear Window*** and sheer terror in *Psycho* (the latter considered by many theatergoers to be Hitchcock's masterpiece of movie-making).

Leave it to the British to get me so ardently conflicted with their findings!

LOST EARLY HITCHCOCK REEL

August 4, 2011

The New Zealand Film Archive and the National Film Preservation Foundation have announced the discovery of the oldest surviving work by Alfred Hitchcock in relation to early cinema. ***The White Shadow*** is a 1924 silent melodrama starring Betty Compson. Only three of six reels are known to exist. The motion picture was produced as a British feature and distributed by Lewis J. Selznick Enterprises, the father of David O. Selznick. The younger Selznick brought the iconic director to America to develop the 1940 Oscar-winning ***Rebecca***.

Hitchcock began his film career in 1920 as a title-card designer in the London branch of what eventually became Paramount Pictures. He worked on the project as an assistant director, art director, editor and writer. Hitchcock debuted as a director just two years later. His contributions to this early work showcase his knack for cinematography, making it an important contribution in the development of modern cinema.

A grant from the Andrew J. Mellon Foundation has led to a number of extraordinary finds, including a lost 1927 feature-length film directed by John Ford, discovered last year. Almost sixty titles were identified in a subsequent search that led to finding the nitrate reels of ***The White Shadow*** in December 2010.

THE SHAKESPEARE CONSPIRACY

April 7, 2018

The Oxford University Press has announced that Christopher Marlowe will be credited as a co-author on a number of William Shakespeare's works in the latest edition of the master's complete works. It is been a much-debated topic among many researchers, professors and literary connoisseurs.

Marlowe was another playwright who penned during the Elizabethan period. Some think his reputation would have trumped Shakespeare if he had lived long enough. He was only twenty-nine when he died. For a time, it was thought that Marlowe was Shakespeare, although the premise has long been dismissed.

Now, Marlowe is being credited as a co-author on the first three parts of *Henry VI*. Since the eighteenth century, it has been suggested that this particular work had at least a co-author working with Shakespeare. Some have suggested George Peele or Robert Greene. Marlowe now seems to be the best fit.

This announcement was based on years of research done in a couple of different studies, including an essay written by Gary Taylor of Florida State University, a contributor to the latest Oxford edition of Shakespeare's works. New tools for analyzing text have added to a confidence in the decision to credit Marlowe. Many experts believe up to seventeen of the master's plays contain work by other authors.

Nobody actually knows whether Marlowe and Shakespeare worked together in person. Marlowe might have been hired to write certain scenes, based on his strengths after William wrote the outline. Or he might have met with Shakespeare to work out the details of the play.

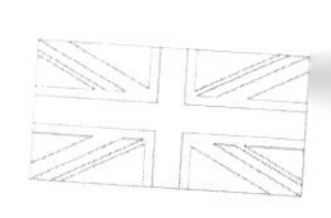

Just because Oxford publishes it does not mean there are not any critics of the analysis. Marlowe's involvement in writing *Henry VI* remains an assumption, albeit, an educated one. And the Oxford University Press has previously made other bold statements about unknown authorship. There are plenty of scholars who disagree.

The conspiracy continues . . .

ORIGINS OF THE CHRISTMAS CARD

December 24, 2014

The Christmas card dates back to Victorian-era England. Sir Henry Cole commissioned John Calcott Horsley to design a card for the holiday in 1843. Two batches totaling over two thousand cards were printed and sold that year for a shilling each. Early English cards rarely showed winter or religious themes, instead favoring flowers, fairies and other fanciful designs that reminded the recipient of the approach of spring. Humorous and sentimental images of children and animals were popular, as were increasingly elaborate shapes, decorations and materials. Official Christmas cards began with Queen Victoria in the 1840s. The British royal family's cards continued to reflect significant personal events of the year.

Festive greeting cards were imported to America from England until 1874, when German-born printer Louis Prang produced the first American-made cards. Nineteenth century designs ranged from depictions of Christmas trees and Nativity scenes to cards shaped like bells and candles or decorated with silk and satin.

By the early twentieth century, sending Christmas cards had become a popular custom in Britain and the United States. The production of Christmas cards became a profitable business for many stationery manufacturers, with the design of cards continually evolving with changing tastes and printing techniques.

The world wars brought cards with patriotic themes. Cartoon illustrations caught on with nostalgic, sentimental and religious images. Of course, movie stars joined in on the tradition, dating back to the Silent Era and into Hollywood's Golden Age.

Have ye a very Merry Christmas!

Until next time . . . *never forget.*

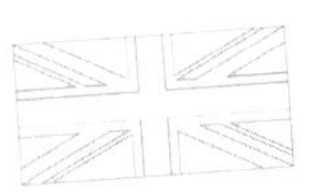

— CHAPTER TEN —

Time Capsule

Break out your shovels, and let us unearth our encapsulated past. Come enjoy a nostalgic excursion through time. These stories are both historical and personal. They paint a vastly universal portrait that traverses a world war, earth-shattering events, indelible legacies and a bit of folklore. Manny likes to refer to some of these narratives as *Hollywood-and-Vine* moments, where Hollywood and Americana intersect. Our journey should prove to be fruitful. A remarkable trip back to the black-and-white of our childhood at the end of this examination should prove the point. When we are finished, let us bury these stories in our hearts where they shall remain as a personal time capsule to be passed onto future generations.

—Virginia Vandewouwer

THE
STAR SPANGLED BANNER
A PARIOTIC SONG.
Baltimore. Printed and Sold at CARRS Music Store 36 Baltimore Street.
Air, Anacreon in Heaven.
Con Spirito
O! say can you see by the dawn's early light, What so
proudly we hail'd at the twilight's last gleaming, Whose broad stripes & bright stars thro' the
perilous fight, O'er the ramparts we watch'd, were so gallantly streaming. And the
Rockets' red glare, the Bombs bursting in air, Gave proof through the night that our
(Adapd. & Arrd. by T.C.)

2d. time Chorus.
Flag was still there, O! say does that star spangled Banner yet wave, O'er the
Land of the free, and the home of the brave
Sym.
L.H.
2
On the shore dimly seen through the mists of the deep,
Where the foe's haughty host in dread silence reposes,
What is that which the breeze, o'er the towering steep,
As it fitfully blows, half conceals, half discloses;
Now it catches the gleam of the morning's first beam,
In full glory reflected new shines in the stream
'Tis the star spangled banner O, long may it wave
O'er the land of the free, and the home of the brave.
(3)
And where is that band who so vauntingly swore
That the havoc of war and the battle's confusion,
A home and a country, shall leave us no more,
Their blood has wash'd out their foul footsteps pollution.
No refuge could save the hireling and slave,
From the terror of flight or the gloom of the grave,
And the star spangled banner, in triumph doth wave,
O'er the Land &c.
(4)
O! thus be it ever when freemen shall stand,
Between their lov'd home, and the war's desolation.
Blest with vict'ry and peace, may the Heav'n rescued land,
Praise the Pow'r that hath made and preserv'd us a nation!
Then conquer we must, when our cause it is just,
And this be our motto_"In God is our Trust";
And the star spangled banner, in triumph shall wave,
O'er the Land &c.
For the Flute.
Con Spirito
Song.
(Adapd. & Arrd. by T.C.)

A STAR-SPANGLED SALUTE

January 8, 2014

Manny P. here . . .

The original handwritten manuscript of *The Star-Spangled Banner* and the flag that inspired the song's lyrics will be displayed together at the Smithsonian in Washington, DC, the first time the historic pieces are believed to have been shown side by side. The manuscript is on display at the Maryland Historical Society in Baltimore, and the flag has been at the Smithsonian since the early 1900s. They will be together from Flag Day, June 14, through July 6. The three-week exhibition starts celebrations, marking two hundred years since the song was written on September 14, 1814.

Francis Scott Key was a thirty-five-year-old lawyer and amateur poet when he wrote the song's words during the War of 1812. Key watched as the British bombarded Baltimore's Fort McHenry for more than twenty-four hours. When he saw the fort's flag flying on the morning after the bombardment, a signal that United States troops had withstood the enemy, he was inspired to write a poem originally called *Defense of Fort McHenry*. It was set to music and later renamed, becoming the country's national anthem in 1931. Key's original manuscript, written with quill and ink, has a surprise for viewers who know the song. His poem has actually four stanzas, though the first stanza is the only one that is traditionally sung.

Folks may be more familiar with the flag, since millions visit each year to the Smithsonian's National Museum of American History. The flag has been at Smithsonian for more than a century after being given to the institution by the family of Major George Armistead. He was the commander of Fort McHenry and the man who commissioned the banner with fifteen stripes and stars, representing the number of states in the Union at the time. Except for a period during World War II, when it was housed in Virginia for safekeeping, the flag has not traveled outside of Washington since coming to the Smithsonian.

RARE VINYL ACCOUNT OF LINCOLN'S DEATH

June 6, 2017

Conjecture filled nationwide periodicals the day after Abraham Lincoln's assassination on Good Friday 1865. Among those people at Ford's Theater who actually witnessed all the chaos unfold was Joseph Hazelton, a stage and cinematic actor who was employed as a program boy. By 1933, Joe was the last living witness of the tragedy. He gave a detailed account at the May Company Exposition Hall in Los Angeles of what he had observed. The only remaining recording of his speech—rare audio of the eyewitness chronicle of President Lincoln's murder—is preserved at the Huntington Library. This is singular treasure complemented by a video, which includes a portion of Hazelton's dramatic account to bring the tragedy to life. His retelling was transferred onto vinyl at Freeman Lang Studios in Hollywood.

Created by the South Pasadena repository's video producer, Aric Allen, the eight-minute clip complements the history behind the sixteen-inch phono record. It is made of shellac, as were many transcriptions from the late 1920s to the early 1930s, and it is incredibly fragile. It resides in the library's most secure, atomic bomb–proof vault. What is fascinating about this account preserved on the recording is how it relates to the memory and mythology of the assassination.

Personal descriptions of that evening survive in the form of correspondence, diary entries, affidavits and similar documents. However, listening to a witness offers a more vivid scene. Those attending the free 1933 lecture would have heard an oral presentation detailing John Wilkes Booth's shooting of Lincoln, then leaping over the railing of the presidential box onto the stage, breaking his leg and stating his declarative exit. Booth made a ready escape on horseback.

Since Hazelton was a thespian, he delivered his narrative as if reading a theatrical script. During his oration, he surmised:

> *I shall never forget to my dying day, the look of anguish and despair on that man's face, as he half dragged and half limped to the center of the stage with a wild maniacal stare, brandished the knife above his head, and cried out . . . "Sic semper tyrannis!"*

BILLY THE CROQUET KID

October 18, 2015

Henry McCarty, known in Wild West lore as *Billy the Kid*, lived a brief and violent life before his death in a gunfight at age twenty-one. He lived with a gun in his hand and, it seems, a croquet mallet in the other. An original Billy the Kid photo would be the holy grail of Western Americana.

BILLY THE KID.—[From a Photograph.]

In a surprising historical moment, a second photo of McCarty ever to be authenticated shows him and his posse, the *Regulators*, playing croquet in New Mexico in 1878. The faded image was among a pile of photos inside a cardboard box at a junk shop in Fresno, California, unearthed by a collector in 2010. Randy Guijarro paid two dollars for the image, which is now estimated to be worth millions of dollars. The only other confirmed photo of Billy the Kid from 1880 sold for over two million dollars in 2011.

The photo was authenticated by a San Francisco-based Americana company, Kagin's Inc., which identified Billy the Kid along with several members of his gang, as well as friends and family. It was taken after a wedding in the summer of 1878, just a month after they took part in the brutal Lincoln County war. Kagin's spent a year investigating the photo and even found the location where it was taken in Chaves County, New Mexico. Kagin's team unearthed the remains of the building in the photo. A related National Geographic Channel documentary is scheduled for broadcast.

Liz Larsson, from the United Kingdom's Croquet Association, said the series of photos from the scene left little doubt what game was being played. The first croquet club in England was founded in 1865, the same year the game was immortalized in Lewis Carroll's *Alice in Wonderland*. Thom Ross, a United States artist specializing in historic scenes, has previously painted Native Americans and cowboys playing croquet. All types of Americans played, including famous folks, such as General George Custer.

I cannot believe this blog contains Billy the Kid, General Custer and croquet in the same story!

GREAT 1906 QUAKE CLAIMS LAST VICTIM

January 14, 2016

When the *Great Earthquake and Fire* hit San Francisco in 1906, three-month-old William Del Monte's family fled the city on a horse-drawn cart. Del Monte was the last known survivor of the 7.8-magnitude quake and fires that killed three thousand people and leveled much of the city.

Of course, Del Monte did not remember any of the family's dramatic escape. His mother bundled him up when the shaking stopped and ran out to the street. His dad commandeered a rig, and they rode down to the waterfront as flames licked at them from all sides. After the earthquake struck on April 18, 1906, fires erupted and raged for almost four days, burning more than twenty-eight thousand structures and leveling three-quarters of the city.

An MGM production was made thirty years later in 1936 that chronicled the days leading to the tragedy. ***San Francisco*** starred Clark Gable, Jeanette McDonald and Spencer Tracy. The film was lauded for great special effects. Del Monte outlived each of the stars by fifty years.

After being forced out of his home in North Beach after the 1906 quake as an infant, Del Monte ultimately witnessed the city's rise from the ashes and watched it rebuilt. He became actively involved in annual earthquake commemoration events. This year, San Francisco's mayor says the city will dedicate the event to him.

The San Fran native embraced the changes in technology that he saw in his life—from gas lamps and horses and buggies all the way through the development of electricity and jet travel to computers. He worked as a stock market trader almost until the day he passed on. William Del Monte died of natural causes at a retirement home, north of San Francisco. He was 109, just eleven days shy of his 110th birthday.

ELIOT NESS IN CONFLICT WITH MYTH

January 29, 2014

Nearly six decades after his passing, Eliot Ness is still so admired that Illinois's two United States senators want to name a federal building after him in Washington, DC. And there are no signs the senators are considering backing down from a resolution to put Ness's name on the Bureau of Alcohol, Tobacco, Firearms and Explosives headquarters.

In lore, Eliot Ness is the prohibition enforcer who brought down Al Capone, the principled lawman and relentless investigator portrayed by actors Robert Stack and Kevin Costner, and he inspired the fellow who created the comic-strip detective *Dick Tracy*. His career has always been imbued with a mix of fact and fiction. He did go after Capone, but his role was less heroic than many Americans imagine.

These facts are undisputed. . . . After graduating from the University of Chicago, Ness took a job as a temporary prohibition agent in 1926. He quickly climbed through the ranks until, according to the ATF website, Eliot put together a squad in 1930 to go after Capone's bootlegging operation. But prosecutors chose to pursue the gangster on tax charges instead. A few years later, Ness's law enforcement career took him to Cincinnati and Cleveland. In 1933, he left his job to become a public safety director. He was widely praised for cleaning up Cleveland corruption. Ness ran unsuccessfully for Cleveland mayor in 1947. He died a decade later but not before co-writing a book about his exploits – *The Untouchables*.

Bob Fuesel, a former Internal Revenue Service agent who knew Mike Malone (inspiration for Sean Connery's character in the 1987 film), did research on the intelligence unit (later becoming the Internal Revenue Service's criminal division) that conducted the investigation. A consultant on the movie, he told Costner that Ness had little to do with the tax-evasion case and men who worked with Ness told stories about his real fear of guns. Costner dismissed the premise.

Standard Form No. 8
(Approved by the President, May 22, 1923)

OATH OF OFFICE

Prescribed by Section 1757, Revised Statutes of the United States

(Department or Establishment) (Bureau or Office)

I, Eliot Ness (Name in full, printed or typed), do solemnly swear (or affirm) that I will support and defend the Constitution of the United States against all enemies, foreign and domestic; that I will bear true faith and allegiance to the same; that I take this obligation freely, without any mental reservation or purpose of evasion; and that I will well and faithfully discharge the duties of the office on which I am about to enter. So help me God.

Eliot Ness (Signature of Appointee)

Subscribed and sworn to before me this 26th day of August A. D. 1926 at Chicago (City or place) Ill. (State)

[SEAL] H. H. Northrust Prohibition agent

Note.—If the oath is taken before a Notary Public the date of expiration of his commission should be shown.

#2500 F7

Position to which appointed Pro. Agent

Date of entrance on duty Pro. Dist. #13

The problem is . . . much of what we think we know about Ness comes from literature, the television show starring Stack a half-century ago and Costner's portrayal of Ness in the motion picture. By the time the story got to Hollywood, the goal was to tell a good story and not give a history lesson.

There is suspicion the virtuous character the public knows may be singularly fabricated because Ness's co-author, Oscar Fraley, applied most of the lawman's qualities from Elmer Irey, a lesser known crimefighter who played a key role in sending the famed gangster to prison. Chicago Alderman Ed Burke, citing a recent Capone biography, concludes Ness had about as much to do with putting the gangster behind bars as *Mrs. O'Leary*'s cow had to do with starting the *Great Chicago Fire*. And he is trying to convince the senators to drop the whole idea. Jonathan Eig, the author of *Get Capone* and a book Burke wants the senators to read, claims that while Ness did investigate bootlegging activities in Chicago, none of what he discovered helped put Al in the clink. And there is no evidence Capone and his supposed nemesis ever even met.

Despite these allegations, Dick Durbin, fellow Illinois Senator Mark Kirk and Senator Sherrod Brown of Ohio believe that back in the era of Prohibition, each man had a price, except for Eliot Ness. His *Untouchables* credo is enough to make him the face for every law enforcement officer of the era who fought crime and corruption. The scribe of an upcoming Ness biography has also weighed in, saying while Elliott was not involved with the income tax case that sent Capone to prison, he was a key figure in the broader battle against Capone in Chicago and his contribution to law enforcement has been misunderstood for too long.

I plan to keep watching ***The Untouchables*** on the small screen each weeknight on ME-TV. I am pretty sure Desi Arnaz, the producer of the iconic television program, and Bob Stack would find this discussion rather amusing. History has a way of singling out a face in the crowd to honor all who have traveled down a well-beaten path.

RARE FDR FILM FOOTAGE FOUND

July 10, 2013

A working scholar at an Indiana college has found movie footage showing President Franklin Roosevelt being pushed in his wheelchair, a secret hidden from the public until after his passing. Ray Begovich, a journalism professor at Franklin College, found the brief clip while doing unrelated research in the National Archives in College Park, Maryland. The National Archives and the FDR Presidential Museum and Library could not say for certain if other comparable footage exists, but both feel it is rare and possible.

The clip shows Roosevelt visiting the *USS Baltimore* at Pearl Harbor in July 1944. Eight seconds of the film show the chief executive exiting a doorway on the ship and being escorted down a likely ramp. The use of the wheelchair is not clearly visible because the view of the president is partially blocked by a row of sailors.

Although Roosevelt's disability was virtually a state secret during his presidency, which spanned the Great Depression and most of World War II, it has become an inspiration to advocates who successfully pushed for a statue of him in his wheelchair to be added to the Roosevelt Memorial in Washington, DC. During his four terms, he often used a wheelchair in private but not for public appearances. News photo journalists cooperated in concealing his disability.

Roosevelt's longstanding clandestine intentions regarding his affliction will be profiled in our Lionel Barrymore documentary. I plan on contacting the National Archives to use the film clip. I believe this footage is an essential piece that should be part of our upcoming screen story.

EPIC ENDING FOR CASABLANCA HANGAR

May 29, 2017

An airport hangar facade from the opening and ending scenes of ***Casablanca*** has found a new home a decade after being saved from the wrecking ball. The arched facade, dating to the 1920s, has been in a parking lot since it was removed during renovations at Van Nuys Airport in 2007.

The hangar, with ninety-five-foot doors, appeared in movies, such as Laurel and Hardy's ***The Flying Deuces***. And *Major Strasser*'s arrival in ***Casablanca*** was filmed at Metropolitan Airport in Van Nuys. Most notably, Humphrey Bogart and Ingrid Bergman stood under the facade during the production's iconic conclusion.

For now, it will be moved to Valley Relics Museum, home to many pop-culture items. The goal is to restore it as part of a Moroccan-themed restaurant at Van Nuys Airport.

A MEMORIAL WEEKEND STORY

May 27, 2017

The iconic World War II bomber *Memphis Belle* is finally going on public display next spring at the National Museum of the United States Air Force, alongside John F. Kennedy's presidential plane, the Wright Brothers' flyer and other national aviation treasures. The journey from flights over occupied France and Germany to restoration and display at the Ohio museum has been problematic for the most celebrated American aircraft to survive the war.

The B-17 *Flying Fortress*, feted as one of the first planes to make it through the required twenty-five bombing missions, arrived at the museum at Wright-Patterson Air Force Base in pieces a dozen years ago. It was in rough shape, having been outside on display for years in Memphis, where it deteriorated from weather and vandalism.

Restoration by an army of volunteers has continued, delayed by major expansion at the museum near Dayton and other restoration projects vying for attention. An unveiling of the restored war bird is scheduled for May 17, 2018, the seventy-fifth anniversary of the crew's twenty-fifth and final mission. The *Memphis Belle* will be the centerpiece of an exhibition on the strategic bombing campaign that broke the back of Germany's wartime production.

Since B-17 parts are no longer manufactured, volunteers have labored painstaking hours, fabricating them from scratch and reassembling the plane inside a cavernous hangar at the museum. The wing tips just went on. But the fuselage skin still needs riveting. And it is still missing the plastic nose cone, a tail section and an authentic paint job.

The four-engine bomber with .50-caliber machine guns was piloted by Lt. Robert Morgan and was given its famous name before leaving the mainland. Morgan, who died in 2004, said its inspiration was his sweetheart, nineteen-year-old Memphis resident Margaret Polk. The actual moniker came from the riverboat in the John Wayne film, ***Lady for a Night***, that Morgan and his co-pilot watched the evening before the crew voted on a name. Prior to flying to Europe, he flew to Memphis, where Polk christened the aircraft with a bottle of champagne amid much fanfare.

The *Memphis Belle*, with a leggy *Esquire* magazine pinup girl painted on the nose, survived six total months of combat in 1942–1943, during missions to bomb submarine pens and munition factories. In doing so, the airplane and its crew beat the odds. Two out of three young men—their average age of twenty—who flew on those B-17 missions from airfields in England did not survive the war. One out of every eighteen planes was lost in combat.

Because the bomber's crew flew in other aircraft, they had actually completed their requisite twenty-fifth mission two days before the *Memphis*, which flew its twenty fifth on May 19, 1943. It was one of the first B-17s to do so. After being honored by army brass and the King and Queen of England, most of the original crew and airplane were reunited in a publicized tour of the United States to help sell war bonds during the summer of 1943, including a trip to the same military base where it will permanently reside. A 1944 William Wyler documentary added to the lore of the *Belle*, while younger generations were introduced to it in a 1990 movie, a fictionalized account of its last wartime mission.

Despite *Memphis Belle*'s final assignment at the air force museum in Ohio, the Tennessee legislature designated it as the state's official airplane earlier this year.

RESTRICTIVE IMMIGRATION POLICY

July 6, 2018

A European family attempts to immigrate to the United States (and later to Cuba), but their efforts are thwarted by America's restrictive immigration policies and the outbreak of World War II. Efforts to get the family out of the Netherlands likely started as early as 1938, the turbulent year when Germany had annexed Austria and part of Czechoslovakia into the Third Reich. On November 9, Nazis terrorized Jews throughout Germany in their violent *Kristallnacht*, also known as the *Night of Broken Glass*.

On May 14, 1940, with this family still on the waiting list for possible visas, the American consulate was devastated in a German bombardment, and necessary papers were destroyed. Even without the loss of their visa application, it would have been difficult to immigrate to the United States. With hundreds of thousands of people seeking refuge each year by the time war broke out in 1939, Washington issued fewer than thirty-thousand annual visas.

The processing of a visa application also lasted several years and included a huge amount of paperwork, such as affidavits from relatives or friends in the United States. Even with the demands fulfilled, applicants could still be turned down. And the war further complicated any immigration efforts. The renewed attempt in 1941 to get the family across the Atlantic failed because American consulates in Germany-occupied Europe, including the Netherlands, were closed by the Nazis.

Eventually, Anne Frank and her family went into hiding in Amsterdam on July 6, 1942, exactly seventy-six years ago to the day. The family hid for over two years during the war, and it was then that Anne wrote her famous diary. On August 4, 1944, the Franks were discovered and deported to Auschwitz.

Only her father, Otto, survived the war. Tragically, Anne and her sister died in Bergen-Belsen concentration camp.

The Anne Frank House in Amsterdam and United States Holocaust Memorial Museum feel a timely reminder is necessary in light of a climate of political provincialism sweeping a number of nations across the globe. . . . Restrictive immigration policies are a morally bankrupt ideal.

THE KISS THAT LAUNCHED FREEDOM

September 11, 2016

She was the woman kissing an ecstatic sailor in Times Square, celebrating the end of World War II in two iconic photographs. Greta Zimmer Friedman fled Austria during the war. She was a twenty-one-year-old dental assistant when she became part of one of the most memorable moments of the twentieth century.

On August 14, known as *V-J Day*, when Japan surrendered to the United States, people spilled into the New York City streets from restaurants, bars and movie theaters and began celebrating the news. That is when George Mendonsa spotted Friedman, spun her around and planted a kiss. The two had never met. In fact, Mendonsa was on a date with a hospital nurse Rita Petry, who later became his wife.

Photos taken by both Alfred Eisenstaedt and United States Navy photo-journalist Victor Jorgensen were titled *V-J Day in Times Square* and *Kissing the War Goodbye*. Today, it is known to most simply as *The Kiss*. In some photos of the scene, Petry could be seen smiling in the background. The former was first published in *Life* magazine, buried deep within its pages, while the latter appeared in the *New York Times*.

Over the years, the photo gained recognition, and several people claimed to be the kissing couple. In an August 1980 issue of *Life*, eleven men and three women said they were the subjects. It was years before Mendonsa and Friedman were confirmed to be the couple. Greta recalled the events happening in an instant. She never thought it was much of a kiss or some kind of romantic event.

Both of Friedman's parents died in The Holocaust. She will be buried in Arlington National Cemetery, next to her late husband. She passed on this week, and she was ninety-two.

OUT OF HIDING

June 4, 2018

Katherine Johnson, the NASA mathematician whose calculations helped astronauts return safely to Earth, will be honored at her alma mater with a bronze statue and an annual scholarship in her name. West Virginia State University is planning a dedication ceremony set for August 25, the day before Johnson's one-hundredth birthday.

Long before the digital age, Johnson performed as a human computer at an agency that would become NASA, working in relative obscurity. Her contributions were later recognized in ***Hidden Figures***, with actress Taraji P. Henson playing her role.

The 1957 launch of the Soviet satellite *Sputnik* changed history and Katherine Johnson's life. In 1962, as NASA prepared for the orbital mission of John Glenn, Johnson was called upon to do the work that she would become most known for.

When asked to name her greatest contributions to space exploration, Johnson refers to the calculations that helped synch project Apollo's lunar lander with a moon-orbiting command and service module. She also worked on the Space Shuttle and Earth resource satellite and authored or co-authored twenty-six research reports.

Katherine retired in 1986. In 2015, at age ninety-seven, she was awarded by President Obama a Presidential Medal of Freedom, America's highest civilian honor. West Virginia State hopes to endow a one-hundred-thousand-dollar scholarship, awarding the money to students majoring in science, technology, engineering and math, targeting aspiring learners who are underrepresented in those fields.

ZAPRUDER FOOTAGE JOURNEY SINCE 1963

November 22, 2016

On November 22, 1963, Abraham Zapruder would video what has become the most famous home movie of all time, a chilling twenty-six-second snippet of film capturing the assassination of President John F. Kennedy. The Russian-born Zapruder was a clothing manufacturer whose office sat across from the Texas School Book Depository in Dallas. On the day of the assassination, he and some of his employees went to Dealey Plaza to get a glimpse of the presidential motorcade. As JFK's limousine passed, Zapruder began filming with his 8mm Bell and Howell camera. He inadvertently captured the most complete record of Kennedy's murder.

Knowing his footage might prove valuable in a future investigation, he developed the 486-frame film and screened it the following day for the Secret Service. He also met with a representative from *Life* magazine and agreed to sell all rights to the footage for the sum of one hundred fifty thousand dollars.

Plagued by nightmares of the film's gruesome content, Zapruder allowed the magazine to publish photos of the assassination footage only on the condition that it remove frame #313—the moment in which Kennedy is shot in the head. The infamous frame would remain excised from all public versions of the film until 1975 when it was shown for the first time on reporter Geraldo Rivera's television program, *Good Night America*.

Zapruder's film has since served as a major piece of evidence for amateur detectives, government investigators and conspiracy theorists. In 1964, the Warren Commission spent weeks examining the footage and conducting tests on the camera during its official investigation of the assassination. Abraham Zapruder died in 1970, but *Life* magazine later sold the film back to his family in 1975 for the token sum of one dollar.

They went on to license the footage to several other sources, including to Oliver Stone, who used it in his 1991 film, ***JFK***. Stone's film helped lead to the creation of the Assassination Records Review Board, which would later decide that the United States government should own all footage related to the Kennedy assassination. As a result, the Justice Department awarded the Zapruder family sixteen million dollars for the original print in 1999.

That same year, the family donated all copyrights of the film to the Sixth Floor Museum at Dealey Plaza. It remains there to this day, a few blocks from where it all was initially recorded.

A REALLY BAD WEEK, A GREAT DAY

April 20, 2014

History buffs might not know this, but April 14 to April 20 appears to be the worst week in American history. May it please the reader . . . the assassination of President Lincoln, the great San Francisco earthquake, the sinking of the *Titanic*, the Bay of Pigs invasion, the Columbine shooting, the Oklahoma City bombing all happened during this seven-day period in history. This year, factor in the events surrounding Good Friday, and you get the point.

Worst Week In American History?
April 14-20

Mon 14	Tue 15	Wed 16	Thurs 17	Fri 18	Sat 19	Sun 20
-1865 Lincoln shot -1935 Black Sunday Storm in the Dust Bowl -1994 Friendly Fire shoot down of army heli-copters, Iraq	-1865 Lincoln Dies -1912 Titanic sinks -1927 Great Miss. Flood of 27 -1969 EC-121 shot down over N. Korea -2013 Boston Marathon bombing	-1947 Texas City Disaster -2007 Virginia Tech Massacre	-1961 Bay of Pigs Invasion -2013 West, Texas Explosion	-1775 British arrive by sea -1906 San Francisco Earthquake -1983 US Embassy Bombing Beriut	-1775 Battles of Lexington and Concord -1989 Iowa Battle-ship turret explosion -1993 Waco Stand-off/raid -1995 OKC Bombing	-1914 Ludlow Mass. Colorado coal miner strike -1999 Columbine HS Shooting -2010 Deepwater Horizons oil spill

Bonus: Civil war start, end, and many battles happen around this time frame, Apollo 13 also happened during this week, and Hitler was born April 20th

Many movies and television programs have alluded to these events in history, what I like to call *Hollywood-and-Vine* moments. The best of these cinematic endeavors: ***San Francisco***, ***Gone with the Wind***, ***The Grapes of Wrath***, ***Abe Lincoln in Illinois***, ***The Red Badge of Courage***, ***A Night to Remember***, ***1776*** and ***Apollo 13***. I am convinced more will follow.

This is my one thousandth blog story, one positive during a troubling week in history. I began this journey into *Forgotten Hollywood* in September of 2009. I never dreamed I would be announcing this milestone over four years later. During this period, I received accolades from the Los Angeles Press Club and a litany of literary critics.

LATINOS OFFERED PLACE FOR PILGRIMAGE

October 2, 2012

President Obama will be on hand to designate the home of labor leader César Chávez as a national monument. The White House has announced plans to establish the *César E. Chávez National Monument* in Keene, CA. The property is nicknamed *Nuestra Señora Reina de la Paz*, or *Our Lady Queen of Peace*. The site served as the headquarters for the United Farm Workers union from the early 1970s until his death in 1993. Chávez is buried there, and his gravesite will be part of the monument.

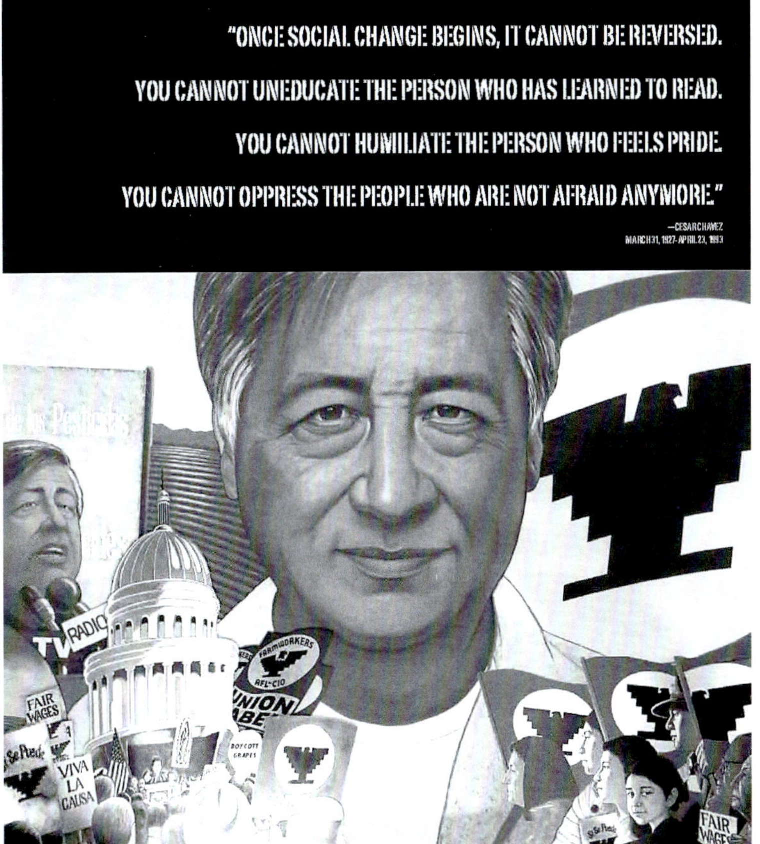

As head of the United Farm Workers, Chávez staged boycotts to raise awareness of the plight of the predominantly Latino farm workers. His efforts were credited with inspiring millions of other Latinos in their fight for educational opportunities, better housing and more political power. Chávez became the best-known Latino American civil rights activist and was strongly endorsed by the American labor movement.

After his passing, he became a major historical icon for the Latino community. His birthday, March 31, has become *César Chávez Day*, a holiday in three states. Many parks, libraries, schools, cultural centers and streets have been named in his honor in cities across the nation. On September 8, 1994, Chávez was posthumously presented with the Presidential Medal of Freedom by Bill Clinton. His likeness hangs in the National Portrait Gallery in Washington, DC.

As a Latino television and radio personality and an award-winning author, I have always felt César Estrada Chávez was a personal hero in my educational journey. His slogan—*Sí se puede* (Yes, you can)—remains the personal call to action by Latin Americans all over the nation in our collective quest for a better life for our families.

GOLDEN AGE OF EAST LOS ANGELES

May 22, 2016

As I prepared for an appearance at the Chicano Resource Center at the East Los Angeles Library on June 23, I recently discovered historic images of the community from the 1930s through the 1970s. The entire *California Light and Sound* collection is part of the County of Los Angeles Public Library's California Audio-Visual Preservation Project.

Among the photos I found were nostalgic shots from the iconic Strand Theatre of Boris Karloff and *Our Gang* stars Darla Hood and Carl *Alfalfa* Switzer (an actor featured in *Son of Forgotten Hollywood Forgotten History*).

Surprisingly, I found a beautiful shot of my mom, Margaret Gloria Pacheco (Zozaya), from her East Los Angeles Garfield High School 1955 class photo and my dad, Manuel Pacheco, as a toddler with my grandmother Sotera Parra and my uncle Robert Pacheco. There are other pictures of my grandma, as well as my aunts, Virginia, Natalie and Dolores.

These photographs were provided by my cousin Richard Armendariz for inclusion in the *Foto East L. A.: A Community History Project* collection. How wonderful that my family are an integral part of a visual retrospective to be enjoyed by all who love the preservation of local history. I am proud of this amazing legacy.

Until next time . . . *never forget.*

Fibber McGee's Closet

Fibber McGee and Molly was a weekly radio program that aired on NBC from 1935 to 1959. They were characters portrayed by real-life husband and wife Jim and Marian Jordan. Their broadcasting careers began in the 1920s. *Fibber McGee's Closet* was their most popular running gag. As you gather from the title, it involved a closet filled with enormous amounts of junk. When the closet door was opened, out poured the barrage of you-name-its! The punchline to the joke was when *Fibber* exclaimed: "*I gotta get this closet cleaned out one of these days*." The audience always roared.

As you have figured out by now, we have a collection of off-the-wall hodgepodge, originally nestled in the bowels of our own cubbyhole. Use extreme caution when opening the door (which we do at the end of the chapter).

~ Virginia Vandewouwer

MOUNT VERNON TO THE POKEY

April 20, 2010

Manny P. here . . .

I monitor newswires (as part of my journalistic routine). Here is one from the *you are not gonna believe this* department . . .

The New York Society Library (one of the Big Apple's oldest locations) found in its ledgers two missing books that were checked out by the *Father of our Country*. You guessed it . . . George Washington is delinquent on returning *Law of Nations* and a volume of debates from Britain's House of Commons.

Needless to say, if he were alive today, Washington would owe a hefty fine, since the books were due back on November 2, 1789! Actually, the library is not concerned about the fines, but would love to have the books returned. By the way, John Jay, Aaron Burr and Alexander Hamilton also checked out books from this historic location. (I wonder what their library cards are worth?)

THE PASSWORD IS "HAROLD AND MAUDE"

May 9, 2015

If you enjoyed the cult classic, ***Harold and Maude***, you will love this story! It takes place in Indiana . . .

A teenager who took his ninety-three-year-old great-grandmother to his junior prom says he had a great time, even though her early bedtime nearly cut the night short. Drew Holm says his classmates thought it was pretty cool that he asked Kathryn Keith to last Friday's Crothersville High School junior prom.

Holm picked Keith up in her Cadillac for the dance in Seymour, about sixty miles south of Indianapolis. Keith, who wore a blue dress, told the *Seymour Tribune* that she is proud that he asked her. The pair hit the dance floor for only one song, sharing a slow dance. Their night ended by 9 p.m. because Keith has an early bedtime. Holm then took his actual girlfriend to an after-prom event at a bowling alley.

Harold and Maude is an unconventional tale about a young man who falls for an octogenarian. Directed by Hal Ashby, the Colin Higgins screenplay featured Ruth Gordon and Bud Cort in the title roles. The 1971 film is ranked #45 on the American Film Institute's list of *One Hundred Funniest Movies of all Time* and was selected in 1997 for preservation in the National Film Registry of the Library of Congress. At the twenty-ninth Golden Globe Awards, Cort and Gordon each received a nomination for Best Actor and Best Actress in a Musical or Comedy.

Colin Higgins later adapted the story into a stage play. The original Broadway production, starring Janet Gaynor as *Maude* and Keith McDermott as *Harold*, closed after just four performances in February 1980. Higgins had expressed interest in 1978 about both a sequel and prequel to ***Harold and Maude***. The sequel, ***Harold's Story***, would have Bud Cort portray *Harold*'s life after *Maude*. Higgins also imagined a prequel showing *Maude*'s life before *Harold*. ***Grover and Maude*** had *Maude* learning how to steal cars from *Grover Muldoon*, the character portrayed by Richard Pryor in Higgins's 1976 film ***Silver Streak***. Higgins wanted Ruth Gordon and Pryor to reprise their roles.

Now, real life captures a celluloid moment . . . minus the auto theft!

ALL ROADS LEAD TO HOLLYWOOD HISTORY

February 8, 2012

Universal City is the community surrounding Universal Studios and Universal *Citywalk*. Until recently, many of the streets were named after pop-singer icons. Geographic tributes to Patsy Cline, Buddy Holly and Muddy Waters are set to be replaced by the names of legendary actors from Hollywood's Golden Age.

To complement James Stewart Drive . . . Bob Hope Avenue, Donald O'Connor Drive and W. C. Fields Drive will be the renamed roads leading to the historic movie studio. Community leaders made the savvy decision to change these street names in recognition of its largest commodity. An added bonus: Hollywood history is carefully honored in the city, sitting along the cusp of Tinsel Town.

I am glad the political fathers at Universal City understand their legacy . . .

A BRIDGE TO EVERYWHERE FOR POITIER

November 3, 2012

The oldest living Oscar-winning Best Actor has received a unique honor. Prime Minister Perry Christie officially renamed the Paradise Island Bridge the *Sir Sidney Poitier Bridge* as part of next month's fortieth anniversary celebration of Bahamian Independence. Hundreds of spectators cheered as the eighty-eight-year-old actor and prime minister arrived for the rechristening.

Though Sidney Poitier was born in Miami, he spent his childhood on Cat Island, a sparsely populated island in the central Bahamas, then a British colony. At age ten, his family moved to Nassau.

Sidney Poitier became the first male black actor nominated for a competitive Academy Award for ***The Defiant Ones*** in 1958. He actually took home the Oscar for ***Lilies of the Field*** in 1963. His breakout part was when he played a member of an incorrigible high school gang in the 1955 classic ***Blackboard Jungle***. The African American actor actively sought non-stereotypical roles throughout his career, and he is credited in altering the landscape in cinema for all minorities.

Sharing dual-citizenship, Poitier was first appointed ambassador of the Bahamas to Japan in 1977, a position he currently holds. He is also the Bahamian ambassador to UNESCO. On August 2009, Sidney Poitier was awarded the Presidential Medal of Freedom, the highest United States civilian honor, by President Barack Obama.

The former Paradise Island Bridge is the largest in the Bahamas. It connects the capital to the Atlantis resort, one of the region's main tourist destinations.

COLD CASE FILE IN OZ

July 12, 2015

An anonymous donor has offered a one-million-dollar reward for credible info leading to a pair of Judy Garland's sequined, ruby-red slippers stolen from a museum in her Minnesota hometown. The late actress wore the slippers in ***The Wizard of Oz***. Three other pairs of shoes still exist, including the ones on display at the Smithsonian Institute in Washington.

John Kelsch, executive director of the Judy Garland Museum in Grand Rapids, Minnesota, says the donor is from Arizona and is a huge fan of Garland and the 1939 movie. The reward offer requires the recovery of the slippers and the perpetrator's name. The ten-year anniversary of the theft is in August. The slippers were insured for one million dollars. Kelsch says they could now be worth two to three million. An actual book was written about the crime.

I can guarantee that the thief did not have a green face or ride a broom!

A FINAL RESTING PLACE FOR TOTO

June 18, 2011

Kudos to J. P. Myers of Diamond Bar, California, for mounting a campaign to establish a gravesite for everyone's favorite dog. The *Orange County Register* reports that today a burial marker will be unveiled for *Toto* at the Hollywood Forever Cemetery at 11 a.m. With the help of Steve Goldstein, author of *L. A. Gravesite Companion*, Myers successfully networked on Facebook, acquiring donations towards the project.

A hundred-thousand-dollar plot near the remains of Rudolph Valentino and Jayne Mansfield was provided by the curator of the cemetery. Expected to attend: Carl Spitz, who owned and trained the dog; an offspring of L. Frank Baum, who penned *The Wizard of Oz*; Mercedes Michalowski, director of the Oz Museum in Wamego, Kansas and one of the remaining *Munchkins*. By the way, the real name of the iconic terrier . . . *Terry*.

J. P. Myers started a similar campaign in 2010 for Jack Norworth, the man who wrote *Take Me Out to the Ballgame*. Because of his efforts, a fan built and donated a two-thousand-pound granite monument to Norworth. Another fan covered burial costs. Hall of Fame pitcher Rollie Fingers appeared at the July 11 ceremony.

What is next for J. P. Myers? The plot thickens . . .

BELOVED UGGIE IS PUT DOWN

August 12, 2015

Uggie, the Jack Russell terrier who became a canine star for his scene-stealing role in the Oscar-winning movie ***The Artist***, has died. The beloved pooch was euthanized after a bout with prostate cancer.

In ***The Artist***, *Uggie* played the canine companion to Jean Dujardin's fading silent-film star character. The movie won Academy Awards for Best Picture, Actor and Director in 2011. His other screen credits included ***Water for Elephants*** and ***Mr. Fix It***. He retired in 2012 in a ceremony at the famous Chinese Theatre in Hollywood and became the first dog to leave his paw prints in concrete alongside the prints of human stars.

Uggie was a rescue dog. His owner made it a point to keep the dog in shape through exercise, including using a treadmill.

Uggie was thirteen.

HOLLYWEED LAND

January 1, 2017

Residents of Los Angeles's well-known neighborhood woke up on New Year's Day to find the world-famous *Hollywood Sign* had been changed to display HOLLYWEED. Police are treating the incident as minor trespassing and are investigating. The sign on Mount Lee is made of forty-five-foot-tall letters.

The prank has not caused lasting damage to the sign, however, as parts of both *O* letters were covered by tarpaulins to make them look like a lowercase letter *E*. A single individual was recorded on security cameras climbing the sign to hang the materials.

The sign was first established in 1923 and originally displayed HOLLYWOODLAND. Its purpose was to advertise the name of a new segregated housing development in the hills above the Hollywood district of Los Angeles. H. J. Whitley had used a sign to advertise his development, Whitley Heights, which was located between Highland Avenue and Vine Street. He suggested to his friend Harry Chandler, the owner of the *Los Angeles Times*, that a land syndicate in which he was involved create a similar placard for advertisement purposes. Real estate developers, Woodruff and Shoults, called the area HOLLYWOODLAND and advertised the properties as a superb environment without excessive cost on the Hollywood side of the hills.

Voters in California approved the legalization of marijuana on the ballot on November 8. The measure is not scheduled to take effect until 2018. A similar prank took place in 1976 to mark a relaxation in the state's marijuana laws.

If caught, the prankster could face time in jail. Why do you think they call it . . . dope?

THE CRAYON CONSPIRACY

March 31, 2017

Dandelion yellow is gone. Crayola announced on *National Crayon Day* it will replace the color in its twenty-four pack with a crayon in the blue family. The company says it will leave it to fans to come up with a name for the replacement color.

It is the third time in Crayola's long history it has retired crayons and just the first instance it swapped out a color in its box of twenty-four. Other colors that previously got the boot include *raw umber*, *lemon yellow*, *maize*, *blue gray*, *orange yellow*, *green blue* and *violet blue*. They were all retired in 1990.

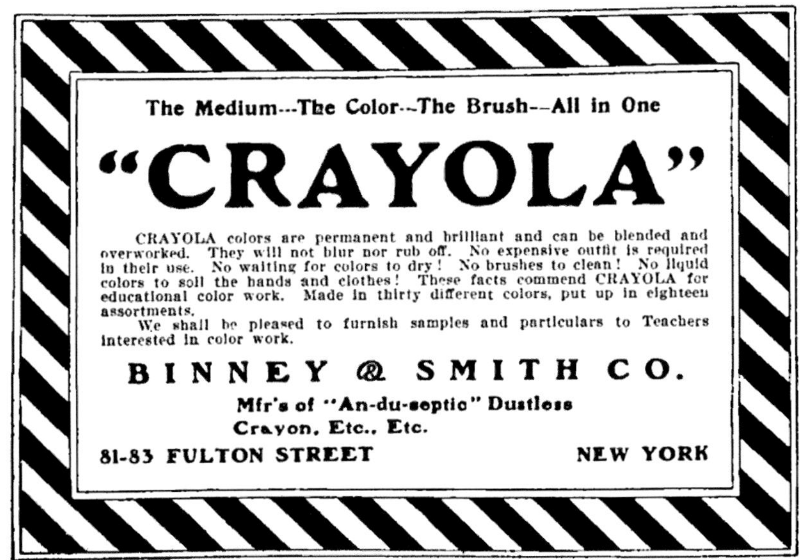

Crayola crayons were first produced by Binney and Smith Co. in 1903. Crayola is based in Easton, Pennsylvania, and is a subsidiary of Hallmark Cards Inc., headquartered in Kansas City, Missouri.

Wait . . . they got rid of raw umber?

MONOPOLY DROPS THIMBLE

February 18, 2017

The classic Monopoly playing piece—the *thimble*—is being dropped from the newest updated version of the board game. It lost out to pieces such as the *Scottie dog*, the *car*, and the *hat* in a worldwide public vote over which tokens to save.

The *thimble* has been a steady staple of Monopoly boards worldwide since the game was launched back in 1935. This is the second time a piece has been removed from play following public consultation. The *iron* made way for the *cat* back in 2013.

The remaining pieces, including the *battleship* and a *boot*, all trace their roots back to the *Great Depression*. A thimble is worn on the middle finger, used to prevent it from being poked when pushing a needle through fabric.

Along with voting out the *thimble*, members of the public were offered the choice of which new playing piece to introduce. The winner of the poll will be announced next month. Among the choices: a *hashtag*, an *emoji*, a *flip-flop* and a *rubber duck*.

Games featuring the new piece will be available in August, 2017. In the meantime, let us take a moment to remember our dear-departed friend—the *thimble*.

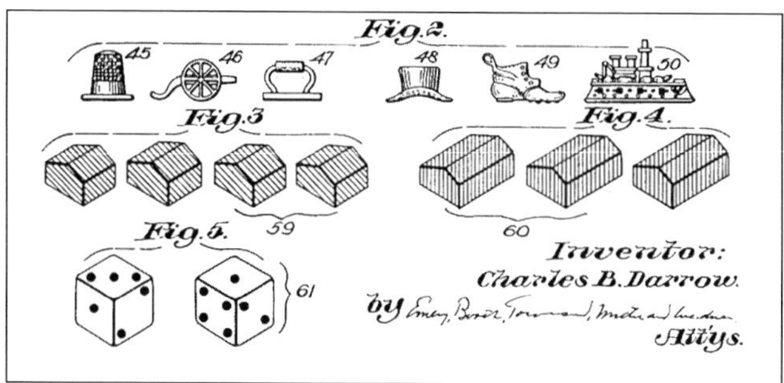

NO NO NECCO

April 9, 2018

New England Confectionary Co., the candy maker behind classic treats such as *Necco Wafers*, *Sweethearts* and *Candy Buttons*, will close its operations in May if it does not find a buyer. Necco is the oldest candy maker in the United States. Its origination dates back to 1847 when Oliver Chase created the first American candy machine. Chase's invention gave birth to the *Necco Wafer*, which became the company's signature treat.

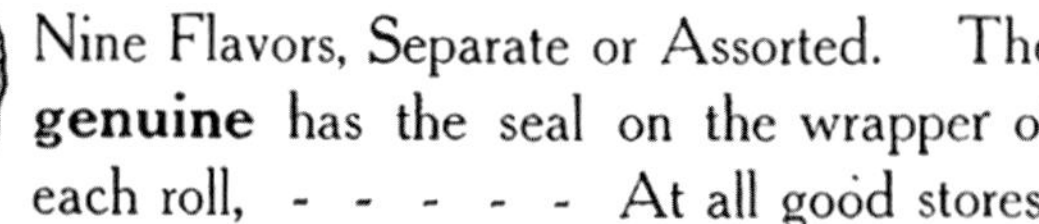

Public opinion on *Necco Wafers* has been divided. A few liken the taste to chalk or drywall, while others consider them a nostalgic treat. That nostalgia runs deep. Necco product sales spiked by fifty percent after the news broke that these candies may disappear forever. Consumers and sellers are stock-piling all the Necco candy they can obtain. One customer even offered to trade a 2003 Honda Accord for an online store's entire stock of wafers. The barter was naturally rejected.

If the company cannot find a buyer, hundreds of jobs will be lost. The company is the largest employer in its hometown of Revere, Massachusetts. CEO Michael McGee notified the state and the mayor of Revere in March that this company may have to lay off almost four hundred workers—a majority of its workforce—if the company is not sold to a new owner.

Candy fans are using the hashtag *SaveNecco* on social media to attempt to protect the beloved treats. A campaign has previously worked in the return of the *Twinkie*. Not bad for the chalky drywall-like confection.

KEY LARGO ABOARD THE AFRICAN QUEEN

April 15, 2012

Talk about mixing your Bogie-metaphors! The *African Queen* has been restored to offer tours along Key Largo, Florida. Set to be scrapped, the steamboat instead was given a heavy facelift to the delight of tourists. It took sixty thousand dollars to fix.

In the motion picture, Humphrey Bogart and Katharine Hepburn travel down the Congo, fighting off alligators, insects, leeches and the rapids to take on a World War I German warship. The *African Queen* was the official set for great scenes between the actors before being transformed into a makeshift torpedo and blowing up their adversary on Lake Tanganyika. Directed by John Huston, Bogart earned his only Oscar for playing *Charlie Allnut*. Robert Morley and Theodore Bikel co-starred in this 1951 movie classic.

The wooden slip was built in 1912 by the British East Africa Railway Company and was the official transport for missionaries, big game hunters and cargo through the Belgian Congo and Uganda. Huston and Sam Spiegel purchased the boat in 1950, giving it a focal personality throughout the classic flick.

It is fantastic to see a national treasure restored and bringing back a bit of cinematic history to a new generation of film lovers.

HAPPY BIRTHDAY, SMOKEY BEAR

August 8, 2014

Smokey Bear is turning seventy on Saturday. As the friendly bruin with the brimmed hat and shovel enters his golden years, his steadfast message of responsible fire prevention has not changed.

Smokey Bear was created in 1944 because of fears that America's enemies would set forest fires while most firefighters were battling overseas. As the war ended, *Smokey* stuck around, and he is at the center of the longest-running public service announcement campaign in United States history. Research shows he is known by 96 percent of American adults and ranks near *Mickey Mouse* and *Santa Claus* for name recognition. His creation was a collaborative effort of the National Association of State Foresters, United States Forest Service and the Ad Council.

Smokey traditionally never spoke in his public service messages except for his signature line—"*Only you can prevent forest fires!*" When he first debuted, television was in its infancy, and posters were hand-drawn. *Smokey Bear*'s ad campaign got a boost in 1950 when a real bear cub that had been rescued from a New Mexico wildfire was nursed back to health and sent to the National Zoo in Washington, DC, as the living *Smokey*.

Now, *Smokey* is a social media connoisseur and a prolific blogger with his own accounts on Facebook, Twitter (*@Smokey_Bear*), Instagram and Flickr. He has more than three hundred thousand friends on Facebook, and twenty-four thousand people follow him on Twitter. Fans can sign a virtual card and upload pictures at www.smokeybear.com. People still enjoy contacting *Smokey* the old-fashioned way, too. He got his own ZIP code, 20252 in 1964, as his popularity soared, and it was reactivated this summer. A series of YouTube videos created around his latest birthday show *Smokey* giving hugs (*#SmokeyBearHug*) to campers who properly build and extinguish camp fires and safely dispose of used barbeque charcoal, among other things.

Happy birthday to the cultural icon of a most reliable campaign . . . *Smokey Bear*!

ORGANIZED CRIME BACK IN VEGAS

March 31, 2011

An interactive attraction examining the sordid roots of Las Vegas has just opened on the Strip. It is called *The Mob Experience*, and visitors can now visit the Tropicana and learn about the history of organized crime's involvement with the rise of Sin City. Tourists can expect to chat with legendary gangsters and, in some cases, get made in mob tradition.

$5,000 REWARD

On November 8, 1937, Homer Cummings, Attorney General of the United States, under authority vested in him by law, offered the following rewards:

$2,500 for information furnished to the Federal Bureau of Investigation resulting in the apprehension of JACOB SHAPIRO;

$2,500 for information furnished to the Federal Bureau of Investigation resulting in the apprehension of LOUIS BUCHALTER.

The photographs and descriptions of the above named persons are hereinafter set out.

Jacob Shapiro was convicted in Federal Court at New York, New York, on November 8, 1936, of violating the Federal Antitrust Laws, and was sentenced to serve two years in a Federal penitentiary and to pay $10,000 fine. On appeal, this conviction was affirmed, and on June 14, 1937, upon his failure to surrender to the United States Marshal, as ordered, his bail in the amount of $10,000 was declared forfeit and a warrant issued for his arrest.

An indictment was returned by the Federal Grand Jury at New York, New York, on November 6, 1933, charging Shapiro and Buchalter, and others, with violating the Federal Antitrust Laws. Both Shapiro and Buchalter failed to appear in Federal Court for trial on July 6, 1937, and bail in the amount of $3,000 for each was forfeited and warrants issued for their arrests on July 7, 1937.

No part of the aforesaid rewards shall be paid to any officials or employees of the Department of Justice. The right is reserved to divide and allocate portions of any of said rewards as between several claimants. The offer provides that all claims to any of the above described rewards and all questions and disputes that may arise as among claimants to the foregoing rewards shall be passed upon by the Attorney General and that his decisions shall be final and conclusive.

Photographs taken February 16, 1936.

JACOB SHAPIRO, with aliases: "GURRAH," CHARLES SHAPIRO, MORRIS FRIEDMAN, SAMUEL DISHOUSE, SAMUEL DISNAHUSEN.

DESCRIPTION: Age, 41 or 42 years (born in Russia about 1895); height, 5' 5¼"; weight, 200 lbs.; build, stocky; nationality, Russian, Jewish; hair, medium chestnut; eyes, blue, wears glasses occasionally; complexion, medium - inclined to be flushed; features, large mouth, thick lips, nose somewhat flattened - appearance of having been broken (possibly remodeled by plastic surgery) - large ears; dress, rather conservative - well tailored; speech, very guttural, Jewish accent; mannerisms, gesticulates with hands when speaking; peculiarities, thick hands and short stubby fingers; fingerprint classification, $\frac{11\ 11\ R\ O\ 7}{26\ R\ 1}$ Ref: $\frac{9}{26}$, $\frac{3}{26}$, $\frac{1}{26}$

Photographs taken June 12, 1933.

LOUIS BUCHALTER, with aliases: "LEPKE," LOUIS BUCKHOUSE, LOUIS BUCKHALTER, LOUIS KAWER, LOUIS COHEN, OUIS BUCKALTER.

DESCRIPTION: Age, 40 years (born February 12, 1897, at New York City); race, white - Jewish; height, 5' 5½"; weight, 160 lbs.; build, medium; hair, dark brown or black; eyes, brown; complexion, dark; peculiarities, nose - large, rather straight and blunt--ears - prominent--eyes - alert and shifting; marital status, married - one son, Harold, aged about 17; fingerprint classification, $\frac{25\ 11\ 17.}{27\ O}$

Information may be communicated in person, or by telephone or telegraph collect, to the undersigned, or to the nearest office of the Federal Bureau of Investigation, United States Department of Justice, the local addresses and telephone numbers of which are set forth on the reverse side of this notice.

JOHN EDGAR HOOVER, DIRECTOR,
FEDERAL BUREAU OF INVESTIGATION,
UNITED STATES DEPARTMENT OF JUSTICE,
WASHINGTON, D. C.
TELEPHONE, NATIONAL 7117.

November 8, 1937.

Highlights include biographies and stories about Benjamin Siegel and Frank Rosenthal, who ran the Stardust, the Fremont and the Hacienda casinos. Furniture from Sam Giancana and a diary from Meyer Lansky are among the historical artifacts to be displayed. Narration is provided by James Caan, Mickey Rourke and Frank Vincent, actors who have played crime figures. The popularity of ***The Godfather***, ***Casino*** and ***Goodfellas*** should guarantee thousands of visitors each year, generating an abundance of tourism dollars.

Downtown Las Vegas also plans to open a publicly funded Mob Museum in December to compliment the Vegas-strip attraction. To lawfully silence critics and raise its academic credibility, the Mob Museum brought in law enforcement officials, historians and acclaimed museum experts to help build its collection. And it will highlight local historic violence and the role organized crime played in the success of casinos.

For example, Bugsy Siegel's troubled and expensive opening of the Flamingo Hotel led to his eventual bloody demise. So much for the so-called glamorous origins of Las Vegas, the planned oasis in the Nevada desert.

SING SING TO OPEN A PRISON MUSEUM

June 22, 2014

An old power plant at Sing Sing that once supplied the juice for the electric chair is being eyed as the site for a museum dedicated to the infamous prison. Supporters envision thousands of tourists streaming up the river from New York to see artifacts, including *Old Sparky* (as the chair was known), a metal cage used when prisoners were transported and a display of prisoners' weapons, from axes made in metal shop to shivs fashioned from forks.

Sing Sing's reputation was burnished by Hollywood, which used it as a setting for such 1930s movies as ***The Big House***, ***20,000 Years at Sing Sing***, ***Manhattan Melodrama*** and ***Angels with Dirty Faces***.

The lockup, thirty miles up the Hudson from New York City, also inspired a saying now synonymous with incarceration, and the title of a 1930 flick . . . ***Up the River***, starring Spencer Tracy and Humphrey Bogart. It was the only time these noted thespians appeared together in a motion picture. The famed prison was also the last stop for many members of the notorious *Murder, Inc.*, which acted as a contract killing squad for the Mafia in the 1930s and 1940s.

There are plenty of prison museums around the country. But most, like Alcatraz in San Francisco Bay and Eastern State Penitentiary in Philadelphia, are at closed facilities. It is rare to have a museum at an active prison. The Angola Museum, just outside the gates of Louisiana State Penitentiary, draws about twenty-six hundred visitors a month. A Sing Sing museum could eventually attract a quarter of a million people each year.

Like Warner Brothers, planners expect to make a killing at this site!

Until next time . . . *never forget.*

— CHAPTER TWELVE —

Year in Memoriam

Let us leave you with lasting memories of those who have departed over the last number of years. Although there were many larger-than-life figures who encompassed all walks of endeavor that died, we were unable to include everyone who left a footprint.

Their legacies could be found in such fields as politics (Nancy Reagan, Nelson Mandela), music (Lena Horne, Prince), cinema (Peter O'Toole, Esther Williams), science (Stephen Hawking, Neil Armstrong), literature (Ray Bradbury, Tom Clancy), sports (Arnold Palmer, Roger Bannister) and pop culture (Robert Osborne, Dr. Joyce Brothers), to name a few.

This chapter takes a look at each month as we have compiled a year-long retrospective of notable icons. Each one, in his or her own unique way, has been able to provide us with indelible memories. Here are their stories . . .

~ Virginia Vandewouwer

DAVID BOWIE, THE ACTOR

January 11, 2016

Manny P. here . . .

A lot will be written over the next week about the legacy of David Bowie. He was unique in the glam-rock era of popular music. And he was a cultural icon for his approach as a musician and song-stylist. Let me also remind you about Bowie's formidable cinematic legacy. His career has been punctuated by his roles in movie and theater productions, earning him acclaim as an actor.

The beginning of David Bowie's film career predates his commercial breakthrough as a musician. Studying avant-garde theatre and mime under Lindsay Kemp, he played *Cloud* in the 1967 theatrical production ***Pierrot in Turquoise*** (later made into the 1970 television film, ***The Looking Glass Murders***). In the black-and-white two-reeler, ***The Image***, he is a ghost who emerges from a troubled artist's painting to haunt him. The same year, ***The Virgin Soldiers*** saw Bowie make a brief appearance as an extra.

In 1976, he earned acclaim for his first major starring role, portraying *Thomas Jerome Newton*, an alien from a dying planet, in ***The Man Who Fell to Earth*** (directed by Nicolas Roeg). For his performance in the science fiction flick, he won a Saturn Award.

Bowie starred in an Anglo-German co-production, ***Just a Gigolo***, as a Prussian officer returning from World War I who is discovered by a baroness (Marlene Dietrich). He is put into her stable of studs. He starred in ***The Hunger***, a revisionist vampire film, with Catherine Deneuve and Susan Sarandon. Bowie had a cameo in ***Yellowbeard***, a 1983 pirate comedy created by Monty Python. And he had a small part as a hitman in ***Into the Night***. Bowie appeared in Jim Henson's dark fantasy, ***Labyrinth***. He played *Pontius Pilate* in Martin Scorsese's 1988 epic, ***The Last Temptation of Christ***. He portrayed physicist *Nikola Tesla* in Christopher Nolan's ***The Prestige*** in 2006. The rock star also appeared as himself in ***Zoolander***. Bowie did decline to play the villain in the *James Bond* film, ***A View to a Kill***.

He took the lead in the Broadway production ***The Elephant Man***, in which he performed wearing no stage make-up and earned high praise for his expressive performance. He played the part 150 times between 1980 and 1981.

In 1999, Bowie was named a *Commander of the Ordre des Arts et des Lettres* by the French government. He declined the royal honor of *Commander of the British Empire* in 2000 and turned down a knighthood in 2003.

One year, I went to a terrific Bowie concert at Dodger Stadium. Also, a personal favorite television moment of mine was when he joined Bing Crosby on his last Christmas special in 1977 (and just five weeks before Crosby's passing from a heart attack after a round of golf), together singing the medley *Peace on Earth/Little Drummer Boy*. The tune has become a seasonal classic.

The innovative performer had just turned sixty-nine on Friday, the day he released his twenty-fifth album. But he continues to influence some of today's top filmmakers with his groundbreaking approach, including Johnny Depp, Nicole Kidman and director Tim Burton. British astronaut Tim Peake tweeted his profound sadness aboard the International Space Station about David Bowie's sudden death from cancer.

"Ground Control to Major Tom . . ."

THE MOCKINGBIRD IS SILENCED

February 20, 2016

Harper Lee, the very elusive novelist of ***To Kill a Mockingbird***, has died. The book, with a child's eye view of racial injustice in a small Southern town, quickly became a bestseller and won the Pulitzer Prize. It was made into a memorable movie in 1962 with Gregory Peck's Oscar-winning portrayal of *Atticus Finch*. His literary daughter, *Scout*, was loosely based on Lee's early life. As the Civil Rights movement grew, the novel inspired a generation of lawyers. It became required reading in high schools all over the country and the consensus assignment for nationwide book-club programs.

Born in Monroeville, Alabama, Lee was known to family and friends as *Nelle*. Like *Atticus*, her father was a lawyer and state legislator. One of her childhood friends was Truman Capote, who lived with relatives next door for several years. Capote became the model for *Scout*'s creative and impish friend *Dill*. Lee's friendship with Capote was evident when she traveled with him to Kansas, beginning in 1959, to help him do research for what became his best-seller, *In Cold Blood*.

Lee attended the University of Alabama, where she wrote and became editor of the campus literary magazine. After studying to be a lawyer like her father and older sister, Lee left the university before graduating and headed to New York to become a writer (as Capote already had done). She worked as an airline reservation clerk in New York City during the early 1950s. Finally, with a Christmas loan from friends, she quit to write full time the first draft of *To Kill a Mockingbird*. She sent it to J. B. Lippincott in 1957. The manuscript, according to the publishing house, arrived under the working title, *Atticus*. Lee worked with editor Tay Hohoff in shaping the book into its final form, a period when Lee was financially strapped and dealing with the difficulties of rewriting.

The title became *To Kill a Mockingbird*, based on the adage:

> *It was all right to kill a blue jay but a sin to kill a mockingbird, which gives the world its music.*

By 2015, the book's sales were reported by HarperCollins to be over forty million, worldwide, making it one of the most widely read American novels of the twentieth century. When the Library of Congress did a survey in 1991 on books that have affected folk's lives, *Mockingbird* was second only to the *Bible*.

Harper became quite mysterious as her book became more famous. At first, she dutifully promoted her work. She spoke frequently to the press, wrote about herself and gave speeches (once to a class of cadets at West Point). Lee began declining interviews in the late 1960s and, until late in her life, firmly avoided making any public comment about her novel or her career. Other than a few magazine pieces for *Vogue* and *McCall's* in the 1960s, she published no other book until stunning the world in 2015 by permitting *Go Set a Watchman* to be released. *Watchman* was written before *Mockingbird* but was set twenty years later, using the same location and many of the same characters. *Watchman* jumped to the top of best-seller lists within a day of its announcement, and it remained there for months.

Parallels were drawn between Lee and Margaret Mitchell, another Southern woman whose only novel, *Gone with the Wind*, became a phenomenon and was made into a beloved movie. But Mitchell's book romanticized the Black-White divide; Lee's work confronted it, although more gently than novels before and since. Mitchell's novel, while hugely popular, was not ranked by scholars in the same category as the work of other Bible-belt authors, such as Eudora Welty or Flannery O'Connor. Some critics called her efforts naive and sentimental. The novel was also considered patronizing for highlighting the bravery of a white man on behalf of Black people.

Lee wrote a letter of thanks in 2001 when the Chicago Public Library chose *Mockingbird* for its initial *One Book One Chicago* program. In 2007, she attended a White House ceremony, receiving the Presidential Medal of Freedom. By 2014, Lee's released novel finally became an eBook. A new production of ***To Kill a Mockingbird*** will head to Broadway during the 2017-2018 season, under the direction of Tony-winner Bartlett Sher and adapted by Oscar-winner Aaron Sorkin.

Friends and Monroeville townsfolk found Lee to be warm, vibrant and witty. She enjoyed life, played golf, read voraciously, ate at McDonald's, fished, fed ducks by tossing seeds out of a Cool Whip tub and frequently enjoyed plays and concerts. She lived in an assisted living facility for years as her health worsened. Two black bows hung on the doors of the old courthouse—now a museum—after her death was announced.

Nelle remained friends with Mary Badham, the actress who was *Scout* on screen, and with Gregory Peck until his passing. The scribe truly believed that the actor was destined to play *Atticus*. Otherwise, she simply abstained from public view in a defiant search for privacy. With her pristine legacy firmly intact, Harper Lee will continue to live on as a literary giant.

Harper Lee was eighty-nine.

THE PASSING OF A LEGEND

March 23, 2011

Much will be written over the next week about the tumultuous life and times of Elizabeth Taylor. She was a true icon from Hollywood's Golden Age. Her personal life was fiery and newsworthy. She lost a great love in a plane crash; she stole a husband away from another screen legend; her relationship with Richard Burton was magically tragic. And her close friends included Roddy McDowell, Montgomery Clift, Rock Hudson and Michael Jackson.

Yet, most will recall Taylor's love affair with the camera. Her violet eyes were striking, even on the black-and-white screen. She effortlessly graduated from the ranks of child actor to adult star. She won two Oscars. Her screen credits include ***Lassie Come Home***, ***National Velvet***, ***Little Women***, ***Father of the Bride***, ***A Place in the Sun***, ***Quo Vadis***, ***Ivanhoe, Giant***, ***Raintree County***, ***Cat on a Hot Tin Roof***, ***Suddenly Last Summer***, ***Butterfield 8***, ***Cleopatra***, ***The V.I.P.s***, ***The Sandpiper***, ***Who's Afraid of Virginia Woolf?***, ***Anne of a Thousand Days*** and ***The Taming of the Shrew***.

It is unfair that Elizabeth Taylor will also be remembered for her many marriages to Richard Burton, Conrad Hilton, Michael Todd, Michael Wilding, Eddie Fisher and Larry Fortensky. Our collective memories should include her unyielding work against the AIDS virus. She was given the *Jean Hersholt Humanitarian Award* from the Academy of Motion Picture Arts and Sciences in 1992. Taylor was appropriately appointed *Dame Commander of the Order of the British Empire*.

She was also a friend to the hospital employees she met while suffering from the many illnesses throughout her life. Gloria Pacheco (my mother) attended to the actress during her various stays at St. John's Hospital in Southern California. She recounted how gracious Taylor was, never treating the staff with anything but dignity. This speaks volumes for the star, known for a well-documented temper. If Liz had been anything but kind, I surely would have heard about it from my mom!

Elizabeth Taylor was seventy-nine and died of congestive heart failure.

THE PASSING OF MICKEY ROONEY

April 7, 2014

One of Metro-Goldwyn-Mayer's greatest stars of the Studio Era has died. Mickey Rooney's film, television and stage appearances spanned nearly his entire lifetime. He became a superstar as a teen for his efforts in the *Andy Hardy* series of movies, and he had one of the longest careers of any actor, spanning ninety-two years, from the 1920s to the 2010s.

Rooney was born in Brooklyn to parents who both were in vaudeville. He began performing at the age of seventeen months as part of his parents' routine, wearing a specially tailored tuxedo. His first screen offer was made by Hal Roach to appear in the *Our Gang* comedies. Fontaine Fox had placed a newspaper ad for a dark-haired child to play the role of *Mickey McGuire* in a series of short films. Rooney got the role and became *Mickey* for seventy-eight of the comedies, running from 1927 to 1936, starting with ***Mickey's Circus***. During the Silent Era and into talkies, he was cast doing bit parts in movies featuring established stars such as Colleen Moore, Clark Gable, Douglas Fairbanks Jr., Joel McCrea and Jean Harlow. Rooney signed with MGM in 1934.

In 1937, he was selected to portray *Andy Hardy* in ***A Family Affair***. He provided comic relief as the son of *Judge James K. Hardy*, portrayed by Lionel Barrymore (although Lewis Stone would play the role in subsequent films). The film was an unexpected success and led to thirty more *Andy Hardy* films between 1937 and 1946 and the final production in 1958. Rooney made his first film with Judy Garland with ***Thoroughbreds Don't Cry***. They became lifelong friends and a very successful song-and-dance team. Besides three *Andy Hardy* flicks, where she portrayed *Betsy Booth*, a young girl with a crush on *Andy*, they were in a string of hit musicals, including the Oscar-nominated ***Babes in Arms***.

Rooney was memorable in ***Manhattan Melodrama*** and ***Captains Courageous***. His breakthrough as a dramatic actor came in ***Boys Town***, opposite Spencer Tracy as *Whitey Marsh*, which opened just before Rooney's eighteenth birthday. He was awarded a Juvenile Academy Award in 1939 and was named the biggest Hollywood box-office draw for three years in 1939, 1940 and 1941. At the height of his popularity, he was cast in ***The Adventures of Huckleberry Finn***, ***Young Tom Edison***, ***Men of Boys Town***, ***Babes on Broadway***, ***A Yank at Eton***, ***A Human Comedy***, ***Girl Crazy*** and ***National Velvet***.

Rooney enlisted in the United States Army. He served more than twenty-one months until shortly after the end of World War II. During and after the war, he entertained the troops in America and Europe and spent part of the time as a radio personality on the American Forces Network. He was awarded the *Bronze Star Medal* for entertaining troops in combat zones and received the *Army Good Conduct Medal*, *American Campaign Medal* and World War II *Victory Medal* for his military service.

His career slumped after the war. Despite a few starring roles, he was assigned smaller parts in ***Words and Music***, ***The Big Wheel***, ***Quicksand***, ***The Bridges at Toko-Ri***, ***The Bold and the Brave***, ***Baby Face Nelson***, ***Breakfast at Tiffany's***, ***Requiem for a Heavyweight*** and ***It's a Mad Mad Mad Mad World***. One of Rooney's fine small-screen moments was playing a jockey in ***The Twilight Zone***. Though he kept working in cinema and television, his comeback was a magnificent Oscar nominated-turn in ***The Black Stallion*** in 1979. The same year, he starred with Ann Miller in the Broadway revue ***Sugar Babies***, which brought him a Tony nomination. Two years later, he garnered an Emmy and Golden Globe for his touching performance in ***Bill***. He received an Academy of Motion Picture Arts and Sciences *Lifetime Achievement Award* in 1983.

The actor was married eight times, most notably to Ava Gardner and Martha Vickers. After a tumultuous personal life, he became an active member of the Church of Religious Science. In September 2010, he celebrated his ninetieth birthday at Feinstein's at the Loews Regency in the Upper East Side of New York City. Among the dignitaries who attended . . . Donald Trump, Regis Philbin, Nathan Lane and Tony Bennett.

Mickey Rooney, the diminutive dynamo, was ninety-three.

SO LONG TO SPECIAL EFFECTS WIZARD

May 8, 2013

The legacy of Ray Harryhausen dates back to the creation of ***King Kong*** in 1933. His mentor, Willis O'Brien, pioneered the technique of stop-motion animation, made famous when he brought his iconic ape to life on screen. An astonished audience truly were amazed by his creation. The work of this pioneering model animator inspired Harryhausen to enter this unique field, and he almost single-handedly kept the technique alive for three decades.

His most important productions include the special effects on ***Mighty Joe Young*** (with O'Brien) that won the Oscar in 1949, ***The 7th Voyage of Sinbad*** (his first color film) and ***Jason and the Argonauts***, featuring the famous sword fight against seven skeleton warriors.

Other inspiration came from friends Ray Bradbury and George Pal, who both became important contributors to the science fiction genre. As a young man, Harryhausen joined a Los Angeles–area *Science Fiction League*, which led to his fortuitous meeting with his idol, Willis O'Brien. He critiqued Harryhausen's early models, and this inspired him to take classes in graphic arts and sculpture to hone his skills.

During World War II, Harryhausen worked for the *Special Services Division* under Colonel Frank Capra. He also collaborated with composer Dimitri Tiomkin and Ted Geisel (Dr. Seuss). In 1947, Ray was brought in by Merian C. Cooper as an assistant animator on what was to become his first major film, ***Mighty Joe Young***.

When ***King Kong*** was rereleased in 1952, it contributed to a revival of a giant monster cinema craze, especially at drive-in theaters. Harryhausen was hired to do the special effects for ***The Beast from 20,000 Fathoms***, based on a story written by Ray Bradbury. Harryhausen's creative method was as old as the motion picture itself. He first used a technique that split the background and foreground of pre-shot live-action footage into two separate images and seemingly integrated live action with models. This style was famously called *dynamation*. Other memorable flicks featuring his special effects include ***It Came from Beneath the Sea***, ***The Three Worlds of Gulliver***, ***Mysterious Island*** and ***One Million Years B.C.*** He worked alone to produce almost all the animation for his films until his last feature film in 1981 . . . ***Clash of the Titans***.

During the 1980s and early 1990s, Harryhausen's growing legion of fans in the film industry, including George Lucas and John Landis, started lobbying the Academy of Motion Picture Arts and Sciences to acknowledge Harryhausen's contribution to cinema. He was finally given a *Gordon E. Sawyer Award* in 1992 for *"Technological contributions [which] have brought credit to the industry."* Tom Hanks and Ray Bradbury presented the award. The Science Fiction Hall of Fame inducted Harryhausen in 2005, the first year it honored non-literary contributors. He also had a comedic cameo role in the 1998 remake of ***Mighty Joe Young***.

There is no question that modern special-effects artists owe a debt of gratitude to this pioneer of live animation.

Ray Harryhausen was ninety-two.

THE GREATEST LOVE OF ALL

June 4, 2016

Originally known as the *Louisville Lip*, Muhammad Ali was a magnificent heavyweight champion, whose fast fists and irrepressible personality transcended sports and captivated the world. Born Cassius Marcellus Clay Jr., a controversial and polarizing figure during his early career, Ali is now remembered for the skills he displayed in the ring, plus the values he exemplified outside of it: religious freedom, racial justice and the triumph of principle over expedience. Ali transformed the role and image of the African American athlete in America by his embrace of racial pride and his willingness to antagonize the white establishment in doing so. He also embodied the savvy concept of self-worth.

Ali was one of the most recognized sports figures of the past one hundred years, and he was crowned *Sportsman of the Century* by *Sports Illustrated*. In 1993, the Associated Press reported that Ali was tied with Babe Ruth as the most recognized athlete out of over eight hundred dead or alive athletes in America. Ali was named the second greatest fighter in boxing history by ESPN.com behind welterweight and middleweight Sugar Ray Robinson. In 2007, ESPN listed Ali the #2 heavyweight of all time, behind Joe Louis. Ali has been the subject of numerous books, films and other creative works. He has appeared on the cover of *Sports Illustrated* on thirty-seven different occasions, second only to Michael Jordan. The brash boxer famously bragged: *"I float like a butterfly, sting like a bee."*

Ali remains the only non-consecutive three-time world heavyweight champion; he won the title in 1964, 1974 and 1978. Nicknamed *The Greatest*, he was involved in several historic boxing matches. Notable among these were the first Sonny Liston fight, three with rival Joe Frazier and one with George Foreman (memorably called *The Rumble in the Jungle*).

After he won the championship from Liston in 1964, the Nation of Islam agreed to recruit him as a member. Shortly after, leader Elijah Muhammad recorded a statement that Clay would be renamed *Muhammad* (worthy of all praises) *Ali*. Only a few journalists (notably Howard Cosell) accepted the new name at the time. Ali would proclaim: *"Cassius Clay is my slave name."* Ali's friendship with Malcolm X ended when there was a radical split within the Nation of Islam a couple of weeks after Ali joined. He later admitted that turning his back on Malcolm X was a mistake he regretted for most of his adult life.

Ali famously met The Beatles during their first visit to the United States. In photos that would become legendary, the boxer is seen knocking the Fab Four down like dominoes and standing over them as they are sprawled out in the ring.

In 1967, just three years after winning his initial heavyweight title, Ali refused to be conscripted into the military, citing his religious beliefs and a personal opposition to American involvement in the Vietnam War. He was eventually arrested, found guilty on draft evasion charges and stripped of his boxing title. He did not fight again for nearly four years, losing a time of peak performance in the athlete's career. Ali's legal appeal worked its way up to the United States Supreme Court. In 1971, his conviction was overturned. Ali's actions as a conscientious objector to the war made him a champion for the counterculture generation. Ali inspired Martin Luther King Jr., who had been reluctant to address the Vietnam War for fear of alienating the Johnson administration and its support of civil rights.

Ali had a cameo role in the 1962 film version of ***Requiem for a Heavyweight***. During his exile, he starred in the short-lived Broadway musical ***Buck White***. Ali appeared in the documentary ***Black Rodeo***, riding both a horse and a bull. The film ***Freedom Road***, made in 1978, featured Ali in a rare acting role as *Gideon Jackson*, an ex-slave in 1870s Virginia who is elected to the Senate.

His autobiography, *The Greatest: My Own Story*, written with Richard Durham, was published in 1975. It was adapted into a film called ***The Greatest***, in which Ali played himself. Ernest Borgnine played *Angelo Dundee* and James Earl Jones played *Malcolm X*. *The Greatest Love of All* was written by composers Michael Masser and Linda Creed. It was the main theme of the 1977 film, with the original version performed by George Benson. Eight years later, the song became even more well-known as a cover version for Whitney Houston. It eventually topped the charts.

When We Were Kings, a 1996 documentary about the *Rumble in the Jungle* boxing match, won an Academy Award. With Jodie Foster and Kevin Spacey wildly applauding, Foreman and Ali both hit the stage to help accept the statuette. And the 2001 biopic ***Ali*** garnered an Oscar nod for Will Smith's portrayal of the champion. The biographical film, directed by Michael Mann, centers on Ali from 1964 to 1974.

His 1996 surprise appearance to light the torch at the *Opening Ceremonies* of the Summer Olympics was considered one of the iconic television moments in sport's history. Ali has a star on the Hollywood Walk of Fame. His star is the only one mounted on a vertical surface, out of deference to his request that his name not be walked upon.

In 2005, President George W. Bush presented the boxer with the Presidential Medal of Freedom. After Ali died, Kentucky's governor ordered the flags at the statehouse to fly at half-staff in Ali's honor. By every measurable account, he was a true gentleman and a real champion in and out of the boxing ring.

On a personal note, I had the distinct honor to be the master of ceremonies at his fiftieth birthday party. Seven years into his diagnosis of Parkinson's disease, he quietly thanked me and shook my hand. I will never forget my opportunity to host this special Hollywood event.

Larger than life, Muhammad Ali was seventy-four.

LIFE AND TIMES OF ERNEST BORGNINE

July 9, 2012

Ernest Borgnine is a true Hollywood legend. The burly Italian with a large smile was quite comfortable playing screen heavies and a variety of characters for over sixty years. And he got a late start after spending a decade in the United States Navy.

He served with distinction on the *USS Lamberton* (DD-119). His numerous military decorations included the *Good Conduct Medal, American Campaign Medal, Asiatic-Pacific Campaign Medal, Defense Service Medal* and a *Victory Medal*. He was discharged as gunner's mate first class.

His mother suggested he learn acting after the war. After graduating from the Barter Theatre in Virginia, he landed his first stage part in ***State of the Union***. Borgnine was good enough to secure roles on Broadway in ***The Glass Menagerie*** and ***Harvey***.

He had a prolific movie career, appearing in ***From Here to Eternity***, ***Vera Cruz***, ***Johnny Guitar***, ***Bad Day at Black Rock***, ***The Dirty Dozen***, ***The Flight of the Phoenix***, ***Ice Station Zebra***, ***The Wild Bunch***, ***The Poseidon Adventure***, ***Red*** and a small film that turned out to be his signature effort. In all, he shared screen time in over two hundred movies.

That little flick, ***Marty***, was a teleplay that was adapted onto the big screen in 1955. Written by Paddy Chayefsky and directed by Delbert Mann, it became an international sensation. Borgnine only got the opportunity to star when Rod Steiger turned down the role because he accepted the chance to appear in ***Oklahoma***, playing *Jud Fry*. Ironically, Borgnine lost the audition to the versatile Steiger to co-star in the Rogers and Hammerstein musical. Beating large-budget films, ***Marty*** won an Oscar for the film, Chayefsky, Mann and Borgnine.

A hard-working actor, Ernest Borgnine never shied away from the small screen. He was rewarded in 1962 by being given the chance to star in ***McHale's Navy***. Though the show poked fun at his early profession, he treasured the opportunity to don his uniform in a laugh-out-loud satire. His character mirrored the actor's personality as a jovial prankster. He remained lifelong friends with his co-star Tim Conway. ***Airwolf*** was another series he starred in. Borgnine was also memorable in ***Little House on the Prairie***; ***Magnum, P.I.***; ***The Love Boat***; ***Walker, Texas Ranger***; ***Murder, She Wrote*** and the final two episodes of ***ER***.

Marty was deemed *"culturally, historically, or aesthetically significant"* by the Library of Congress and selected for preservation in the National Film Registry in 1994. His later career was interspersed with many well-deserved accolades. Borgnine became the oldest actor to be nominated for an Emmy, when he was ninety-two. Last year, he received the *Lifetime Achievement Award* from the Screen Actors Guild.

His personal life was turbulent. He married five times, including to actress Katy Jurado and, briefly, to Ethel Merman. When the latter wrote about the six-week union in her memoirs, the chapter was maliciously a blank page! Borgnine countered that he thought he had wed Rosemary Clooney!

The durable cinematic icon and a real gentleman, Ernest Borgnine was ninety-five.

REMEMBERING A COMEDIC PIONEER

August 20, 2017

In the wake of the passing of comedian and social activist Dick Gregory, a legend of the stage and screen has died. Admittedly an acquired taste, Jerry Lewis was a major star for seven decades. He trail-blazed a path in early television. Along with Dean Martin, they inherited the comedy-duo mantle made popular by the screen antics of Laurel and Hardy and Abbott and Costello. Lewis raised money for *Jerry's kids* to end muscular dystrophy, and he had a memorable cinematic career. His son formed Gary Lewis and the Playboys, and they had a string of hits in 1965-1966.

Jerry Lewis's career spanned a colorful history of show business throughout the twentieth century, beginning with his parents' vaudeville act when he was just five years of age. At twenty, his pairing with Martin made them international stars. Martin and Lewis delighted audiences with their stage antics and on television on ***The Colgate Comedy Hour***. Newspaper columnists Walter Winchell and Ed Sullivan raved over the sexy singer and the berserk clown. Hollywood producer Hal Wallis saw them at New York's Copacabana and signed them to a film contract. Together, they appeared in supporting roles in ***My Friend Irma*** and ***My Friend Irma Goes West***. Both would eventually star in a series of light comedies throughout the mid-1950s.

Martin grew tired of playing the straight man and the dizzying pace of their work. He began openly sparring with Lewis on stage. In 1956, the team dissolved. They remained apart for twenty years until Frank Sinatra brought them together as part of a surprise appearance during one of Jerry's live telethons in 1976.

After the team split up, Lewis went on to star in ***The Bellboy***, ***Cinderfella***, ***The Disorderly Orderly*** and ***The Nutty Professor***. He was featured in Martin Scorsese's ***The King of Comedy*** and appeared as himself in Billy Crystal's ***Mr. Saturday Night***. Retaining complete control of his own productions, Lewis pioneered the playback device that is still used in cinema

to this day. In the 1990s, he scored a stage hit as the *Devil* in a Broadway revival of ***Damn Yankees***.

Lewis was the face of the Muscular Dystrophy Association Labor Day Telethon, joking and reminiscing, introducing guests, sharing stories and concluding with his personal anthem, *You'll Never Walk Alone*. From the 1960s, his telethons raised one and a half billion dollars, including over sixty million dollars in 2009. He stepped down as official host in 2011. Jerry's MDA fundraising efforts earned him the *Jean Hersholt Humanitarian Award* at the 2009 Oscars.

France embraced the humor of Jerry Lewis. The French government awarded the comedian a *Chevalier de la Légion d'Honneur* in 1983 and *Commander of Arts and Letters* the following year. He also had his detractors. However, they never troubled Lewis's outlook on comedy. He remained true to his brand of humor.

He influenced scores of comedians, including Jim Carrey and many of the television stars of ***Saturday Night Live***. In Las Vegas, a message honoring the comedian is being featured on a marquee at Caesars Palace where Lewis was once a headliner and where he also hosted his telethons. In Los Angeles, fans gathered at Lewis's two Hollywood Walk of Fame stars, one for television and one for film.

Larger than life, Jerry Lewis was ninety-one.

PASSING PARADE CLAIMS A PLAYBOY

September 27, 2017

Playboy founder Hugh M. Hefner was an unabashed hedonist, who revved up the sexual revolution in the 1950s and built a multi-media empire of clubs and mansions. His brand is symbolized by women wearing bunny suits. Hef was an ardent supporter of classic films, American standards and pop culture. Hugh Hefner and *Playboy* remain iconic names worldwide.

Hefner was born in Chicago on April 9, 1926, to devout Methodist parents. As a youngster, he began publishing a neighborhood newspaper, which he sold for a penny a copy. He spent time writing and drawing cartoons and in middle school, he began reading *Esquire*, a magazine of among other things . . . innuendo!

Hefner would help slip sex out of the confines of brown wrappers and into our mainstream conversation. In 1953, when states could legally ban contraceptives and the word *pregnant* was not allowed to be uttered on ***I Love Lucy***, Hefner published the first issue of *Playboy*, featuring nude photographs of Marilyn Monroe and an editorial promise of humor, spice and sophistication. *Playboy* became forbidden fruit for teens and a bible for men with time and money. The magazine prescribed nights of dim lights, hard drinks, soft jazz and hidden desires. Within a year, circulation neared two hundred thousand. After five years, it topped one million.

Hef was a strong advocate of the First Amendment, civil rights and reproductive issues. Censorship was inevitable. *Playboy* was outlawed in China, India, Saudi Arabia and Ireland. For years, 7-Eleven stores did not sell the magazine. Retail outlets that sold *Playboy* made sure to stock it on a higher shelf.

The magazine contained more than centerfolds. *Playboy* serialized Ray Bradbury's *Fahrenheit 451* and later published fiction by John Updike, Doris Lessing and Vladimir Nabokov. It also featured candid interviews from Fidel Castro, Frank Sinatra and Marlon Brando to presidential candidate Jimmy Carter, who confided in an article that he committed adultery in his heart. John Lennon spoke to *Playboy* in 1980 right before he was murdered.

Hefner ran *Playboy* from elaborate mansions and became a flamboyant symbol of the lifestyle he espoused. For decades, he was the pipe-smoking, silk-pajama-wearing center of a constant party with celebrities and *Playboy* models. Drew Barrymore, Farrah Fawcett and Linda Evans are among those who posed for the cover of the magazine. By the 1970s, the magazine had over seven million readers and inspired raunchy imitations, such as *Penthouse* and *Hustler*. The internet reduced magazine circulation to under three million by the twenty-first century.

Hefner was host of a television show, ***Playboy After Dark*** and, in 1960, opened a string of clubs around the world where waitresses wore revealing costumes with bunny ears and fluffy white bunny tails. *Playboy*'s venues influenced culture, giving breaks to such entertainers as George Carlin, Rich Little, Dick Gregory and Redd Foxx. Some bunnies became celebrities, including singer Deborah Harry and model Lauren Hutton, both of whom had fond memories of their time at *Playboy*. One bunny was a journalist. Feminist Gloria Steinem got hired in the early 1960s and turned her brief employment into an article for *Show* magazine that described the clubs as pleasure havens for men. She surmised that bunnies tended to be poorly educated, overworked and underpaid. The last of the clubs closed in 1988.

An advocate for the arts, Hef lent his name and donated time and money to a pet project established by Michael Feinstein . . . *The Great American Songbook Foundation*. Hefner appeared with Feinstein on PBS in a documentary promoting their collaborative effort. At the mansion, Hefner frequently screened classic movies, including his favorite, ***Casablanca***. USC currently houses the Hugh M. Hefner Moving Image Archive, comprising over seventy thousand motion picture negatives, prints, magnetic sound elements and moving image materials in digital formats.

On a personal note, I visited the *Playboy Mansion* in 1987 to do a live radio broadcast that helped raise money for the John Tracy Clinic. Joining me that day was actor and fellow high school classmate, Vince Van Patten. I met Hefner, and he was in his familiar robe and slippers. He was also a complete gentleman.

Though he married numerous times, Hef advocated the *Playboy* lifestyle for his entire adult life. Hugh M. Hefner died peacefully in his sleep, surrounded by his current flock. He was ninety-one.

IRISH EYES SMILING FROM HEAVEN

October 24, 2015

Maureen O'Hara was the Irish beauty who appeared in such classic films as ***Miracle on 34th Street***, ***The Quiet Man***, ***The Hunchback of Notre Dame*** and ***How Green Was My Valley***. Her pals were the biggest names in Hollywood, including John Wayne and director John Ford. She could stand up to *The Duke*, both on and off screen. She was proud when he remarked in an interview that he preferred to work with men—except for Maureen O'Hara . . . *"she's a great guy."* She joins Myrna Loy as the only actresses ever to receive an Academy Award without a previous nomination.

The famous redhead, O'Hara was known for playing fiercely passionate heroines with a highly sensible attitude. She trained in drama, music and dance. At the age of ten, she joined the Rathmines Theatre Company and worked in amateur theatre in the evenings. Maureen enrolled in a business school and became a proficient bookkeeper and typist.

Those skills proved helpful years later when she took and transcribed production notes dictated by John Ford for the screen adaptation of Maurice Walsh's short story ***The Quiet Man***.

Her initial champion was Charles Laughton. O'Hara was offered a seven-year contract with his new company, Mayflower Pictures. Her first major film was ***Jamaica Inn***, directed by Alfred Hitchcock. Laughton was so pleased with O'Hara's performance he decided to cast her in the role of the gypsy girl, *Esmeralda*, opposite him in ***The Hunchback of Notre Dame***. One person not happy with this decision was Elsa Lanchester, Laughton's wife, who was fiercely jealous of O'Hara's beauty. The popularity of ***How Green Was My Valley*** confirmed O'Hara's status as a Hollywood star. RKO and Twentieth Century Fox shared her contract, and her most successful films were made at Fox. During her movie heyday, she became known as the *Queen of Technicolor* because of the camera's love affair with her vivid hair, pale complexion and spunky nature.

John Wayne and his favorite leading lady starred together in five fine motion pictures, including ***The Quiet Man***, ***Rio Grande***, ***Big Jake*** and ***McLintock!*** Other screen credits are ***The Black Swan***, ***The Parent Trap***, ***Our Man in Havana***, ***Spencer's Mountain*** and ***Mr. Hobbs Takes a Vacation***. In addition to her acting skills, O'Hara had a soprano voice and described singing as her first love. The studio heads never capitalized on her musical talent as she was already a big box-office draw in other genres of film. However, she was able to channel her love of singing through television. O'Hara was a frequent guest on variety shows with Perry Como and Andy Williams.

She was inducted into the Western Performers Hall of Fame at the National Cowboy and Western Heritage Museum in Oklahoma. In 1999, O'Hara was asked to be Grand Marshal of New York City's St. Patrick's Day Parade. In addition to her Oscar, she was honored with a *Lifetime Achievement Award* from the Irish Film and Television Academy in her native Dublin. She was formally inducted into the Irish America Hall of Fame in 2011. After her third husband died in a plane crash, she became the CEO of the airline company he owned, Antilles Air Boats. O'Hara released her autobiography, *'Tis Herself*, co-authored with Johnny Nicoletti and published by Simon and Schuster.

She made a public appearance at the 2013 *John Wayne Birthday Tribute to Maureen O'Hara* celebration in Winterset, Iowa. The occasion was the groundbreaking for the John Wayne Birthplace Museum. The festivities included an official proclamation from Iowa Governor Terry Branstad, declaring May 25, 2013, as *Maureen O'Hara Day* in Iowa.

Because of her roles in ***Miracle on 34th Street*** and, more recently, a Hallmark television movie, ***The Christmas Box***, the actress has a firm legacy to new generations of holiday viewers of the small screen. The latter film is based on a best-selling book.

The fiery Maureen O'Hara died peacefully in her sleep. She was ninety-five.

THE DEMISE OF HELTER SKELTER

November 19, 2017

Charles Manson was a wannabe entertainer who directed a most horrific murder spree in American history during the raucous 1960s. His lasting infamy rivaled any career launched in show business. His brush with Hollywood painted a nightmare etched in blood, a hippie cult leader with the wide-eyed face of evil.

Manson was born to a woman with dubious credentials, and he was in reform school by the time he was eight. He served a ten-year sentence for check forgery in the mid-1960s. He was released in San Francisco in the Haight-Ashbury district during the sexy heyday of the hippie movement.

He was in his mid-thirties by then and began collecting his family—mostly women—who likened him to *Jesus Christ*. Many were teens that came from good homes but were at odds with their parents. A petty criminal, the charismatic, guru-like Manson surrounded himself with runaways and other lost souls. He then sent his disciples to butcher some of Hollywood's rich and famous in what prosecutors said was a bid to trigger a race war, an idea he got from a twisted interpretation of The Beatles song *Helter Skelter*.

His victims included actress Sharon Tate (the pregnant bride of director Roman Polanski), coffee heiress Abigail Folger, celebrity hairdresser Jay Sebring,

Polish movie director Voityck Frykowski, Steven Parent (the friend of the estate's caretaker) and, the next evening, a wealthy grocer and his wife, Leno and Rosemary LaBianca. Other intended victims were Hollywood power brokers that earlier dismissed Manson's talent . . . Steve McQueen, Dennis Wilson of The Beach Boys and music producer Terry Melcher, the son of Doris Day.

Polanski and Tate rented the Hollywood Hills estate Terry Melcher had previously owned. The evening of the multiple slaughter, Polanski was out the country. Manson was later convicted of slaying musician Gary Hinman and stuntman Donald *Shorty* Shea. This marked the symbolic ending of what was known as the *Summer of Love*.

After a trial that lasted nearly a year, Manson and three followers—Susan Atkins, Patricia Krenwinkel and Leslie Van Houten—were found guilty of murder and sentenced to death. Another defendant, Charles Tex Watson, was convicted later. All were spared execution and given life sentences after the California Supreme Court struck down the death penalty in 1972. Vincent Bugliosi was the Los Angeles prosecutor who put Manson behind bars. The state's star witness, Linda Kasabian, who was granted immunity, testified that Manson tied up the LaBianca couple and then ordered his followers to kill and leave grizzly messages in blood. Another Manson devotee, Lynette Squeaky Fromme, was unsuccessful in her attempt when she tried to assassinate President Gerald Ford in 1975. She served thirty-four years in prison.

The trial spawned movies, television programs and documentaries. Bugliosi wrote a best-selling book about the killings, *Helter Skelter*. The macabre shock rocker Marilyn Manson borrowed part of his stage name from Charlie. The Manson case remains one of the most chilling in crime history. Over the decades, Manson's followers appeared sporadically at parole hearings, where their bids for freedom have been repeatedly rejected. Manson, however, stopped attending, saying prison had become his home. One may assume that *Dante's Inferno* will be his new digs for eternity, a most appropriate curtain call.

The utterly monstrous Charles Manson was eighty-three.

MAY THE FORCE BE WITH CARRIE FISHER

December 27, 2016

Carrie Fisher found enduring fame as *Princess Leia* in the initial entry of the ***Star Wars*** trilogy. In 1987, her autobiography, *Postcards from the Edge*, became a best-seller. It became a 1990 motion picture starring Shirley MacLaine and Meryl Streep. Her parents were Hollywood royalty: Eddie Fisher and Debbie Reynolds.

She made her movie debut opposite Warren Beatty in ***Shampoo***. The actress co-starred in ***The Blues Brothers***, ***When Harry Met Sally***, ***Hannah and Her Sisters***, ***Charlie's Angels***, ***Austin Powers*** and ***Scream 3***. Last year, Carrie reprised her recurring part as *Leia* in ***Star Wars: The Force Awakens*** and ***Episode VIII*** (2017).

Her one-woman show, *Wishful Drinking*, which she had performed across the country since 2006, was adapted into a book, made its way to Broadway in 2009 and became a production for HBO in 2010. Carrie was not coy in revealing details about her mental illness, drug addiction or failed relationships. In fact, she was relentless in efforts to destigmatize mental health issues.

She co-hosted *The Essentials* on TCM with Robert Osborne in 2007. Harvard College gave Fisher its annual *Outstanding Lifetime Achievement Award in Cultural Humanism*. Her memoir, *The Princess Diarist*, was released in November 2016. The book is based on the diaries she kept during filming of the original ***Star Wars*** trilogy in the late 1970s and early 1980s. A new documentary, ***Bright Lights: Starring Carrie Fisher and Debbie Reynolds***, will screen at the upcoming Palm Springs Film Festival. It first debuted at Cannes Film Festival in May and is set to air on HBO in early 2017.

With a thriving career left intact, Carrie Fisher was taken prematurely at age sixty.

DEBBIE REYNOLDS STRICKEN AND DIES

December 28, 2016

The death of her child was simply just too tough to comprehend. Debbie Reynolds was rushed to the hospital just a day after the passing of her daughter, Carrie Fisher. Debbie and Carrie were quite close, and the legendary actress became distraught over her latest personal tragedy. The family was in the process of making funeral arrangements.

Debbie Reynolds was one of Hollywood's brightest stars during the 1950s and 1960s and is best known for her part in ***Singing in the Rain*** in 1952. She was nominated for an Oscar for her role in ***The Unsinkable Molly Brown***. Other films include ***How the West Was Won*** and ***The Singing Nun***. Reynolds also had several hit records and one went #1: *Tammy* from ***Tammy and the Bachelor***. She continued to stay active by preserving memorabilia. And she made sure MGM costumes and artifacts would end up in appropriate Hollywood museums.

Reynolds was married to Eddie Fisher from 1955 to 1959, and they had two children. He left her to wed Elizabeth Taylor. Two other husbands made foolish business deals and cost Debbie millions of dollars, leaving her almost broke and, eventually, thrice divorced.

She received the *Jean Hersholt Humanitarian Award* but was too weak to attend the event. Reynolds was recognized for her decades-long commitment to various charities, including the mental-health organization she founded, *The Thalians*. Debbie was a benefactor of a *Lifetime Achievement Award* from the Screen Actors Guild. On a personal note, I interviewed her in 2012 on my *Forgotten Hollywood* radio program and podcast.

The Los Angeles Fire Department confirmed the transport of an adult female in fair-to-serious condition at 1 p.m. to Cedars Sinai Medical Center. Reynolds may have suffered stress-induced cardiomyopathy, or takotsubo syndrome. She died just thirty-two hours after the loss of her beloved Carrie. My thoughts and prayers to her family for enduring extraordinary adversity, an unbelievable turn of tragic events.

Debbie Reynolds was eighty-four, a singularly buoyant personality that graced the silver screen.

Until next time . . . *never forget.*

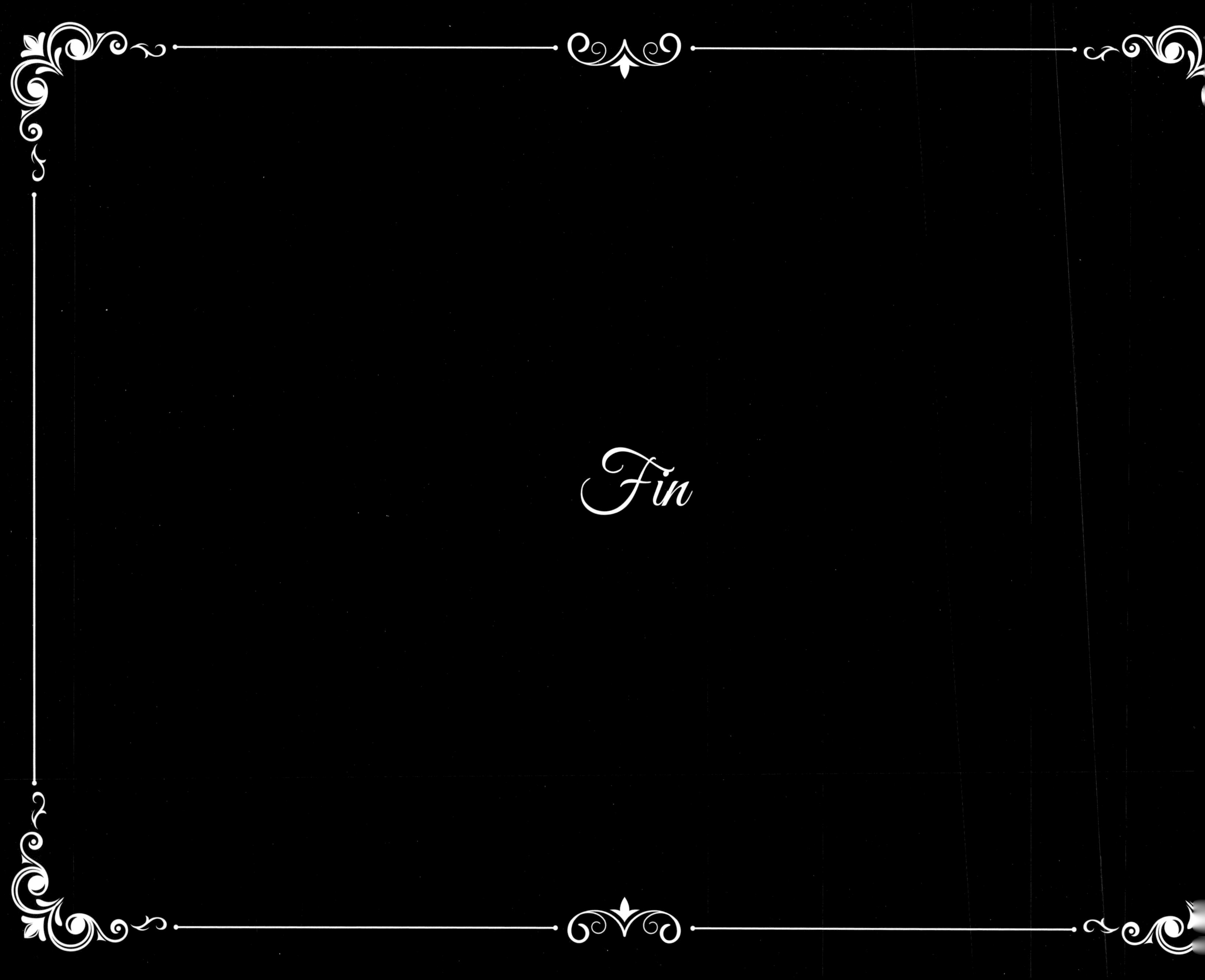
Fin

DOCUMENTARY PRODUCTION BEGINS

June 5, 2013

Manny P. here . . .

After four months of fundraising through *Indiegogo*, we have begun principal production of our *Forgotten Hollywood* documentary with Lionel Barrymore as our primary subject. Nervousa Films captured first-person interviews of Academy Award–winning actress Margaret O'Brien and Scott Essman, the creative director of Visionary Media and a public relations rep for Universal Studios. He will be our go-to historian with issues related to Hollywood's Silent Era and subsequent Golden Age. Miss O'Brien worked on two MGM productions with Barrymore, and she was a poster child and advocate for the *March of Dimes* campaign.

Essman and O'Brien were engaging and informative. I am confident their contributions were original and uniquely fresh in the cinematic storytelling process. Each guest provided a valuable first-person narrative and personal assessment relating to Lionel Barrymore's quest to continue working, despite a degenerative disability due to arthritis, the relationship between President Franklin D. Roosevelt and Hollywood during the origins of the March of Dimes and the movie studio maturation process in the presentation of disease and disability.

Michelle Merker is a co-producer of the documentary project, and together, we conducted the day-long interviews. Dan Donley was our director of photography. This first day of production took place at the Granada Pavilion, a multi-purpose facility in the San Fernando Valley. Virginia Vandewouwer was in charge of craft services.

The next step is to catalog the interview footage, collect the appropriate still photos to help us tell the story and create narration. The finished trailer will be used in conjunction with a pitch package to garner potential major investment opportunities. This overall process is quite exciting!

FRIEND TO SOUTHERN CALIFORNIA RADIO

April 10, 2013

Suffice to say, this is the most difficult blog story I have ever written . . .

My dear, dear friend Gary Lycan has passed on. Part of the fabric of Southern California, he was the award-winning radio columnist of the *Orange County Register* since his initial assignment in 1968. Gary was also my cherished co-host on *Forgotten Hollywood*, a weekly radio program that airs on the Financial News and Radio Network. And he wrote the *Foreword* and *Introduction* to my first two works in the *Forgotten Hollywood* book series.

Though we have been like brothers working on the *Forgotten Hollywood* franchise for these past five years, I am smart enough to know that he had a really keen friendship with every Southern California broadcaster who has cracked a microphone during the Golden Age of Format Radio. He was inspired by the disc jockeys, radio personalities and news-related folks who worked at KFWB, KRLA and KHJ back in the 1960s. He wanted desperately to join this fraternity. But his unparalleled talent lay in the written, not spoken, word. Through his weekly radio column, he became an elder statesman of this so-called fraternity. Orange County folks learned about the business of broadcasting in digestible, easy-to-read and friendly bites, which made his readers feel that they were all part of the inner circle.

Never to rest on his laurels, Gary Lycan also had longtime allies who fought for animal rights (a particular passion of his) and, ultimately, the Golden Age of Hollywood community. During one of our programs, he secured an interview for us with the legendary Debbie Reynolds.

On his birthday in 2012, the Los Angeles Press Club honored Gary Lycan with its *National Entertainment Journalist Award* in the *Print Columnist of the Year* category. He was really astounded at the fine outpouring of congratulations by radio broadcasters throughout Southern California on his Facebook page. Of course, I was not surprised at all. I knew what he meant to our community. His words transcended Orange County even after the advent of the *dot.com* and social media craze.

Knowing that his time on earth was short, Gary wrote me a wonderful email on October 30. I seldom share my personal correspondence. I am compelled to offer this:

> *These have been the best days of my life—working with you, collaborating on ideas, hanging out with you, applauding YOUR work as a writer on the radio show and the blog. I want you to know how much I treasure all that. It just sucks to be saddled with illness at the same time, but I will keep on keeping on, as they say. I just want you and your family to know how much I value your talents and how much I enjoy our relationship. It puts a smile on my face every day.*
>
> Best,
>
> Gary

Until next time . . . *never forget.*

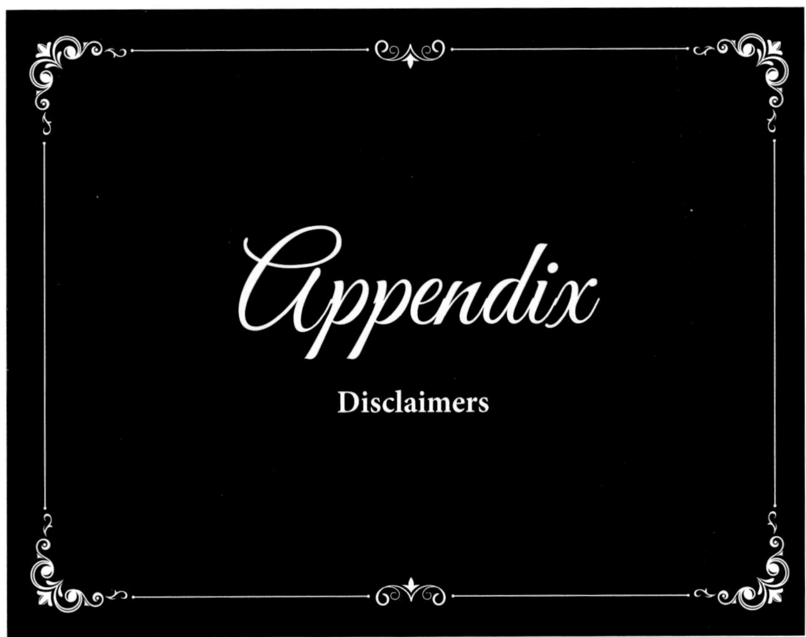

Wikipedia and Freebase

Some text facts and photos were found on wikipedia.org and freebase.com. Full articles on chapter subjects and themes might be found on wikipedia.org.

Wikipedia content is licensed under the GNU Free Documentation License (GFDL), which is a copyleft license for free documentation, designed by the Free Software Foundation (FSF) for the GNU Project. It is similar to the GNU General Public License, giving readers the rights to copy, redistribute and modify a work, and requires all copies and derivatives to be available under the same license. Copies may also be sold commercially, but if produced in larger quantities (greater than one hundred), the original document or source code must be made available to the work's recipient. Freebase Content is "freely licensed" under the GFDL or Creative Commons Attribution (BY), which allows one to share and remix (creative derivative works), even for commercial.

Photos found on the above website were confirmed in the public domain (PD-US). Specific reasons can be found here in the appendix.

Pacheco Family

The authors, Manny Pacheco and Virginia Vandewouwer, have a collection of photos used in this work. All rights allowed. No restrictions.

Academy Awards and Oscar

Academy Awards and Oscar are registered trademarks and service marks of the Academy of Motion Picture Arts and Sciences (AMPAS). The copyrighted Award of Merit (Oscar) statuette is identified as copyr. AMPAS. In addition, the Oscar statuette and depictions thereof are trade names of AMPAS.

Movie Trailers

Most trailers prior to 1976 were created as new works, which contained new material (such as *Coming Soon*) as well as scenes from the films they were advertising. Trailers did not contain copyright notices, nor were they registered in the Copyright Office or the Library of Congress. Consequently, the new material at the very least went into the public domain. Many of these trailers also contained material that appeared to be from the movie, but actually, they were made for the trailer. That material, since it did not contain a copyright notice, falls into public domain. The major argument has been that the scenes from the film itself were protected by the copyright on the complete film. However, one could argue that once you cut a clip from a film, it is a separate entity, and without a complete and separate copyright and notice, it, too, becomes public domain by its publication. In any event, industry custom and practice have been to use trailers prior to 1972 based on the above information.

Furthermore, trailers prior to 1960 offer an additional incentive since, under Screen Actors Guild rules, theatrical feature films prior to 1960 do not require residuals be paid to actors, writers and directors when the trailer is broadcast. Consequently, writers and directors in clips and trailers do not have to be paid, and actors do not have to be cleared or paid as long as the trailer clearly identifies the film on screen over the clip as it is played or it is identified verbally. This information is not contained in the Screen Actors Guild Code Book, but can be obtained from a SAG representative via a telephone call.

Publicity Photos

Several sources provide guidance about copyrights—whether copyright laws apply, how to discover if they apply, and how to indicate copyright. The following sources were used.

United States Copyright Office, page 2

The notice for visually perceptible copies should contain all three elements described below. They should appear together or in close proximity on the copies.

1. The symbol ©, the word "Copyright"; or the abbreviation "Copr."
2. The year of first publication. If the work is a derivative work or a compilation incorporating previously published material, the year date of first publication of the derivative work or compilation is sufficient. Examples of derivative works are translations or dramatizations; an example of a compilation is an anthology. The year may be omitted when a pictorial, graphic, or sculptural work, with accompanying textual matter, if any, is reproduced in or on greeting cards, postcards, stationery, jewelry, dolls, toys, or useful articles.
3. The name of the copyright owner, an abbreviation by which a name can be recognized, or a generally known alternative designation of owner (example © 2007 Jane Doe).

The Complete Film Production Handbook by Eve Light Honthaner

"According to the old copyright act, such production stills were not automatically copyrighted as part of the film and required separate copyrights as photographic stills. Most studios never bothered to copyright these stills because they were happy to see them pass into public domain to be used by as many people in as many publications as possible."

Film Study and the Copyright Law by Gerald Mast, page 87

"If any copyright was secured for this image under the terms of the 1909 Copyright Act (law until 1978) it would have had to be renewed in the twenty-eighth year following registration."

Presidential Libraries

The presidential libraries of Franklin D. Roosevelt, John F. Kennedy, Lyndon Johnson, Richard Nixon and Ronald Reagan have given specific permission for photographs obtained for use.

Library of Congress

Selected photographs and pictures from the Library of Congress Prints and Photographs Division had no known copyright restrictions on publication. In some cases, the copyright had expired or was given specific permission for use as a gift of the photographer, artist, or owner of the material (including National Photo Company, Carol Highsmith, George Grantham Bain, William P. Gottleib, John Margolies and *New York World-Telegram* and the *Sun* newspaper). Some photos may require the condition that they not be altered or cropped. They include Vivien Leigh (wax figure), Louis Armstrong, Ella Fitzgerald, Frank Capra, Dean Martin (mural), Abraham Lincoln (actor Frank McGlynn Sr.), Brooklyn Dodgers, Joe DiMaggio, Cleveland

Indians, Charlie Chaplin, Prang American Christmas and New Year Cards, President Abraham Lincoln Assassination (illustration), San Francisco 1906 Earthquake, Franklin D. Roosevelt Memorial, *The African Queen*, Louis Buchalter and Jacob Shapiro (FBI wanted poster), Muhammad Ali, Lena Horne, *The Diary of Anne Frank* (poster), Grauman's Chinese Theatre, Jerry Lewis, Phyllis Diller and Henry Fonda (footprints).

National Archives and Records Administration

Photos and pictures from the National Archives and Records Administration were given specific permission for use in this book. They have been confirmed "use unrestricted." They include Teddy Roosevelt *Rough Riders* (illustration), Arthur Godfrey, Eliot Ness, Maureen O'Hara and V-J Day *The Kiss.*

Miscellaneous/Specific Use Conditions

Wikipedia/Freebase Images

United States government images may enter the public domain under the terms of Title 17, Chapter 1, Section 105 of the US Code. The photographs that fall into this category include *The Battle of Midway* (documentary), President Ronald Reagan, Nancy Reagan, Jacqueline Kennedy Onassis, Bing Crosby (U S Army V-Disc No. 441), Brigadier General James M. Stewart, USAF Reserve, Will Rogers (WPA dedication poster), Alexander Hamilton (engraved portrait), Major General Edwin Anderson Walker, Jackie Robinson (gold medal), Dalton Trumbo, Rock Hudson, Harrison Ford, Audie Murphy, HMS *Bounty*, *Intrusion Kill Chain* (diagram), Eliot Ness, *The Memphis Belle*, César Chávez (poster), Passengers from SS *St. Louis*, Sidney Poitier, Smokey Bear, Mickey Rooney (2), President Richard Nixon, Pat Nixon, Debbie Reynolds, Carrie Fisher, Northern Mockingbird and Playboy Bunnies.

Pre-1929 photographs may enter the public domain because of copyright expiration. The photos that fall into this category include *Good Morning to All* (music and lyrics), Stan Laurel, *In the Clutches of the Gang* (with Fatty Arbuckle), Adolf Hitler, Hans Christian Andersen (illustration), Holland Amerika (poster), Damon Runyon (caricature), *Le voyage dans la lune* (illustration), Movie Palace, Abraham Lincoln and Cabinet, Ruby Murder's Posse, Baseball Players (illustration), Chicago Cubs, William Randolph Hearst, *Le Retour de la Jonde* (illustration), *Mona Lisa*, Wedding of Prince of Wales and Alexandra of Denmark, Big Ben (illustration), Henry VI of England (illustration), *The Star-Spangled Banner*, Billy-the-Kid (illustration), *The Wizard of Oz*, Necco Wafers and Crayola Crayons.

Disclaimers (by Chapter)

Chapter One

Van Nuys High School logo: Van Nuys High School allowed me use of logo with no conditions.

Lauren Bacall: Swedish photograph in the public domain in Sweden because one of the following:

- The work is non-artistic (journalistic, etc.) and has been created before January 1, 1970 (SFS 1960:729, § 49a).
- The photographer is not known and cannot be traced, and the work has been created before January 1, 1950 (SFS 1960:729, § 44).

Spencer Tracy and Elizabeth Taylor: MGM *Father's Little Dividend*, 1951. American film in public domain.

William Holden: This photograph is in the public domain in Finland because a period of fifty years has elapsed from the year of creation or the photograph was first published before 1966. Material already released to public domain according to the previous 1961 law remains in the public domain, and therefore all photographs released before 1966 are in the public domain.

Chapter Two

Swan Theatre: Aernout Van Buchel, artist. Utrecht University Library. This is a faithful photographic reproduction of a two-dimensional, public domain work of art.

Author Craig Inglis, the creator of the *Lucky* series of books: Craig Inglis owns the total rights to *Lucky.* I printed my blog story about *Lucky* as a tribute to Craig Inglis.

Carol Lombard: Paul Hesse, photographer, January 1940. Photoplay copyright not renewed.

Chapter Three

Vivien Leigh: Roloff Beny, photographer, 1958. This image is available from Library and Archives Canada under the reproduction reference number PA-193748 and under the MIKAN ID number 3535726. The copyright holder of this work allows anyone to use it for any purpose including unrestricted redistribution, commercial use and modification.

Harold Robbins: Rob Croes, Anefo photo collection, 1979. This is an image from the Nationaal Archief, the Dutch National Archives, donated in the context of a partnership program. This file is made available under the Creative Commons CC0 1.0 Universal Public Domain Dedication. The person who associated a work with this deed has dedicated the work to the public domain by waiving all their rights to the work worldwide under copyright law, including all related and neighboring rights, to the extent allowed by law. You can copy, modify, distribute and perform the work, even for commercial purposes, all without asking permission.

Robert Redford *The Great Waldo Pepper*: Photograph from San Diego Air and Space Museum, 1975. According to the museum, there are no known restrictions on the publication of photos.

Chapter Four

The Ambassador Theatre: *OptimumPX* own work, 2010. I, the copyright holder of this work, release this work into the public domain. This applies worldwide. I grant anyone the right to use this work for any purpose, without any conditions, unless such conditions are required by law.

Fiddler on the Roof: Robert C. Croes, photographer. Anefo Photo Collection, Nationaal Archief, October 21, 1971. Access number 2.24.01.05. File number 925-0675. This file is made available under the Creative Commons CC0 1.0 Universal Public Domain. The person who associated a work with this deed has dedicated the work to the public domain by waiving all their rights to the work worldwide under copyright law, including all related and neighboring rights, to the extent allowed by law. You can copy, modify, distribute and perform the work, even for commercial purposes, all without asking permission.

Paul Muni: University of California Libraries. The uploading organization may have various reasons for determining that no known copyright restrictions exist. Files are available under licenses specified on their description page. All structured data from the file and property namespaces is available under the Creative Commons CC0 License.

Clint Eastwood: Zarateman, March 10, 2019. This file is made available under the Creative Commons CC0 1.0 Universal Public Domain. The person who associated a work with this deed has dedicated the work to the public domain by waiving all their rights to the work worldwide under copyright law, including all related and neighboring rights to the extent allowed by law. You can copy, modify, distribute and perform the work, even for commercial purposes, all without asking permission.

Sonja Henie: *Toronto Star*, 1942. This Canadian work is in the public domain in Canada because its copyright has expired due to the following: (1) It was subject to Crown copyright and was first published more than fifty years ago, or it was not subject to Crown copyright, and (2) It is a photograph that was created prior to January 1, 1949, or (3) Creator died over fifty years ago.

Chapter Six

Mr. Smith Goes to Washington: Work for hire on behalf of Columbia Pictures. The poster included a defective copyright notice. The notice omits the year of publication, 1939. Even if the notice is deemed sufficient, the copyright for the artwork was not renewed as was required by American copyright law to extend/maintain protection for works published 1963 or earlier. In order to maintain copyright protection, the poster would have had to be renewed twenty-eight years after publication in 1966 or 1967. Because it was not renewed, copyright lapsed at that time.

Andy Griffith: State Archives of North Carolina, 1950s. This image was originally posted by State Archives of North Carolina. The uploading organization may have various reasons for determining that no known copyright restrictions exist.

Sinclair Lewis: This Swedish photograph is in the public domain in Sweden because the photographer is not known and cannot be traced and the work has been created before January 1, 1950 (SFS 1960:729, § 44).

Bells Are Ringing: Incorporates artwork by Reynold Brown, 1960. US Copyright Office did not find a copyright renewal. In the absence of renewal of the US copyright, this poster art entered the public domain twenty-eight years after its US publication date.

Chapter Seven

Baseball wall art: Two-dimensional work of art in the public domain.

Vin Scully: Mural in front of Toro Grill in Los Angeles. Original photo of Vin Scully by Dominic DiSaria. Mural by Alex Ali Gonzalez.

Henry Aaron (autographed jersey): Smithsonian National Museum of African American History and Culture, 1968 or 1969. All items are released explicitly into the public domain. You can copy, modify, distribute and perform the work, even for commercial purposes, all without asking permission. CC0 1.0.

Chapter Eight

Gone with the Wind: Acme News Photos, December 15, 1939. A search for original registrations was done in artwork for the year 1939. There were no listings containing "Acme." There is no evidence of original copyright for this photo.

Anti-Communist literature: Myron Coureval Fagan, circa 1950-1956.

Susan Sarandon: This file or its source was published by Press Information Bureau on behalf of Ministry of Information and Broadcasting, Government of India under ID 50974 and CNR 53760. This image was originally posted in https://pib.gov.in/newsite/photo.aspx?photoid=50974. Following the mandate of the National Data Sharing and Accessibility Policy (NDSAP) of the government of India that applies to all shareable non-sensitive data available either in digital or analog forms, but generated using public funds by various agencies of the government of India, all users are provided a worldwide, royalty-free, non-exclusive license to use, adapt, publish (either in original or in adapted and/or derivative forms), translate, display, add value and create derivative works (including products and services) for all lawful commercial and non-commercial purposes, and for the duration of existence of such rights over the data or information. Ministry of Information and Broadcasting (GODL-India.)

Joan Crawford: *CINEGRAF* magazine, 1937. This image is in the public domain because the copyright of this photograph, registered in Argentina, has expired.

Chapter Nine

Royal Crown Jewels: *Illustrated* magazine, December 13, 1952. This work created by the United Kingdom government is in the public domain because it is a photograph that was taken before June 1957. HMSO has declared that the expiry of Crown copyrights applies worldwide.

William Shakespeare (bench): National Literacy Trust, Book about Town Literacy Campaign, 2014. The National Literacy Trust a registered charity in England, Wales (1116260), and in Scotland (SCO42944).

Jane Austen: Courtesy of the University of Texas Libraries, the University of Texas at Austin, Perry Castaneda Library, Noel Collection. Duychinick, Evert A. Portrait Gallery of Eminent Men and Women in Europe and America (New York: Johnson, Wilson and Company, 1873). The image is in the public domain, and no permission is needed to use it.

Agatha Christie Memorial: Diagram Lajard, photographer 2103. The photographic reproduction of this work is covered under United Kingdom law (Section 62 of the Copyright, Designs and Patent Act 1988), which states that it is not an infringement to take photographs of buildings or of sculptures, models for buildings or works of artistic craftsmanship in public place or premises open to the public.

Queen Elizabeth II and Prince Phillip: This work created by the United Kingdom government is in the public domain because it is a photograph that was taken before June 1957. HMSO has declared that the expiry of Crown copyrights applies worldwide.

Chapter Ten

Katharine Johnson: NASA copyright policy states, "NASA material is not protected by copyright unless noted."

John F. Kennedy: Walt Cisco, *Dallas Morning News*, November 22, 1963. Copyright expired in 1991 without renewal. From US Copyright Information Circular, 15t: "Copyright whose first twenty-eight-year term between January 1, 1950 to December 31, 1963 . . . still had to be renewed within strict time limits in order to receive the maximum statutory duration . . . if renewal registration was not made within the statutory time limits, these copyrights expired at the end of their first terms and protection was lost permanently."

Memphis Belle: By Manassehkatz – Own work, CC BY-SA 3.0

Chapter Eleven

Fibber McGee and Molly: Dell Publications, 1948 magazine photo. There is no evidence Dell Publications continues to claim copyright on this magazine. Copyright not renewed.

George Washington: Open Clipart Library. All items are released explicitly into the public domain. You can copy, modify, distribute and perform the work, even for commercial purposes, all without asking permission. CC0 1.0

Universal City (aerial view): Los Angeles Public Library, 1956. photos.lapl.org. No known copyright info.

Hollywood Sign: Johnny Blu was Twitter name of person who took Hollywood Sign photo and posted on January 1, 1977. No copyright protection.

Chapter Twelve

Harper Lee: Photo credited to Truman Capote, 1960. The photo is a mechanical scan/photocopy of the original cover and does not qualify for independent copyright protection. The photo was first published prior to 1978 without a valid copyright notice. *To Kill a Mockingbird* was first published in 1960; the hardcover book itself carried a copyright notice, so its contents remain copyrighted. However, the first-edition dust jacket did not carry a separate copyright notice. The Compendium of US Copyright Office Practices: Chapter 2200, § 2207.1(C) at p. 15. The photo has no copyright markings on it.

Muhammad Ali: Zarateman, 2012. All items are released explicitly into the public domain. You can copy, modify, distribute and perform the work, even for commercial purposes, all without asking permission. CC0 1.0 The photographical reproduction of this work is covered under the article 35.2 of the Spain Royal Legislative Decree 1/1996 of April 12, 1996, and amended by Law 5/1998 of March 6, 1998, which states: "Works permanently located in parks or on streets, squares or other public thoroughfares may be freely reproduced, distributed and communicated by painting, drawing, photography and audiovisual processes."

Ray Harryhausen: Photographer Art Kirsch. Courtesy of Art Kirsch.

Charles Manson: California Department of Corrections and Rehabilitation, 1968. This work was created by a government unit (including state, county, city and municipal government agencies) that derives its powers from the laws of the state of California and is subject to disclosure under the California Public Records Act (Government Code § 6250 et seq.). It is a public record that was not created by an agency that state law has allowed to claim copyright and is therefore in the public domain in the United States.

THIS WORK IS LOVINGLY DEDICATED TO:

MANUEL NUNEZ PACHECO

HUSBAND – FATHER – BROTHER

"PAPA" "DURPY"

1938 – 2021

He was always so supportive to the singular and combined efforts of his children. We miss him every single day.

Manny Pacheco

Manny Pacheco has been one busy scribe. He has appeared at book signings and given oral presentations in support of his *Forgotten Hollywood* franchise in various cities, including Calgary, Chicago, Las Vegas, Los Angeles, Manhattan, Miami, Milwaukee, Orange County, Portland, San Diego and Seattle. All this he does while working as a weekend traffic anchor on KNX 97.1 FM/1070 AM News Radio in Los Angeles and as an adjunct faculty (providing a curriculum in various aspects of radio, television and cinema) on the campuses of Mt. San Antonio College in Walnut, California; Rio Hondo College in Whittier and Long Beach City College.

The *Forgotten Hollywood* journey is a family affair, with Manny's sister, Virginia Vandewouwer, offering sage advice in the development and promotion of the *FH* book series and award-winning blog at www.forgottenhollywood.com. Manny's nephew and godson developed the *Forgotten Hollywood* blog site and acts as co-administrator for the social media repository. This collaborative effort is successful due to the close bond of the family. Manny's childhood nickname for his sister is *Vigi.*

The *Forgotten Hollywood* franchise includes a weekly podcast on Spotify. Manny is also a guest contributor of content on ***Celebrating Act 2***, a cable podcast on the YouTube platform. Manny is the executive producer of a *Forgotten Hollywood* documentary, currently in production. In 2015, Carl Rollyson, the advisory editor of the *Hollywood Legends* series from University Press of Mississippi and author of several biographies, referenced Manny Pacheco's literary work in his book, *A Real American Character: The Life of Walter Brennan*.

Virginia Vandewouwer

Virginia Vandewouwer continues to lead a very interesting life. As a teen, she studied karate at the Chuck Norris Studios, receiving lessons from the action star. As an adult, she catered a documentary film shoot for Oscar-winning actress Margaret O'Brien. And she took a class with renowned master chef Fabio Viviani.

A native Angelino, Virginia grew up in the heart of the San Fernando Valley and has embraced her lifelong entrepreneurial spirit. She worked in the lending industry before transitioning to help create a nonprofit organization with her husband of forty-plus years and business partner, Roland Vandewouwer. Virginia also belonged to the Southern California ballroom dancing community. The couple is retired, and she has decided to dabble in the literary field (with her brother). Virginia and Roland have a son, Matthew, who is a successful advertising director and the proud father of a beautiful baby girl named Violet.

In her spare time (which is limited), you can find Virginia and Roland managing or renovating one of their many rental properties. In the kitchen, Virginia cooks international delicacies and bakes gourmet goodies. And she loves to landscape her picturesque half-acre garden. Her landscape design work was part of a public tour and has been featured in a brochure about the beauty of ponds. While in her twenties, she took flying lessons, culminating in a solo flight a week before her wedding! Virginia also has a motorcycle license. She continues to extensively travel abroad. Her favorite cinema includes ***Cool Hand Luke***, ***Dead Poet's Society*** and ***The Shawshank Redemption***.

Virginia and her husband live in Thousand Oaks. It was also home to their terrier-mix pooch, Milou. His name was a tribute to the *Tintin* stories by Hergé and his internationally acclaimed Belgian books. In his writings, the hero owns a terrier-mix named *Milou*.